PRAISE FOR

NO IS NOT ENOUGH

"Naomi Klein is magnificent, and in *No Is Not Enough*, she has forged a courageous coruscating counter-spell against the hegemonic nightmare that, if left unchecked, will devour us all."
—Junot Díaz, author, *The Brief Wondrous Life of Oscar Wao*

"Naomi Klein is a critically important thought-leader in these perilous times, a necessary voice as a courageous movement of movements rises from the ashes of the last election cycle. *No Is Not Enough* tells a compelling story about where we are, how we got here, and what we should do now. The book is a genuine page-turner—highly engaging and provocative—and provides a fascinating lens through which we can view our current moment. Klein is not preaching to the choir, but framing the moment, connecting necessary dots, and outlining the challenge that lies ahead in clear terms that anyone can understand."
—Michelle Alexander, author, *The New Jim Crow: Mass Incarceration in the Age of Colorblindness*

"Naomi Klein is one of the few revolutionary public intellectuals of great integrity and vision. This new book confirms her crucial relevance and essential pertinence."
—Cornel West, author, *Race Matters*

"Urgent, timely, and necessary."
—Noam Chomsky, Institute Professor (Emeritus), MIT

"If you're wondering how Naomi Klein has managed to produce an essential and gripping book so early in the Trump presidency, it's because she's spent her whole intellectual life preparing for

just this moment. Trump is the ultimate logo. Every day we watch him try to exploit yet another shock to the system. So this is the book to read—not just the first word on Trump, but in powerful ways the last word as well."
—Bill McKibben, author, *Radio Free Vermont*

"Naomi Klein has written an ordinary person's guide to hope. Read this book."
—Arundhati Roy, author, *The End of Imagination*

"Saying No to their shock doctrine is essential but insufficient. Naomi Klein's new book incites us brilliantly to stiffen our lip, to overcome quickly their calculated shocks, and to interweave our No with a programmatic Yes. It is a manual for emancipation by means of the only weapon we have against orchestrated misanthropy: constructive disobedience."
—Yanis Varoufakis, former Finance Minister of Greece

"Naomi Klein shows us that the monstrosity of Donald Trump has not occurred in a vacuum but is the culmination of decades of unchecked economic inequality, racism, militarism, and war. As the shock of Trump as president gives way to anger and the determination to fight, *No Is Not Enough* makes an urgent intervention in emerging movements. It will take more than 'resistance' to beat Trumpism. We need history, politics, strategy, and, most importantly, the optimism that another world is possible. Klein has made a critical contribution to the developing opposition to Trump and the economic disorder that produced him."
—Keeanga-Yamahtta Taylor, author,
From #BlackLivesMatter to Black Liberation

"Naomi Klein's books are ceaselessly illuminating, daring, and indispensable. As accessible as it is brilliant, *No Is Not Enough* is an essential blueprint for a worldwide counter-attack against right-wing corporate hegemony."

—Owen Jones, author, *The Establishment:*
And How They Get Away with It

"From *No Logo* to *The Shock Doctrine* to *This Changes Everything,* Naomi Klein's books have charted the harmful impact of surging corporate power on culture, jobs, peace, and the planet. In our current hellish situation, who better than Naomi to make sense of this madness, and help us find a way out? This book is a top-of-the-stack summer must-read."

—Michael Stipe, musician

"*No Is Not Enough* is Naomi Klein 2.0. It is the accumulation of years of brilliant and layered analysis applied with lightning precision to an understanding of how we got to Trump, and how we can use this moment to bring about another system and world. It is a potent stand for No—and a compelling vision of the Yes to come."   —Eve Ensler, author, *In the Body of the World*

"Naomi Klein has written a compelling book that we all need to read and act on. *No Is Not Enough* is an essential handbook for all people, especially young people, who want to understand the economic, social, and political forces that produced the current crisis we are facing—and how we can effectively organize to win a better world."   —Danny Glover, actor

"Naomi Klein constructs a common story that allows us to sustain the effects of being shocked. We can act upon that, with intelligence and happiness, to recover our world."

—Gael García Bernal, actor

NO

IS NOT

NAOMI KLEIN

ENOUGH

RESISTING TRUMP'S SHOCK POLITICS AND WINNING THE WORLD WE NEED

Haymarket Books
Chicago, IL

Published in 2017 in the United States by Haymarket Books,
and simultaneously in Canada by Alfred A. Knopf, a division of
Penguin Random House Canada Limited, and in Great Britain by
Allen Lane, a division of the Random House Group Limited.

Haymarket Books
P.O. Box 180165, Chicago, IL 60618
www.haymarketbooks.org

Issued in print and electronic formats.
ISBN 978-1-60846-890-4
eBook ISBN 978-1-60846-891-1

Distributed in the United States by
Consortium Book Sales and Distribution, www.cbsd.com.

This book was published with the generous support
of Lannan Foundation and the Wallace Action Fund.

Book design by CS Richardson.

Printed on 100 percent post-consumer recycled paper
by union labor in Canada.

Library of Congress Cataloging-in-Publication Data is available.

2 4 6 8 10 9 7 5 3 1

For my mother, Bonnie Sherr Klein,
who teaches me more about shock resilience every day.

I'm not looking to overthrow the American government,
the corporate state already has.
—JOHN TRUDELL
Santee Dakota activist, artist, and poet (1946–2015)

CONTENTS

PART IV | **HOW THINGS COULD GET BETTER**

INTRODUCTION

Shock.

It's a word that has come up again and again since Donald Trump was elected in November 2016—to describe the poll-defying election results, to describe the emotional state of many people watching his ascent to power, and to describe his blitz-krieg approach to policy making. A "shock to the system," in fact, is precisely how his adviser Kellyanne Conway has repeatedly described the new era.

For almost two decades now, I've been studying large-scale shocks to societies—how they happen, how they are exploited by politicians and corporations, and how they are even deliberately deepened in order to gain advantage over a disoriented popula-tion. I have also reported on the flip side of this process: how societies that come together around an understanding of a shared crisis can change the world for the better.

Watching Donald Trump's rise, I've had a strange feeling. It's not just that he's applying shock politics to the most powerful and heavily armed nation on earth. It's more than that. In books, documentary films, and investigative reporting, I have docu-mented a range of trends: the rise of Superbrands, the expanding power of private wealth over the political system, the global imposition of neoliberalism, often using racism and fear of the "other" as a potent tool, the damaging impacts of corporate free trade, and the deep hold that climate change denial has taken on the right side of the political spectrum. And as I began to research Trump, he started to seem to me like Frankenstein's monster, sewn together out of the body parts of all of these and many other dangerous trends.

Ten years ago, I published *The Shock Doctrine: The Rise of Disaster Capitalism*, an investigation that spanned four decades of history, from Chile after Augusto Pinochet's coup to Russia after the collapse of the Soviet Union, from Baghdad under the US "Shock and Awe" attack to New Orleans after Hurricane Katrina. The term "shock doctrine" describes the quite brutal tactic of systematically using the public's disorientation following a collective shock—wars, coups, terrorist attacks, market crashes, or natural disasters—to push through radical pro-corporate measures, often called "shock therapy."

Though Trump breaks the mold in some ways, his shock tactics do follow a script, one familiar from other countries that have had rapid changes imposed under the cover of crisis. During Trump's first week in office, when he was signing that tsunami of executive orders and people were just reeling, madly trying to keep up, I found myself thinking about the human rights advocate Halina Bortnowska's description of Poland's experience when the US imposed economic shock therapy on her country in the midst of Communism's collapse. She described the velocity of change her country was going through as "the difference between dog years and human years," and she observed that "you start witnessing these semi-psychotic reactions. You can no longer expect people to act in their own best interests when they're so disoriented they don't know—or no longer care—what those interests are."

From the evidence so far, it's clear that Trump and his top advisers are hoping for the sort of response Bortnowska described, that they are trying to pull off a domestic shock doctrine. The goal is all-out war on the public sphere and the public interest, whether in the form of antipollution regulations or programs for the hungry. In their place will be unfettered power and freedom for corporations. It's a program so defiantly unjust and so manifestly corrupt that it can only be pulled off with the assistance of divide-and-conquer racial and sexual politics, as well as a nonstop spectacle of media distractions. And of course it is being backed up with a massive increase in war spending, a dramatic escalation of military conflicts on multiple fronts, from Syria to North Korea, alongside presidential musings about how "torture works."

Trump's cabinet of billionaires and multimillionaires tells us a great deal about the administration's underlying goals. Exxon-Mobil for secretary of state. General Dynamics and Boeing to head the department of defense. And the Goldman Sachs guys for pretty much everything that's left. The handful of career politicians who have been put in charge of agencies seem to have been selected either because they do not believe in the agency's core mission, or do not think the agency should exist at all. Steve Bannon, Trump's apparently sidelined chief strategist, was very open about this when he addressed a conservative audience in February 2017. The goal, he said, was the "deconstruction of the administrative state" (by which he meant the government regulations and agencies tasked with protecting people and their rights). And "if you look at these Cabinet nominees, they were selected for a reason, and that is deconstruction."

Much has been made of the conflict between Bannon's Christian nationalism and the transnationalism of Trump's more establishment aides, particularly his son-in-law Jared Kushner. And Bannon may well get voted off this gory reality show entirely before long (perhaps by the time you read these words). Which is why it's worth underlining that when it comes to deconstructing the state, and outsourcing as much as possible to for-profit corporations,

Bannon and Kushner are not in conflict but in perfect alignment.

As this has been unfolding, it struck me that what's happening in Washington is not the usual passing of the baton between parties. It's a naked corporate takeover, one many decades in the making. It seems that the economic interests that have long since paid off both major parties to do their bidding have decided they're tired of playing the game. Apparently, all that wining and dining of elected officials, all that cajoling and legalized bribery, insulted their sense of divine entitlement. So now they're cutting out the middlemen—those needy politicians who are supposed to protect the public interest—and doing what all top dogs do when they want something done right: they are doing it themselves.

Which is why serious questions about conflicts of interest and breaches of ethics barely receive a response. Just as Trump stonewalled on releasing his tax returns, so he has completely refused to sell, or to stop benefiting from, his business empire. That decision, given the Trump Organization's reliance on foreign governments to grant valuable trademark licenses and permits, may in fact contravene the United States Constitution's prohibition on presidents receiving gifts or any "emolument" from foreign governments. Indeed, a lawsuit making this allegation has already been launched.

But the Trumps seem unconcerned. A near-impenetrable sense of impunity—of being above the usual rules and laws—is a defining feature of this administration. Anyone who presents a threat to that impunity is summarily fired—just ask former FBI director James Comey. Up to now in US politics there's been a mask on the corporate state's White House proxies: the smiling actor's face of Ronald Reagan or the faux cowboy persona of George W. Bush (with Dick Cheney/Halliburton scowling in the background). Now the mask is gone. And no one is even bothering to pretend otherwise.

BRANDING

This situation is made all the more squalid by the fact that Trump was never the head of a traditional company but has, rather, long been the figurehead of an empire built around his personal brand—a brand that has, along with his daughter Ivanka's brand, already benefited from its merger with the US presidency in countless ways. The Trump family's business model is part of a broader shift in corporate structure that has taken place within many brand-based multinationals, one with transformative impacts on culture and the job market, trends that I wrote about in my first book, *No Logo: Taking Aim at the Brand Bullies*. What this model tells us is that the very idea that there could be—or should be—any distinction between the Trump brand and the Trump presidency is a concept the current occupant of the White House cannot begin to comprehend. The presidency is in fact the crowning extension of the Trump brand.

As I explored Trump's inextricable relationship with his commercial brand, and its implications for the future of politics, I began to see why so many of the attacks on him have failed to stick—and how we can identify ways of resisting him that will be more effective.

The fact that such defiant levels of profiteering from public office can unfold in full view is disturbing enough. As are so many of Trump's actions in his first months in office. But history shows us that, however destabilized things are now, the shock doctrine means they could get a lot worse.

The main pillars of Trump's political and economic project are: the deconstruction of the regulatory state; a full-bore attack on the welfare state and social services (rationalized in part through bellicose racial fearmongering and attacks on women for exercising their rights); the unleashing of a domestic fossil fuel frenzy (which requires the sweeping aside of climate science and the gagging of large parts of the government bureaucracy);

PREZ GOALS

and a civilizational war against immigrants and "radical Islamic terrorism" (with ever-expanding domestic and foreign theaters).

In addition to the obvious threats this entire project poses to those who are already most vulnerable, it's also a vision that can be counted on to generate wave after wave of crises and shocks. Economic shocks, as market bubbles—inflated thanks to deregulation—burst; security shocks, as blowback from anti-Islamic policies and foreign aggression comes home; weather shocks, as our climate is further destabilized; and industrial shocks, as oil pipelines spill and rigs collapse, which they tend to do when the safety and environmental regulations that prevent chaos are slashed.

All this is dangerous. Even more so is the way the Trump administration can be relied upon to exploit these shocks to push through the more radical planks of its agenda.

A large-scale crisis—whether a terrorist attack or a financial crash—would likely provide the pretext to declare some sort of state of exception or emergency, where the usual rules no longer apply. This, in turn, would provide the cover to push through aspects of the Trump agenda that require a further suspension of core democratic norms—such as his pledge to deny entry to all Muslims (not only those from selected countries), his Twitter threat to bring in "the feds" to quell street violence in Chicago, or his obvious desire to place restrictions on the press. A large-enough economic crisis would offer an excuse to dismantle programs like Social Security, which Trump pledged to protect but which many around him have wanted gone for decades.

Trump may have other reasons for upping the crisis level too. As the Argentine novelist César Aira wrote in 2001, "Any change is a change in the topic." Trump has already proven head-spinningly adept at changing the subject, using everything from mad tweets to Tomahawk missiles. Indeed, his air assault on Syria, in response to a gruesome chemical weapons attack, won him the most laudatory press coverage of his presidency (in some quarters, it sparked an ongoing shift to a more respectful tone). Whether in response to further revelations about Russian connections or scandals related to his labyrinthine international business dealings, we can expect much more of this topic changing—and nothing has the ability to change the topic quite like a large-scale shock.

We don't go into a state of shock when something big and bad happens; it has to be something big and bad *that we do not yet understand*. A state of shock is what results when a gap opens up between events and our initial ability to explain them. When we find ourselves in that position, without a story, without our moorings, a great many people become vulnerable to authority figures telling us to fear one another and relinquish our rights for the greater good.

This is, today, a global phenomenon, not one restricted to the United States. After the coordinated terrorist attacks in Paris in November 2015, the French government declared a state of emergency that banned political gatherings of more than five people—and then extended that status, and the ability to restrict public demonstrations, for months. In Britain, after the shock of the Brexit vote, many said they felt as though they'd woken up in a new, unrecognizable country. It was in that context that the UK's Conservative government began floating a range of regressive reforms, including the idea that the only way for Britain to regain its competitiveness is by slashing regulations and taxes on the wealthy so much that it would effectively become a tax haven for all of Europe. It was also in this context that Prime Minister Theresa May called a snap election against her low-polling rival, clearly in the hope of securing another term in office before the public has a chance to rebel against new austerity measures that are the antithesis of how Brexit was originally sold to voters.

For each of my previous books I spent five or six years deeply researching the subject, examining it from many angles, and reporting from the regions most impacted. The results are hefty tomes, with a whole lot of endnotes. In contrast, I've written this book in just a few months. I've kept it brief and conversational, knowing that few of us have time these days for tomes, and that others are already writing about parts of this intricate story that they grasp far better than me. But I've come to realize that the research I've done over the years can help shed some light on crucial aspects of Trumpism. Tracing the roots of his business model and of his economic policies, reflecting on similar destabilizing moments from history, and learning from people who found effective ways to resist shock tactics can go some way toward explaining how we ended up on this dangerous road, how we can best withstand the shocks to come, and, more importantly, how we can quickly get to much safer ground. This, then, is the beginning of a road map for shock resistance.

Here's one thing I've learned from reporting from dozens of locations in the midst of crisis, whether it was Athens rocked by Greece's debt debacle, or New Orleans after Hurricane Katrina, or Baghdad during the US occupation: these tactics *can* be resisted. To do so, two crucial things have to happen. First, we need a firm grasp on how shock politics work and whose interests they serve. That understanding is how we get out of shock quickly and start fighting back. Second, and equally important, we have to tell a *different* story from the one the shock doctors are peddling, a vision of the world compelling enough to compete head-to-head with theirs. This values-based vision must offer a different path, away from serial shocks—one based on coming together across racial, ethnic, religious, and gender divides, rather than being wrenched further apart, and one based on healing the planet rather than unleashing further destabilizing wars and pollution. Most of all, that vision needs to offer those who are hurting—for lack of jobs, lack of health care, lack of peace, lack of hope—a tangibly better life.

I don't claim to know exactly what that vision looks like. I am figuring it out with everyone else, and I am convinced it can only be birthed out of a genuinely collaborative process, with leadership coming from those most brutalized by our current system. In the final chapters of this book, I'll explore some early and very hopeful grassroots collaborations between dozens of organizations and thinkers who have come together to begin to lay out that kind of agenda, one capable of competing with rising militarism, nationalism, and corporatism. Though still in its early stages, it is becoming possible to see the outlines of a progressive majority, one grounded in a bold plan for the safe and caring world we all want and need.

All this work is born of the knowledge that saying no to bad ideas and bad actors is simply not enough. The firmest of no's has to be accompanied by a bold and forward-looking yes—a plan for the future that is credible and captivating enough that a great many people will fight to see it realized, no matter the shocks and scare tactics thrown their way. No—to Trump, to France's Marine Le Pen, to any number of xenophobic and hypernationalist parties on the rise the world over—may be what initially brings millions into the streets. But it is *yes* that will keep us in the fight.

Yes is the beacon in the coming storms that will prevent us from losing our way.

This book's argument, in a nutshell, is that Trump, extreme as he is, is less an aberration than a logical conclusion—a pastiche of pretty much all the worst trends of the past half century. Trump is the product of powerful systems of thought that rank human life based on race, religion, gender, sexuality, physical appearance, and physical ability—and that have systematically used race as a weapon to advance brutal economic policies since the earliest days of North American colonization and the trans-atlantic slave trade. He is also the personification of the merger of humans and corporations—a one-man megabrand, whose wife and children are spin-off brands, with all the pathologies and conflicts of interest inherent in that. He is the embodiment of the belief that money and power provide license to impose one's will on others, whether that entitlement is expressed by grabbing women or grabbing the finite resources from a planet on the cusp of catastrophic warming. He is the product of a business culture that fetishizes "disruptors" who make their fortunes by flagrantly ignoring both laws and regulatory standards. Most of all, he is the incarnation of a still-powerful free-market ideological project—one embraced by centrist parties as well as conservative ones—that wages war on everything public and commonly held, and imagines corporate CEOs as superheroes who will save humanity. In 2002, George W. Bush threw a ninetieth-birthday party at the White House for the man who was the intellectual architect of that war on the public sphere, the radical free-market economist Milton Friedman. At the celebration, then US secretary of defense Donald Rumsfeld declared, "Milton is the embodiment of the truth that ideas have consequences." He was right—and Donald Trump is a direct consequence of those ideas.

In this sense, there is an important way in which Trump is *not* shocking. He is the entirely predictable, indeed clichéd outcome of ubiquitous ideas and trends that should have been stopped long ago. Which is why, even if this nightmarish presidency were to end tomorrow, the political conditions that produced it, and which are producing replicas around the world, will remain to be confronted. With US vice president Mike Pence or House speaker Paul Ryan waiting in the wings, and a Democratic Party establishment also enmeshed with the billionaire class, the world we need won't be won just by replacing the current occupant of the Oval Office.

About that word *we*: as you read, you may notice that I sometimes say *we* about the United States and sometimes about Canada. One reason for that is pretty simple. I am a citizen of both countries, with deep ties and relationships on both sides of the border. My parents are American, and my extended family all lives in the United States. But I was raised in Canada, and I choose to live here. (On election night, I got a text from my father: "Aren't you glad we already moved to Canada?") Most of my journalism, however, and much of my political work, is in the States, where I've participated in countless meetings and debates about how we can collectively rise to the responsibility of this moment.

Another reason I sometimes say *we* about the US has nothing to do with passports. The fact is, the US presidency impacts everyone on earth. No one is fully protected from the actions of the world's largest economy, the planet's second-largest emitter of greenhouse gases, and the nation with the world's largest military arsenal. Those on the receiving end of Trump's missiles and monstrous bombs bear the greatest burdens and risks by far. But with powers so vast and policies so reckless, everyone on this planet is potentially in the blast zone, the fallout zone, and certainly in the warming zone.

There's no one story that can explain everything about how we arrived at this juncture, no one blueprint for how to fix things—our world is far too braided and complicated for that. This is but one attempt to look at how we got to this surreal political moment; how, in concrete ways, it could get a lot worse; and how, if we keep our heads, we might just be able to flip the script and arrive at a radically better future.

To get started, we first need to understand what we're saying no to—because that *No* on the cover is not just to an individual or even a group of individuals (though it is that too). We're also saying no to the *system* that has elevated them to such heights. And then let's move to a *yes* — a yes that will bring about change so fundamental that today's corporate takeover will be relegated to a historical footnote, a warning to our kids. And Donald Trump and his fellow travelers will be seen for what they are: a symptom of a deep sickness, one that we decided, collectively, to come together and heal.

Note: A small portion of the writing here has appeared in previous essays, books, and speeches; the vast majority, however, is appearing for the first time. Please visit noisnotenough.org for a list of ways to plug into the movements described in these pages, and to connect with many more organizations and theorists.

A full list of sources for all quotes and statistics in this book can also be found there.

PART I

HOW WE GOT HERE: RISE OF THE SUPERBRANDS

We must rapidly begin the shift from a thing-oriented society to a person-oriented society. When machines and computers, profit motives and property rights are considered more important than people, the giant triplets of racism, materialism, and militarism are incapable of being conquered.

—MARTIN LUTHER KING JR.
"Beyond Vietnam," 1967

CHAPTER ONE

HOW TRUMP WON BY BECOMING THE ULTIMATE BRAND

The night Donald Trump was declared the winner of the 2016 election and forty-fifth president of the United States was particularly disorienting for me because it wasn't a night at all. I was in Sydney, Australia, on a lecture tour, and because of the time difference, it was late morning on Wednesday, November 9, where I was. For almost everyone in my life, it was Tuesday night, and friends were sending texts from drunken election-night viewing parties. But for Australians, it was the start of a normal workday, which for me just contributed to the overall feeling of vertigo when the results started coming in.

At the time, I was in a meeting with around fifteen heads of various Australian environmental, labor, and social justice organizations. We were having a discussion that circled around a key insight. Up to now, the fights against global warming, racism, inequality, violations of Indigenous, migrant and women's rights, as well as many other progressive battles, have often been broken up into their own boxes or silos. But we had been asking, as so many movements are today: how do they intersect? What root causes connect them? How can these issues be tackled in tandem, at the same time? What values would govern such a movement? And how could it translate into political power? With a group of colleagues, I had been working on how to build that kind of cross-movement "people's platform" in North America through a project called the Leap Manifesto—which I'll come back to in the final chapter—and there were many Australian groups who were interested in exploring a similar approach.

For the first hour or so, it was a pretty upbeat meeting, with lots of excitement about what was possible. People were feeling totally relaxed about the US elections. Like many progressives and liberals, and even many traditional conservatives, we were sure Trump would lose.

Then everyone's phones started to buzz. And the room grew quieter and quieter, and everyone around the light-filled boardroom began to look increasingly panicked. All of a sudden, the reason for gathering—the idea that we could help spark an integrated leap forward on climate action, racial justice, decent jobs, and more—felt utterly absurd. It was as if everyone instantly understood, without even having to speak, that we were about to be blasted backward by a gale-force wind and all we could do now was try to hold our ground. The idea of forward momentum on any one of the pressing crises on the table seemed to evaporate before our eyes.

Then, without anyone calling it to a close, the meeting dispersed, with colleagues barely saying goodbye to one another. CNN was calling out like some sort of irresistible homing device and we all silently went in search of bigger screens.

Most US voters did not cast a ballot for Donald Trump; Hillary Clinton received nearly 2.9 million more votes, a fact that continues to torment the sitting president. That he won at all is the result of an electoral college system originally designed to protect the power of slave owners. And on the rest of the planet, overwhelming majorities of people told pollsters that if they had been magically able to vote in this pivotal election, they would have cast a ballot for Clinton. (A notable exception to this global trend was Russia, where Trump enjoyed strong support.)

Within this very large anti-Trump camp, we all have different stories about how we felt on that night/day. For many, the defining emotion was shock that this could happen in the United States. For a great many others, it was grief at seeing long-held knowledge about the depth of US racism and misogyny so vividly confirmed. For others, the feeling was one of loss at watching the first female candidate for United States president lose her chance to become a role model for their children. Still others were flooded with feelings of rage that such a compromised candidate was ever put forward against Trump in the first place. And for millions inside the US and out, the primary emotion was fear—a raw bodily knowledge that Trump's presidency would act as a catalyst to unleash extreme acts of racism, violence, and oppression. Many people experienced a mixture of these emotions, and more.

And many also understood that this election result was not only about one man in one country. Trump is but one strand of a seemingly global contagion. We are seeing a surge of authoritarian, xenophobic, far-right politics—from Marine Le Pen in France, to Narendra Modi in India, to Rodrigo Duterte in the Philippines, to the UK Independence Party, to Recep Tayyip Erdoğan in Turkey and all of their counterparts (some explicitly neo-fascist) threatening to take power around the world.

The reason I am sharing my own experience of election day/night in Sydney is that I can't shake the feeling that there is something important to learn from the way Trump's win was able to cut short our conversation, how it severed plans for a forward-looking agenda without so much as a debate. It was perfectly understandable that we all felt that way on election day. But if we accept the premise that, from here on in, the battles are all defense, all about holding our ground against Trump-style regressive attacks, then we will end up in a very dangerous place indeed. Because the ground we were on before Trump was elected is the ground that produced Trump. Ground many of us understood to constitute a social and ecological emergency, even without this latest round of setbacks.

Of course the attacks coming from Trump and his kindred demagogues around the world need resisting fiercely. But we cannot spend the next four years only playing defense. The crises are all so urgent, they won't allow us that lost time. On one issue I know a fair amount about, climate change, humanity has a finite window in which to act, after which protecting anything like a stable climate becomes impossible. And as we'll see in Chapter 4, that window is closing fast.

So we need, somehow, to fight defense and offense simultaneously—to resist the attacks of the present day *and* to find space to build the future we need. To say no and yes at the same time.

But before we can get to what we want instead of Trump and all that he and his administration represent, we need to take an unflinching look at where we are and how we got here, as well as how things will likely get a lot worse in the short term. And, with respect to the latter, be advised: the doom is pretty persuasive. But we can't let it be debilitating. Mapping this territory is tough, but it's the only way to avoid repeating past mistakes and arrive at lasting solutions.

Not a Transition, but a Corporate Coup

What Donald Trump's cabinet of billionaires and multimillionaires represents is a simple fact: the people who already possess an absolutely obscene share of the planet's wealth, and whose share grows greater year after year—the latest figure from Oxfam shows eight men are worth as much as half the world—are determined to grab still more.

According to NBC News in December 2016, Trump's picks

for cabinet appointments had a staggering combined net worth of $14.5 billion (not including "special adviser" Carl Icahn, who's worth more than $15 billion on his own). Moreover, the key figures who populate Trump's cabinet are more than just a representative sample of the ultrarich. To an alarming extent, he has collected a team of individuals who made their personal fortunes by knowingly causing harm to some of the most vulnerable people on the planet, and to the planet itself, often in the midst of crisis. It almost appears to be some sort of job requirement.

There's junk banker Steve Mnuchin, Trump's Treasury secretary, once chairman and lead investor in "foreclosure machine" OneWest, which kicked tens of thousands of people out of their homes after the 2008 financial collapse. There's Trump's secretary of state, Rex Tillerson, former CEO of ExxonMobil, the largest private oil company in the world. The company he headed bankrolled and amplified junk climate science for decades, and lobbied fiercely, behind the scenes, against meaningful international climate action, all while figuring out how Exxon could profit from a warming world. And there are also military and surveillance contractors and paid lobbyists who make up a staggering number of Trump's defense and Homeland Security appointments.

We Were on a Roll

It can be easy to forget, but before Trump's election upset, regular people were standing up to battle injustices represented by many of these very industries and political forces, and they were starting to win. Bernie Sanders's surprisingly powerful presidential campaign, though ultimately unsuccessful, had Wall Street fearing for its bonuses and had won significant changes to the official platform of the Democratic Party. Black Lives Matter and Say Her Name were forcing a national debate about systemic anti-Black racism and militarized policing, and had helped win a phase-out of private prisons and reductions in the number of incarcerated Americans. By 2016, no major sporting or cultural event—from the Oscars to the Super Bowl—could take place without some recognition of how the conversation about race and state violence had changed. Women's movements were turning sexual violence into a front-page issue, shining a spotlight on "rape culture," changing the conversation about high-profile men accused of sexual crimes like Bill Cosby, and helping force the ouster of Roger Ailes from the top job at Fox News, where he was accused of sexually harassing more than two dozen women (allegations he denies).

The climate movement was also on a roll, winning victory after victory against oil pipelines, natural gas fracking, and Arctic drilling, very often with resurgent Indigenous communities in the lead. And more victories were on the way: the climate accord negotiated in Paris in 2015 contained commitments to keep temperatures at a level that would require trillions of dollars' worth of extremely profitable fossil fuel assets to stay in the ground. For a company like ExxonMobil, a realization of those goals was an existential threat.

And as the meeting I attended in Sydney suggested, there was a growing understanding, in the United States and beyond, that the pressing task ahead was to connect the dots among these movements in order to build a common agenda, and with it a winning progressive coalition—one grounded in an ethic of deep social inclusion and planetary care.

The Trump administration, far from being the story of one dangerous and outrageous figure, should be understood partly in this context—as a ferocious backlash against the rising power of overlapping social and political movements demanding a more just and safer world. Rather than risk the possibility of further progress (and further lost profits), this gang of predatory lenders, planet-destabilizing polluters, war and "security" profiteers joined forces to take over the government and protect their ill-gotten wealth. After decades of seeing the public sphere privatized in bits and pieces, Trump and his appointees have now seized control of the government itself. The takeover is complete.

Granting the Corporate Wish List

In the face of his total lack of government experience, Trump sold himself to voters with a somewhat novel two-pronged pitch. First: I'm so rich that I don't need to be bought off. And second: You can trust me to fix this corrupt system because I know it from the inside—I gamed it as a businessman, I bought politicians, I dodged taxes, I outsourced production. So who better than me and my equally rich friends to drain the swamp?

Not surprisingly, something else has occurred. Trump and his cabinet of former executives are remaking government at a startling pace to serve the interests of their own businesses, their former businesses, and their tax bracket as a whole. Within hours of taking office, Trump called for a massive tax cut, which would see corporations pay just 15 percent (down from 35 percent), and pledged to slash regulations by 75 percent. His tax plan includes a range of other breaks and loopholes for very wealthy people like the ones inhabiting his cabinet (not to mention himself). He appointed his son-in-law, Jared Kushner, to head up a "swat team" stacked with corporate executives who have been tasked with finding new regulations to eliminate, new programs to privatize, and new ways to make the US government "run like a great American company." (According to an analysis by Public Citizen, Trump met with at least 190 corporate executives in less than three months in office—before announcing that visitor logs would no longer be made public). Pushed on what the administration had accomplished of substance in its first months, budget director Mick Mulvaney cited Trump's hail of executive orders and stressed this: "Most of these are laws and regulations getting rid of other laws. Regulations getting rid of other regulations."

That they are. Trump and his team are set to detonate programs that protect children from environmental toxins, have told gas companies they no longer need to report all of the powerful greenhouse gases they are spewing, and are pushing dozens and dozens of measures along the same lines. This is, in short, a great unmaking. Which is why Trump and his appointees are laughing at the feeble objections over conflicts of interest—the whole thing is a conflict of interest. That's the point.

And for no one more than Donald Trump, a man who has merged so completely with his corporate brand that he is clearly unable to tell where one stops and the other begins. One of the most remarkable aspects of the Trump presidency so far is the emergence of Mar-a-Lago, Trump's personal resort in Palm Beach, as a carnivalesque, members-only, all-for-profit "Winter White House" (it was even briefly advertised as such on state department websites). One club member told the *New York Times* that going to Mar-a-Lago was like "going to Disneyland and knowing Mickey Mouse will be there all day long"—only in this exercise in full-contact branding, it's not Disneyland but Americaland, and the President of the United States is Mickey Mouse.

The Ultimate Brand Bully

When I read that quote, I realized that if I was going to try to understand this presidency, I'd have to do something I'd resisted for a long time: delve back into the world of corporate marketing and branding that was the subject of my first book, *No Logo*.

The book focused on a key moment in corporate history—when behemoths such as Nike and Apple stopped thinking of themselves primarily as companies that make physical products, and started thinking of themselves first and foremost as manufacturers of brands. It was in the branding—which manufactured a sense of tribal identity—that they believed their fortunes lay. Forget factories. Forget needing to maintain a huge workforce. Once they realized that their biggest profits flowed from manufacturing an image, these "hollow brands" came to the conclusion that it didn't really matter who made their products or how little they were paid. They left that to the contractors—a development with devastating repercussions for workers at home and abroad, and one that was also fueling a new wave of anticorporate resistance.

Researching *No Logo* had required four years of total immersion in branded culture—four years of watching and rewatching Super Bowl ads, scouring *Advertising Age* for the latest innovations in corporate synergy, reading soul-destroying business books on how to get in touch with your personal brand values, making excursions to Niketowns, visiting Asian sweatshops, going to monster malls, to branded towns, heading out on nighttime billboard raids with ad-busters and culture jammers.

Some of it was fun—I'm far from immune to the allure of good marketing. But by the end, it was as if I had passed some kind of tolerance threshold and developed a condition close to a brand allergy. If Starbucks had come up with a new way to "unbrand" their stores, or Victoria's Secret had appropriated Indigenous headdresses on the runway, I didn't want to write about it—I had moved on and left that rapacious world behind. The trouble is, to understand Trump you really have to understand the world that made him what he is, and that, to a very large extent, is the world of branding. He reflects all the worst trends I wrote about in *No Logo*, from shrugging off responsibility for the workers who make your products via a web of often abusive contractors to the insatiable colonial need to mark every available space with your name. Which is why I decided to delve back into that glossy world to see what it could tell us about how Donald Trump rose to the world's most powerful job, and maybe even what it was saying about the state of politics more broadly.

Transcending the World of Things

The rise of the Superbrands, like the one Trump built around his brash persona, has its roots in a single, seemingly innocuous idea developed by management theorists in the mid-1980s, that to be successful, corporations must primarily produce brands as opposed to products.

Until that time, although it was understood in the corporate world that bolstering one's brand name through advertising was important, the primary concern of every solid manufacturer was the production of goods. As a 1938 editorial in *Fortune* magazine put it, "the basic and irreversible function of an industrial economy is the making of things . . . It is in the factory and on the land and under the land that purchasing power originates."

But by the 1980s, sales of classic brand-name goods like Tide, Levi's, and Marlboro had begun to falter. The problem seemed to be that the market was flooded with nearly identical products and, with the economy in recession, many were making decisions based on price, not brand name. The old tricks—billboards, TV ads—didn't seem to be working anymore; it was as if consumers had built up some sort of resistance. (Or, as ad executive David Lubars memorably put it, consumers "are like roaches—you spray them and spray them and they get immune after a while.")

At around this same time, a new kind of corporation began to rival the traditional all-American manufacturers for market share. These were the Nikes and Apples and, later, the Tommy Hilfigers and Starbucks and so on. These pioneers had a different model: Create a transcendent idea or brand surrounding your company. Use it to connect with consumers who share its values. Then charge a steep premium for products that are less about the objects themselves than about the profound human desire to be part of a tribe, a circle of belonging.

So when kids lined up all night to buy $250 Nike sneakers, they weren't exactly buying the sneakers; they were buying the idea of "Just Do It" and the dream of Michael Jordan, who had become a one-man Superbrand, a term first used to describe the athlete's growing empire. When their parents bought Apple computers, they were bringing home a piece of a deeply optimistic vision of the future, captured in the slogan "Think Different." (The aura of authenticity increased with each revolutionary and artistic icon, living or dead, whose face graced the campaign: Gandhi, Martin Luther King, Picasso, Mandela, the Dalai Lama.) And when commuters were suddenly paying four times what they used to for a cup of coffee, it was because Starbucks wasn't really selling coffee; it was selling, according to its CEO, the idea of the "third place," not home, not work. (The third place used to be actual community spaces where people would gather without the help of corporations, but those spaces were fast disappearing.)

Another key development in this period was the notion that, since the true product was the brand, it could be projected onto any number of seemingly unconnected physical commodities. Ralph Lauren launched a line of paints, Virgin went into wedding dresses and colas, Starbucks had a line of jazz CDs. The possibilities seemed endless.

Many of these highly branded companies made the (then) bold claim that producing goods was only an incidental part of their operations, and that, thanks to recent victories in trade liberalization and labor law reform, they could have their products produced for them at bargain-basement prices by contractors and subcontractors, many of them overseas. It didn't really matter who did the physical work, because the real value lay not in manufacturing but in design, innovation, and of course marketing.

A consensus soon emerged at the management level that a great many corporations that did not embrace this model were bloated, oversized; they owned too much, employed too many people, and were weighed down with too many things. The old-fashioned process of producing—running one's own factories, being responsible for tens of thousands of full-time, permanent employees—began to look less like the route to success and more like a clunky liability. The goal was to become a hollow-brand— own little, brand everything.

Pretty soon, multinationals were competing in a race toward weightlessness: whoever owned the least, had the fewest employees on the payroll, and produced the most powerful images as opposed to things, won the race.

No Space, Few Jobs

The meteoric rise of this business model had two immediate impacts. Our culture became more and more crowded with marketing, as brands searched out fresh space and new "brand extensions" with which to project their big ideas and reach their target markets. Work and workers, on the other hand, experienced a sharp discounting and were treated as increasingly disposable.

Brands like Nike and Adidas competed fiercely in the marketing sphere, and yet they manufactured their products in some of the same factories, with the same workers stitching their shoes. And why not? Making stuff was no longer considered a "core competency." Head offices (now increasingly being called "campuses") wanted to be as free as possible to focus on what they considered the real business at hand: creating a corporate mythology powerful enough to project meaning onto pretty much any object, simply by stamping their brand on it.

In the press, this phenomenon was often reported as Company X or Y deciding to move their factories to a part of the world where labor was cheaper. But as I found when I visited sweatshops producing name-brand goods like Gap clothing and IBM computers in Indonesia and the Philippines, the truth was somewhat different. In most cases, these companies were not moving their factories in North America and Europe and reopening them in Asia, but rather closing them down and never reopening them, anywhere. This period saw a proliferation of very complex supply chains, where it became increasingly difficult to sort out where a product was being produced and by whom. It also saw a wave of scandals: again and again intrepid investigative journalists and labor groups would reveal that, say, a Michael Jordan–branded Nike shoe or a Disney-branded t-shirt was being made under horrific sweatshop conditions in Haiti or Indonesia. But when journalists or consumers tried to hold the brand accountable, the company would almost invariably declare, "We're as horrified as you are. Which is why we're going to stop doing business with that contractor."

It's no secret why this model took off. If you did it right—if you made beautiful commercials, invested heavily in design, and tried to embody your brand identity through countless sponsorship arrangements and cross-promotions—many people were willing to pay almost anything for your products. Which is why the success of what came to be called "lifestyle brands" set off a kind of mania, with brands competing with one another over who had the most expansive network of brand extensions, or who could create the most immersive 3-D experiences—chances for customers to crawl inside and merge with their favorite brands.

So what does all this 1990s history have to do with Donald Trump? A great deal. Trump built an empire by following this formula precisely. And then, as a candidate, he figured out how to profit from the rage and despair it left behind in communities that used to do the kind of well-paid manufacturing that companies like his long ago abandoned. It's quite a con.

The Trump Show

In the eighties, when Trump first became a national figure, he was still a fairly traditional real estate developer who happened to have a bottomless desire to see his own name in print and pretty much everywhere else. He splashed his name on buildings around New York and Atlantic City; he worked the press relentlessly; and he turned his relationship with his wife and mistress into a live-action soap opera. As a result, Trump punched above his weight in terms of visibility: His face gazed off the cover of magazines, from *Time* to GQ. He landed cameos in Hollywood films and TV shows. And he understood something essential about branding early on. As he told *Playboy*: "The show is Trump, and it is sold-out performances everywhere." Even so, the core of his business remained conventional: acquiring real estate and running those buildings, whether hotels or condo towers or casinos.

In the nineties, that started to change, mostly because Trump had so mismanaged his Atlantic City casinos that his bankers were taking over more and more of his business, even before he had his first few bankruptcies under his belt. He didn't lose total control over his properties, though. Investors appeared to be convinced that they needed the Trump name—his personal brand—to keep the house of cards from crashing down. And that proved an important lesson in the real-world value of a studiously promoted name.

Even though he was still primarily a builder, Trump had seen the way companies like Nike were making a killing on the hollow-brand model. And gradually, he followed suit. At the start, his innovation was that he branded a part of the economy that had never been branded before: high-end real estate. Obviously, there were global branded hotel and resort chains before. But Trump pioneered the idea that where you work (an office tower), where you live (a condominium), and where you play (your golf club or vacation destination) would all be franchises of a single global luxury brand. Much like Celebration, Florida—Disney's fully branded town—Trump was selling the opportunity for people to live inside his brand, 24/7.

The real breakthrough, however, came when Mark Burnett, head of a reality TV empire, pitched Trump on the idea of *The Apprentice*. Up until then, Trump had been busy coping with the fallout from his bankruptcies and the impatience of his bankers. Now, out of the blue, he was being offered a chance to leap into the stratosphere of Superbrands, those rarefied companies earning their enormous profits primarily by building up their brand meaning and then projecting it hither and yon, liberated from the burden of having to make their own products—or, in Trump's case, build his own buildings.

He understood the potential immediately. Because the show would put the brightest possible spotlight on his gilded lifestyle, with long, lingering shots of his palatial homes and his luxury jets, it would do wonders to solidify his decades-long mission to equate the name Trump with material success. Before the first episode even aired, he was already lining up deals to license his name for a menswear line. He told the network's publicist that, even if *The Apprentice* "doesn't get ratings, it's still going to be great for my brand."

But it did get ratings—impressive ones. And pretty soon he had launched a complete menu of spinoff brands—from Trump cologne to Trump water to Trump eyewear to Trump mattresses to Trump University. As far as the current president of the United States was concerned, there was no category of product that couldn't be brought into the Trump-branded bubble.

Most importantly, with *The Apprentice*, Trump wasn't paying, as other brands do, to have his brand featured in a hit network TV show; he was getting paid a fortune for priceless free advertising.

More than that, his shows collected millions by promoting other brands. In April 2011, for example, *The Celebrity Apprentice* was paid to promote more products on the air than any other show, 120 product placements in all. This is the mark of a true Superbrand: Trump built a brand that contains brand multitudes. (And in bringing his children into the show, he even began to *breed* brands.)

After you have pulled off a feat like that, what's your next trick? Merge your brand with the ultimate symbol of power and authority: the White House.

Oligarch Chic

But before that could happen, Trump needed one more thing to complete his transformation. He radically changed the core of his business: real estate. Rather than building and owning the structures himself, as he had earlier in his career, Trump realized that he could make far easier money simply by selling his name to developers around the world, who would use his celebrity to attract buyers and customers for their office buildings, condos, and hotels. The outside developers would do the construction and carry all the liabilities. If the projects failed (as they frequently did), Trump still collected his licensing fee. And the fees were enormous. According to the *Washington Post*, on a single hotel-condo project in Panama, "Trump has earned at least $50 million on the project on virtually zero investment."

He still owns a few flagship properties, including Trump Tower in New York and Mar-a-Lago in Florida. But if you look at the broader network of a great many Trump-branded properties — from the Trump International Golf Club in Dubai to the many other Trump properties in India, Canada, Brazil, South Korea, and New York City—what you see is that Trump either doesn't

Leasing his brand

own them himself or owns just a piece of them. His revenue comes from leasing his name.

A large part of Trump's international success was timing. He entered the global high-end real estate market at a time when an unprecedented amount of untaxed private wealth was sloshing around looking for safe places to park, as it still is. According to James S. Henry, a senior advisor with the UK-based Tax Justice Network, in 2015 the estimated private financial wealth of individuals stashed unreported in tax havens around the globe was somewhere between $24 trillion and $36 trillion. Gilded condos, with a flashy aesthetic pitched perfectly to newly minted oligarchs from Moscow to Colombia, fit the bill perfectly.

But Trump's market wasn't just the rich. His *Apprentice*-era brand empire allowed him to appeal to wealthy and middle-income consumers simultaneously. For the well-heeled and flashy, there was membership at his beach and golf clubs, or a unit in a Trump-branded tower, with furnishings from the Trump homeware collection. For the masses who don't have that kind of cash, Trump auctioned off little pieces of the dream—a glossy red Trump tie, a Trump steak, a Trump book.

You Are All Fired!

Trump won the White House on a campaign that railed ceaselessly against the loss of manufacturing jobs—the same kind of jobs he has outsourced at virtually every opportunity. As a businessman, he took full advantage of the outsourcing economy, as does Ivanka's company. And, unsurprisingly, there have been major investigative reports detailing the appalling conditions under which Trump's ties are made in Shengzhou, China, for instance, and the even worse conditions in the Chinese factories producing Ivanka's line of footwear. In April 2017, the Fair Labor Association, a watchdog that grew out of the sweatshop scandals in the nineties, issued a report disclosing that workers in a factory in China producing for a major supplier of Ivanka's dresses and blouses put in close to 60 hours a week, and earned what works out to a little over $1 an hour (well below the average wage for urban Chinese manufacturing workers). Most employees also lacked health and maternity benefits—not a good look for an advocate of women in the workforce.

The construction of many Trump-branded hotels and towers has been plagued with similar controversies, in the US and abroad. An investigation by *Vice*, for instance, revealed that the treatment of migrant workers constructing a Trump-branded golf course in Dubai stood out even in a city notorious for slave-like labor conditions. Ben Anderson, who produced the report, describes worker dorms in which "guys live 21 to a room with rats running around above them" and bathrooms that "didn't look fit for human beings."

The Trump Organization issued a statement about its "zero tolerance policy for unlawful labor practices at any project bearing the 'Trump' name." Needless to say, this particular project was being built by an outside company; Trump had just leased his name.

Some brands would have been badly battered by these types of revelations. The Trump Organization just shrugs them off. And that has everything to do with the big branding idea around which Donald Trump chose to build his empire.

Immune to Scandal

Trump publicly defines his brand identity as quality and luxury. But that's a sleight of hand: Trump hotels and resorts don't even make it into the top ten luxury accommodation brands in the world, lists that reliably include names such as Four Seasons and Oberoi (as if to underline the point, Mar-a-Lago was cited for nearly a dozen food safety violations in January 2017). The truth, which doesn't sound nearly as glamorous, is that the Trump brand stands for wealth itself—or, to put it more crassly, money. That's why its aesthetics are *Dynasty*-meets-Louis XIV. It's why Trump's relationship to gold is the inverse of Superman's relationship to kryptonite: Trump crumples when he is more than three feet away from something big and shiny.

Donald Trump's personal brand is slightly different but intimately related. His brand is being the ultimate boss, the guy who is so rich he can do whatever he wants, whenever he wants, and to whomever he wants (including grabbing whichever woman he wants, by whichever body part he wants).

This helps explain why signifiers of Trump's wealth are so important to him. Gold curtains and shots of his private jets are how Trump constantly reinforces his brand as the ultimate capitalist success story—power and wealth incarnate. It's why he placed his personal wealth (however exaggerated) at the center of his campaign for president.

It's also why no labor scandal is ever going to stick to him. In the world he has created, he's just acting like a "winner"; if someone gets stepped on, they are obviously a loser. And this doesn't only apply to labor scandals—virtually every traditional political scandal bounces off Trump. That's because Trump didn't just enter politics as a so-called outsider, somebody who doesn't play by the rules. He entered politics playing by a completely different set of rules—the rules of branding.

According to those rules, you don't need to be objectively good or decent; you only need to be true and consistent to the brand you have created. That's why brand managers are so obsessed with discipline and repetition: once you have identified what your core brand is, your only job is to embody that brand, project that brand, and repeat its message. If you stay focused, very little can touch you.

That's a problem when applied to a sitting US president, especially because over many, many years, and with a startling level of consistency, Donald Trump created a brand that is entirely amoral. On the campaign trail, Trump was able to shrug off almost every conventional "gotcha." Caught dodging federal taxes? That's just being "smart." Wouldn't reveal his tax returns? Who's going to make him? He was only half joking on the campaign trail when he said, "I could stand in the middle of Fifth Avenue and shoot somebody and I wouldn't lose any voters." In Trump's world, impunity, even more than lots of gold, is the ultimate signifier of success.

This has grave implications for any hope of preventing this administration from acting as an open kleptocracy. But as we will see in the next chapter, there *are* ways to pierce Trump's brand bubble. You just have to know where to place the needle.

CHAPTER TWO

THE FIRST FAMILY OF BRANDS

Donald Trump may never have thought he had a chance of winning the White House; very few people did. But after he won the Republican nomination, he clearly realized he had the ultimate branding tool within reach: the US presidency. Every single minute he is president, his brand value and the value of his ongoing businesses is increasing, and he is therefore directly and significantly profiting from public office—precisely what conflict-of-interest rules are designed to prevent.

So now we are in entirely uncharted territory, because let's face it: human megabrands are a relatively new phenomenon. There's no rulebook that foresaw any of this. People keep asking—is he going to divest? Is he going to sell his businesses? Is Ivanka going to? But it's not at all clear what these questions even mean, because their primary businesses are their names. You can't disentangle Trump the man from Trump the brand; those two entities merged long ago. Every time he sets foot in one of his properties—a golf club, a hotel, a beach club—White House press corps in tow, he is increasing his overall brand value, which allows his company to sell more memberships, rent more rooms, and increase fees.

The logic of how the Trump family sees the relationship between branding and political office was laid bare in the lawsuit

Melania Trump launched just before she became First Lady. She demanded $150 million in damages from the company that owns the *Daily Mail* website for falsely implying she worked in the past as an escort. And she had every right to sue for damages for that. But what was the basis for saying she had lost a staggering $150 million, given that she barely has a business of her own? The core of her legal case was that, as First Lady, she would have built—in the future—a valuable brand "in multiple product categories, each of which could have garnered multimillion-dollar business relationships for a multi-year term during which Plaintiff is one of the most photographed women in the world." (The *Daily Mail* settled, apologizing to Trump and paying out an undisclosed sum.)

It's not unprecedented for first wives to parlay their political profile into a lifestyle brand. Samantha Cameron, wife of David, waited just five months after her husband stepped down as British prime minister before announcing her own "working women" clothing line. But what is striking about Melania's now-settled lawsuit is that she seemed to be trying to skip the stage of actually launching a serious brand and instead went straight to claiming the money. Moreover those original court filings make plain how the Trumps see public office: as a short-term investment to enormously swell the value of your commercial brand in the long run.

We can also see this with Ivanka, whose products have notoriously been hawked by taxpayer-funded public employees, including her father via Twitter, and his adviser Kellyanne Conway, who went on national television to do what she described as a "commercial," telling viewers to "Go buy Ivanka's stuff!" The conflicts tipped into self-parody on April 6, 2017, when, the *Associated Press* reported, "Ivanka Trump's company won provisional approval from the Chinese government for three new trademarks, giving it monopoly rights to sell Ivanka brand jewellery, bags and spa services in the world's second-largest economy." But that's not the only thing that happened that day. "That night, the first daughter and her husband, Jared Kushner, sat next to the president of China and his wife for a steak and Dover sole dinner at Mar-a-Lago." A political summit whose details had been arranged by none other than Jared Kushner. Asked about these kinds of conflicts, Ivanka invariably stresses that just as her father has supposedly distanced himself from the Trump Organization by putting it in the hands of his sons (while he still collects the profits), Ivanka has put her company in the hands of "independent trustees"—her husband's brother and sister (while she still collects the profits). This goes well beyond nepotism; it's the US government as a for-profit family business.

We know that Trump's presidency has made the family of brands more valuable because Ivanka's business reported record sales after Kellyanne Conway made her televised pitch. Mar-a-Lago has already increased its membership fees, to $200,000 a year from $100,000. And why not? Now, for your fee, you might find yourself witnessing a high-stakes conversation about national security over dinner. You might get to hobnob with a visiting head of state. You might even get to witness Trump announcing that he has just launched an air assault on a foreign country. And, of course, you might even get to meet the President himself, and have the chance to quietly influence him. (No public records are kept of who comes and goes from the club, so who knows?) For decades, Trump has been selling the allure of proximity to wealth and power—it is the meaning of his brand. But now he's able to offer, to his paying customers, the real deal.

Trump's ownership of Mar-a-Lago is telling in itself. A decade before Trump purchased the property in 1985, the owner of the estate, socialite Marjorie Merriweather Post, had bequeathed it to the US government in the hopes that it could be used as a presidential retreat or a "Winter White House." But no president used it and it was eventually returned. Long before the 2016 election, Trump had enjoyed boasting about the fact that he lived in a house intended for presidents. Indeed, in retrospect it is as if he was playing at being president for three decades. And now, with the 2016 elections, that fantasy has become a reality— or is it reality that has been swallowed whole by Trump's fantasy? As with all things Trump, it's genuinely difficult to tell. Trump may call his Palm Beach estate the "Winter White House" or the "Southern White House," but it is, of course, no such thing. The White House is a public institution; Mar-a-Lago remains a private, for-profit, members-only club with the proceeds flowing directly to Trump and his family.

Any president who refused to sell his business would face potential conflicts of interest, since the actions of the US government can impact everything from stock prices to, as we will see in a couple of chapters, the price of oil. But brand-based companies like Trump's are different beasts entirely. The conflicts of interest are not only tied to specific policies or actions. Rather, the conflicts are omnipresent and continuous, embedded in the mere fact of Trump being president. That's because the value of lifestyle brands fluctuates wildly depending on the space they occupy in the culture. So anything that increases Donald Trump's visibility, and the perception of him as all-powerful, actively increases the value of the Trump brand, and therefore increases how much clients will pay to be associated with it—to slap it on their new condo development, say, or, on a smaller scale, to play on his golf courses or buy one of his ties.

And there is no sign that Trump is backing off exploiting that fact to its fullest advantage. According to a *New York Times* report in April 2017, "Mr. Trump's enterprise, now run by his two adult sons, has 157 trademark applications pending in 36 countries."

What Exactly Are the Trump Boys Selling?

In January 2017, Donald Trump's son Eric went on a trip to Uruguay to meet with a developer who is buying the right to use the Trump name on his new tower. At the time, the public scandal was how much US taxpayers' money went to pay for the Secret Service and other government staff who traveled with Eric on that trip: around $100,000 in hotel costs, a direct public subsidy to Trump's private dealings. But the deeper scandal is what they were in Uruguay to promote: the Trump brand, which had just been made so much more valuable by the fact that its owner was about to be sworn in as US president.

And this says nothing about the potential for corruption, which is dizzying. Given that what the Trump sons—Eric and Donald Jr.—are selling is ephemeral (a name), a buyer could pay $6 million for it or could pay $60 million. Who's to judge what constitutes a fair market-value price? More worryingly, who's to say what services are being purchased when a private company pays millions to lease the Trump brand? Do they really think it's that valuable to their condo tower, or do they think that by throwing in an extra $5 million, they might be looked on more favorably in other dealings that require a friendly relationship with the White House? It's very difficult to see how any of this can be untangled. A brand is worth whatever buyers are willing to pay for it. That's always been the appeal of building a business on this model—that something as ephemeral as a name could be vested with such real-world monetary value.

The Trump Organization has said it will not make any new deals for foreign properties, to prevent an appearance of impropriety. But this isn't just an international question. If a US city or state government grants a Trump development a break on taxes or regulations, are they really doing it because they think this particular business will help their community—or because they want something from the White House? Same goes for any government or business—foreign or domestic—that chooses a Trump property for an event or as a place for employees to stay. Do they really think it's the best option, or are they trying to curry favor?

What's fascinating about these ethics questions is that they are so similar to the scandals surrounding the Clinton Foundation, which may well have contributed to Hillary's electoral loss. There were many thorny questions about what a private company or foreign government thought they were getting when they made a hefty donation to the Clinton Foundation. Were they being purely philanthropic, moved by the scourge of infectious diseases and childhood obesity? Or were they also making a calculation that their donation would pay some dividends because Hillary Clinton was secretary of state and looked likely to become the next US president?

US. Clinton Foundation

Those were valid concerns, and Trump didn't hesitate to raise them about his rival. But with the money the Trump sons are collecting from leasing their father's name, and the favors they are negotiating, the potential for influence peddling is of a different order: we now have money flowing to the family of a sitting president, not a projected president, and with not even the pretext of philanthropy, which the Clinton Foundation at least had. This is not to exonerate the Clintons—far from it. The decades Bill and Hillary spent blurring ethical lines at the Foundation are part of what set the stage for Trump to annihilate those lines altogether (more on that in Chapter 6).

Reagan's Prophecy Fulfilled

A few months into the new administration, the cover of the *New Yorker* featured an illustration of Trump whacking golf balls at the White House, shattering window after window. It's a striking image, in large part because it slowly dawns that the broken windows are not at Mar-a-Lago or Trump Tower but the publicly owned building where Trump's own family has assiduously avoided living.

And this points to a difficult truth. With every alleged ethics violation, with every brazen lie, with every deranged tweet, this administration leaves the public sphere more broken and degraded. Even if corruption (or treason) ultimately costs Trump the White House, what will be left behind will be wreckage—proof of the fundamental premise of Trump's political project: that government is not just a swamp, it's a burden. That there is nothing worth protecting. That private is better than public. And if that's all true, why not wreck the place before you leave—figuratively if not literally.

It's a reminder that Trump's political career would have been impossible without the degradation of the whole idea of the public sphere, which has been unfolding over decades. It could never have happened without the idea that "government is not the solution, it is the problem," as Ronald Reagan famously put it. And it could never have happened had that message not been followed up with decades of deregulation that essentially legalized bribery, with outrageous sums of corporate money flowing into politics.

It's absolutely true that the system is corrupt. It *is* a swamp. And people know it. They know that the rewriting of the rules in favor of a small group of corporate interests and the one percent has been a bipartisan process—that it was Bill Clinton who deregulated the banks, setting the stage for the 2008 collapse, and it was Obama who chose not to prosecute the bankers, and that the Democratic candidate running against Trump would almost surely have done no different.

Sure, it's preposterous for a self-described billionaire sitting on a golden throne to pass himself off as a savior of the working class. But a pitch as patently irrational as "Trust me *because* I cheated the system" could only have sold to a significant portion of the American public because what passed for "business as usual" in Washington well before Trump looked a whole lot like corruption to everyone else.

That's why so many people have been happy to treat electoral politics as macabre entertainment. Once politics has reached such a debased state, why bother protecting it from a boor like Trump? It's a cesspool anyway, so let the games begin. As a resident of Toronto, this is a pathology that I've lived through before. Our former mayor, Rob Ford, was something of a municipal rehearsal for Trump. Ford, who died in 2016, created a performance-based image that was impossible to shame—because his brand was being shameless. Even when he was caught on tape smoking crack, it didn't finish him off, because it was still the wacky Rob Ford show, and his supporters were his semi-ironic loyal audience, taking it all in like a *Saturday Night Live* sketch. But, as with Trump, the over-the-top performance and the personal scandals distracted from a sinister agenda, a pseudopopulism that specialized in handouts to corporations, a blank check for police, and eroded services for the most vulnerable.

I didn't foresee branding culture going this far when I started writing about it twenty years ago. But I'm also not surprised. Back then, I saw branding as a colonial process: it seeks to absorb ever more space and real estate and create a self-enclosed bubble. What's extraordinary about Donald Trump's presidency is that now we are all inside the Trump branded world, whether we want to be or not. We have all become extras in his for-profit reality TV show, which has expanded to swallow the most powerful government in the world.

Is there any escape? The essential immorality of Trump's brand does present unique barriers to holding this administration accountable. And yet there is hope. In fact, Trump's animating life force—the quest for money—may actually make him more vulnerable than any president before.

Jam the Trump Brand

Back when I published *No Logo*, we used to call it "culture jamming," and the trick was always the same: identify the big bold idea a company is selling and then expose the dirty reality behind the shine. The ability of consumers and activists to impact the behavior of a commercial brand has been demonstrated many times, most recently by the successful campaign to push Bill O'Reilly off the air at Fox News, following revelations that he and his employer had paid out $13 million to settle sexual harassment allegations (without admission of guilt).

Realizing that there was no shaming the O'Reilly brand, Color of Change, a racial justice organization, alongside several women's groups, took a backdoor approach: they went after the show's advertisers, informing them that they were now considered accomplices in what seemed to be a long-term strategy of buying women's silence. The advertisers heard the same from thousands of customers, online and off, and they began fleeing from the show in droves. Within less than three weeks of the settlement revelations breaking in the *New York Times*, and despite having the highest rated show on US cable news, O'Reilly was off the air (though with a golden handshake reportedly worth as much as $25 million).

The campaign showed that any brand can be jammed, even one as defiantly amoral as Trump's—you just need to understand its weak points.

Since Trump's personal brand is being "the boss" who does what he wants, one way to mess with it is to make him look like a puppet. It doesn't really matter who is yanking the strings. Once they're exposed, Trump's carefully nurtured image begins to slip. And this tactic clearly works: Trump was driven so mad by the persistent jokes about #PresidentBannon that he took to Twitter to proclaim himself the supreme decider, and the status of his once all-powerful chief strategist seemed to rapidly decline.

Since the Trump brand is all about having bags and bags of money, the other way to jam it is to make him less rich. And as with the O'Reilly strategy, the best way to do that is by sending his branding empire into crisis. #GrabYourWallet, the clearinghouse for boycotts of Trump's web of brands, has been on this since before Trump was elected, and has successfully helped to pressure several chains to drop various Trump brands.

In the grand scheme of Trump's branding empire, these are dents. The main source of revenue for the Trump Organization is selling and renting office and condo units and leasing Trump's name to real estate companies around the world. Trump was clearly betting that being president would drive up the price. But what if he is proven wrong? What if he starts losing commercial renters because they are coming under pressure for their association with his brand (several boycott campaigns like this are already under way)? And what if developers come under so much public pressure that they decide having Trump's name on their façade is actually costing them revenue? Already, in New York City, tenants of Trump Place demanded that their building manager take the Trump name off their home. As one resident said, she was tired of feeling "disgust" each time she walked into her building. The manager complied and Trump's name was removed.

And when the Trump sons went to Vancouver to celebrate the opening of the latest Trump temple, they were met with protests and boycotts from local politicians. If these kinds of protests spread, more developers could decide to de-Trump themselves. And it's a fair bet that if his golden name starts disappearing off giant phallic symbols from Vancouver to Manila, Trump would not take it well, nor would his sons, who are reportedly already worried about the damage that senior advisors like Steve Bannon may have done to the family name.

In a parallel tactic, when the White House closed down its call-in comment lines in January 2017, one group—whitehouseinc.org—suggested voters phone Trump hotels and resorts and tell whoever answered that they were upset about the president's plans to take away their health insurance, or any other policy grievances they had. It was a smart tactic. Tens of thousands reportedly made the calls, and one month later the White House reopened the lines.

If any of this seems unfair, consider this: The whole reason we expect politicians to divest their financial holdings, or put them in a real blind trust, is that having active business holdings while serving in office creates all kinds of opportunities for conflicts of interest and backdoor influence. Trump has chosen not to divest. His adviser-daughter has made the same choice. Which is why it's perfectly legitimate to use those choices to try to influence the hell out of them.

If his branding empire loses enough revenue, and his personal boss image is sufficiently battered, Trump might just course-correct on some of his more inflammatory policies. At the very least, jamming his central pitch to voters—"trust me, I'm a successful billionaire"—will hurt his chances in 2020.

But before we get there, we are all going to be subjected to a lot more of the Trump show.

CHAPTER THREE

THE MAR-A-LAGO HUNGER GAMES

Ronald Reagan was once asked what it was like to be president after being an actor, and he reportedly said, "How can a president not be an actor?" You can imagine Trump thinking the same thing about being a reality TV star.

Trump's mastery of the genre was pivotal in the construction of his branded empire and it was essential to his successful run for president. And now Trump is using those same skills he learned on *The Apprentice*—the belief that he can cut, edit, and reshape reality to fit a largely pre-scripted, self-aggrandizing outcome—to transform not just the White House, but large parts of the world.

The King of Live-Action Trickle-Down

The colonization of network television by reality TV at the turn of the millennium happened at a speed that few could have predicted. In very short order, North Americans went from deriving entertainment from scripted shows with the same recurring characters and dramas week after week, season after season, to watching seemingly unscripted shows where the drama came from people's willingness to eject one another from whatever simulation of reality happened to be on display. Tens of millions were glued to their sets as participants were voted off the island on *Survivor*, voted out of the mansion on *The Bachelor*—and, eventually, fired by Donald Trump.

The timing makes sense. The first season of *Survivor*—so wildly successful that it spawned an army of imitators—was in 2000. That was two decades after the "free-market revolution" had been kicked into high gear by Ronald Reagan and Margaret Thatcher, with its veneration of greed, individualism, and competition as the governing principles of society. It was now possible to peddle as mass entertainment the act of watching people turn on each other for a pot of gold.

The whole genre—the alliances, the backstabbing, the one person left standing—was always a kind of capitalist burlesque. Before *The Apprentice*, however, there was at least the pretext that it was about something else: how to survive in the wilderness, how to catch a husband, how to be a housemate. With Donald Trump's arrival, the veneer was gone. *The Apprentice* was explicitly about the race to survive in the cutthroat "jungle" of late capitalism.

The first episode began with a shot of a homeless person sleeping rough on the street—a loser, in other words. Then the camera cut to Trump in his limo, living the dream—the ultimate winner. The message was unmistakable: you can be the homeless guy, or you can be Trump. That was the whole sadistic drama of the show—play your cards right and be the one lucky winner, or suffer the abject humiliation of being berated and then fired by the boss. It was quite a cultural feat: after decades of mass layoffs, declining living standards, and the normalization of extremely precarious employment, Mark Burnett and Donald Trump delivered the coup de grâce: they turned the act of firing people into mass entertainment.

Life's a Bitch

Every week, to millions of viewers, *The Apprentice* delivered the central sales pitch of free-market theory, telling viewers that by unleashing your most selfish and ruthless side, you are actually a hero—creating jobs and fueling growth. Don't be nice, be a killer. That's how you help the economy and, more importantly, yourself.

In later seasons, the underlying cruelty of the show grew even more sadistic. The winning team lived in a luxurious mansion—drinking champagne in inflatable pool loungers, zipping off in limos to meet celebrities. The losing team was deported to tents in the backyard, nicknamed "Trump trailer park."

The tent-dwellers, whom Trump gleefully deemed the "have-nots," didn't have electricity, ate off paper plates, and slept to the sounds of howling dogs. They would peek through a gap in the hedge to see what decadent wonders the "haves" were enjoying. In other words, Trump and Burnett deliberately created a microcosm of the very real and ever-widening inequalities outside the show, the same injustices that have enraged many Trump voters—but they played those inequalities for kicks, turning them into a spectator sport. (There was a slight *Hunger Games* quality to it, though hemmed in by network television restrictions on non-simulated violence.) On one show, Trump told the tent team that "life's a bitch," so they'd better do everything possible to step over the losers and become a winner like him.

What's interesting about this particular piece of televised class warfare, which aired in 2007, is that the pretense sold to a previous generation—capitalism was going to create the best of all possible worlds—is completely absent. No: this is a system that generates a few big winners and hordes of losers, so you'd better make damn sure you are on the winning team.

This reflects the fact that, for well over a decade now, the ideological and intellectual side of the neoliberal project has been in severe crisis. In 2016, Credit Suisse estimated that there is roughly $256 trillion in total global wealth—with a staggeringly unequal distribution: "While the bottom half collectively own less than 1 percent of total wealth, the wealthiest top 10 percent own 89 percent of all global assets." Which is why there just aren't many serious people left who are willing to argue, with a straight face, that giving more to the wealthy is the best way to help the poor. Trump's pitch has always been different. From the start, it was: I will turn you into a winner—and together we can crush the losers.

In a Real-World Nightmare, Dreams Sell

It's worth remembering that Trump's breakthrough to national celebrity status came not via a real estate deal, but a book about making real estate deals. *The Art of the Deal*, marketed as holding the secrets to fabulous financial wealth, was published in 1987—the peak of the Reagan era. It was followed up over the years with crasser variations on the same theme: *Think Like a Billionaire, Think Big and Kick Ass, Trump 101*, and *How to Get Rich*.

Trump first started selling the notion that he held the ticket to joining the top one percent of income earners at the precise moment when many of the ladders that provided social mobility between classes—like free quality public education—were being kicked away, and just as the social safety net was being shredded. All of this meant that the drive to magically strike it rich, to win big, to make it to that safe economic stratum, became increasingly frantic.

Trump, who was born wealthy, expertly profited off that desperation across many platforms, but most infamously through Trump University. In one ad for the scandal-plagued and now-defunct "university" (actually a series of dodgy seminars in hotel meeting rooms), Trump declared, "I can turn anyone into a successful real estate investor, including you."

And then there were the casinos, a large chunk of Trump's US real estate portfolio. The dream at the center of the casino economy is not so different from the dream for sale at Trump University or in *How to Get Rich*: you may be on the verge of personal bankruptcy today, but if you (literally) play your cards right, you could be living large by morning.

This is central to how Trump built his brand and amassed his wealth—by selling the promise that "you too could be Donald Trump"—at a time when life was becoming so much more precarious if you weren't in the richest one percent. He then turned around and used that very same pitch to voters—that he would make America a country of winners again—exploiting those deep economic anxieties and using all the reality-simulation skills that he had picked up from years at the helm of a top-rated TV show. After decades of hawking how-to-get-rich manuals, Donald Trump understands exactly how little needs to be behind the promise—whether on renegotiating trade deals or bringing back manufacturing—if the desperation is great enough.

Reveling in the Fake on the Road to the White House

Well before Trump's rise, elections had already crossed over into ratings-driven infotainment on cable news. What Trump did was to exponentially increase the entertainment factor, and therefore the ratings. As a veteran of the form, he understood that if elections had become a form of reality TV, then the best contestant (which is not the same thing as the best candidate) would win. Maybe they wouldn't win the final vote, but they would at least win wall-to-wall coverage, which from a branding perspective is still winning. As Trump said when he was contemplating a presidential run in 2000 (he decided against it): "It's very possible that I could be the first presidential candidate to run and make money on it."

Since the election, we've heard a few mea culpas from media executives acknowledging that they helped Trump's electoral rise by giving him such an outsized portion of their coverage. And that's true, they helped enormously, but the hand-wringing doesn't go nearly far enough. They are also responsible because the biggest gift to Trump was not just airtime but the entire infotainment model of covering elections, which endlessly plays up interpersonal dramas between the candidates while largely abandoning the traditional journalistic task of delving into policy specifics and explaining how different candidates' positions on issues such as health care and regulatory reform will play out in voters' lives.

The Tyndall Report found that, through the entire election, the three major nightly network news shows combined spent a total of just 32 minutes on "issues coverage"—down from an already paltry 220 minutes in the 2008 election. The rest was the reality show of who said what about whom, and who was leading which poll where. For millions of viewers, the result was highly entertaining. (Which is likely why French media followed a markedly similar formula to cover its high-stakes 2017 elections.)

This is worth underlining: Trump didn't create the problem—he exploited it. And because he understood the conventions of fake reality better than anyone, he took the game to a whole new level.

Fake Fights, Real Stakes

Trump didn't just bring reality TV expertise to electoral politics—he mashed that up with another blockbuster entertainment genre that is also based on a cartoonishly fake performance of reality:

professional wrestling. It's hard to overstate Trump's fascination with wrestling. He has performed as himself (the ultrarich boss) in World Wrestling Entertainment (WWE) appearances at least eight times, enough to earn him a place in the WWE Hall of Fame. In a "Battle of the Billionaires," he pretended to pound wrestling kingpin Vince McMahon and then celebrated victory by publicly shaving McMahon's head in front of the cheering throngs. He also dropped thousands of dollars in cash into the audience of screaming fans. Now, he has appointed the former CEO of WWE, Linda McMahon (wife of Vince), to his cabinet as head of the Small Business Administration, a detail that has largely been lost amidst the daily deluge.

As with *The Apprentice*, Trump's side career in pro wrestling exposed and endeared him to a massive audience—in stadiums, on TV, and online. Pro wrestling might be largely invisible as a cultural force to most liberal voters, but WWE generates close to a billion dollars in annual revenue. And Trump did more than pick up votes from this experience—he also picked up tips.

As Matt Taibbi pointed out in *Rolling Stone*, Trump's entire campaign had a distinctly WWE quality. His carefully nurtured feuds with other candidates were pure pro wrestling, especially the way he handed out insulting nicknames ("Little Marco," "Lyin' Ted"). And most wrestling-like of all was the way Trump played ringmaster at his rallies, complete with over-the-top insult-chants ("Lock her up!" "Killary") and directing the crowd's rage at the arena's designated villains: journalists and demonstrators. Outsiders would emerge from these events shaken, not sure what had just happened. What happened is that they had just been to a bizarre cross between a pro-wrestling match and a white supremacist rally.

What reality television and professional wrestling have in common is that they are forms of mass entertainment that are relatively new in American culture, and they both establish a curious relationship with reality—one that is both fake and still somehow genuine at the same time.

With WWE, every fight is fixed, everybody knows that it's rehearsed. But that doesn't lessen the enjoyment in any way. The fact that everyone is in on the joke, that the cheers and boos are part of the show, increases the fun. The artifice is not a drawback— it's the point.

Wrestling and reality TV both thrive on the spectacle of extreme emotion, conflict, and suffering. They both involve people screaming at each other and pulling each other's hair out and, in the case of wrestling, beating the crap out of each other. But at the same time as you're watching it, you know it's not real, so you don't have to care; you get to be part of the drama without having to feel any empathy. Nobody cries when wrestlers get slammed and humiliated, any more than we were meant to cry for *The Apprentice* contestants when Trump fired or humiliated them. It's a safe place to laugh at suffering. And it was all part of preparing the ground for that Igor of all things fake, Donald Trump. Fake body parts, fake wrestling, fake-reality TV, fake news, and his whole fake business model.

And now Trump has grafted this same warped relationship to reality onto his administration. He announces that Obama wiretapped him in the same way that a wrestler declares he's going to annihilate and humiliate his opponent. Whether or not it's true is beside the point. It's part of rousing the crowd, part of the theater. *The Apprentice* may be off the air, and Trump may have retired his WWE career, but the show is still on. Indeed, it never stops.

Newt Gingrich, who has been a pretty faithful cheerleader of Donald Trump, was asked shortly before inauguration what he thought of the president-elect's decision to keep his position as executive producer of *Celebrity Apprentice*. His answer was quite revealing. He said Trump was making a mistake because he "is going to be the executive producer of a thing called the American government. He's going to have a huge TV show called 'Leading the World.'"

And that's exactly what's happening. The Trump Show is now broadcasting live from the Oval Office. And from Mar-a-Lago, which is even more like a TV show because its well-heeled members provide a built-in live studio audience. And it's clear that this is precisely how Trump sees his presidency too, as the executive producer of a country, always with an eye on the ratings. Responding to the suggestion that he might fire his gaffe-machine of a press secretary, he reportedly said, "I'm not firing Sean Spicer. That guy gets great ratings. Everyone tunes in."

RATINGS

It's with the same brash showmanship that Trump is now navigating—or failing to navigate—the promises he made to bring back the bygone days of booming factories and blue-collar jobs that paid middle-class wages, promises that he would impose a "Buy American, Hire American" policy (never mind that his own empire is built on outsourcing and exploited labor).

This posture is as authentic as the violence he enacted when he appeared to take on a WWE wrestler in the ring, or when he was choosing from among contestants on *Celebrity Apprentice*. Trump knows as well as anyone that the idea of American corporations returning to 1970s-style manufacturing is a cruel joke. He knows this because, as his own business practices attest, a great many US companies are no longer manufacturers at all, but hollow shells, buying their own products from a web of cheap contractors. He may be able to bring back a few factories, or claim that he did, but the numbers will be minuscule compared with the need. (There is a real way to create a great many well-paying jobs—but it looks nothing like the Trump approach. It requires looking to the future, not the past, as we'll see in the final chapter.)

Trump's game plan, which is already under way, is to approach the unemployment and underemployment crisis in the same way he approaches everything—as a spectacle. He will claim credit for a relatively small number of jobs—most of which would have been created anyway—and then market the hell out of those supposed success stories. It won't matter one bit whether the job numbers support his claims. He'll edit reality to fit his narrative, just as he learned to do on *The Apprentice*, and just as he did on his very first day as president, insisting, against all objective evidence, that his inauguration crowds had been historic.

This is what Trump does, and has always done. In 1992, when his empire was teetering on the edge of bankruptcy thanks to a series of bad investment decisions, he didn't deal with the situation by getting his finances in order. Instead, he threw an elaborate "comeback party" for his investors and financiers at the Trump Taj Mahal in Atlantic City, which culminated in Trump—wearing satin boxing shorts and red boxing gloves—punching through a paper wall to the theme song from *Rocky*. This is a man who thinks he can solve anything with the right stage-managed performance, and very often in the past he's been proven right. So just as he spun and performed his way out of bankruptcy, he is convinced he can do the same with the country's economy.

Fake News, Alternative Facts, and the Big Lie

If we know anything for certain, it's that hard facts don't matter in Donald Trump's world. With Trump, it's not so much the Big Lie as the Constant Lies. Yes, he tells big ones, like the time he implied Ted Cruz's dad had a role in assassinating JFK, and his years of lies about Obama's place of birth. But it's the continuous stream of lies—notoriously offered to us as "alternative facts"—that is most dizzying. According to a *Politico* investigation, this is quite deliberate: "White House staffers do much of their lying for sport, rather than to further any larger agenda," even competing over who can "smuggle the biggest whoppers into print." Though these claims are based on anonymous sources, and so may themselves be lies, the story fits with what we know about Trump: what good is reaching the pinnacle of power if you can't bend reality to your will? In Trump's world, and according to the internal logic of his brand, lying with impunity is all part of being the big boss. Being tethered to fixed, boring facts is for losers.

And so far it seems to be working, at least with his base. Some liberals have seized upon this apparent tolerance for "alternative facts" to dismiss his working-class voters as "suckers." But it's worth remembering that a large portion of Barack Obama's base was quite happy to embrace the carefully crafted symbols his administration created—the White House lit up like a rainbow to celebrate gay marriage; the shift to a civil, erudite tone; the spectacle of an incredibly appealing first family free of major scandals for eight years. And these were all good things. But, too often, these same supporters looked the other way when it came to the drone warfare that killed countless civilians, or the deportations of roughly 2.5 million immigrants without documents during Obama's term, or his broken promises to close Guantanamo or shut down George W. Bush's mass-surveillance architecture. Obama positioned himself as a climate hero, but at one point bragged that his administration had "added enough new oil and gas pipelines to encircle the Earth and then some."

In Canada, many liberals are displaying the same kind of selective blindness. Dazzled by the progressive messaging of our handsome prime minister, they are letting him hang on to many of his predecessor's disastrous policies, from the indefinite detention of many immigrants to ramming through tar sands pipelines (more on that later). Politically, Justin Trudeau is very different from Donald Trump, but for his staunchest supporters—who often behave a lot like fans—his celebrity has a similarly distorting effect. This new "Trudeaumania" reminds us that conservatives aren't the only ones capable of confusing engaged citizenship with brand loyalty.

Of course, Trump's successful attempt to sell his white working class voters on the dream of a manufacturing comeback will eventually come crashing down to earth. But what is most worrying is what Trump will do then, once it's no longer possible to hide the fact that coal jobs aren't coming back, and neither are the factory jobs that paid workers enough to provide their families with a middle-class life. In all likelihood, Trump will then fall back on the only other tools he has: he'll double down on pitting white workers against immigrant workers, do more to rile up fears about Black crime, more to whip up an absurd frenzy about transgendered people and bathrooms, and launch fiercer attacks on reproductive rights and on the press.

And then, of course, there's always war.

The Apocalypse Show

Acknowledging that Trump's presidency is being produced like a reality show in no way diminishes the danger it represents — quite the opposite. People have already died in this show — in Yemen, in Afghanistan, in Syria, in the United States — and many more will meet the same fate before it goes off the air. In March alone, a UK-based monitoring group recorded allegations of more than 1,500 civilian deaths from US-led coalition airstrikes in Iraq and Syria, higher than ever recorded under Obama.

But that doesn't mean it's not a show. Blood-sport reality TV is, after all, a science-fiction cliché. Think of *The Hunger Games*, with its reality TV spectacle in which all the players die but one. Or *The Running Man*, another film about a televised event where the stakes are life or death. (Wilbur Ross, Trump's commerce secretary, reportedly described the bombing of Syria as Mar-a-Lago's "after-dinner entertainment.")

The most chilling part is that, as I write, Trump has only just started playing his version of *The Mar-a-Lago Hunger Games* with the full arsenal of US military power as his props—and he is getting plenty of encouragement to keep upping the ante. When Trump launched Tomahawk missiles on Syria, MSNBC host Brian Williams declared the images "beautiful." Just one week later, Trump went for more spectacle, dropping the largest non-nuclear weapon in the US arsenal on a cave complex in Afghanistan, an act of violence so indiscriminate and disproportionate that analysts struggled to find any rationale that could resemble a coherent military strategy. Because there was no strategy—the megatonnage is the message. Mass communication through bombs.

Given that Trump ordered the use of a weapon that had never been deployed in combat before, and given that he did this just twelve weeks into his presidency and with no obvious provocation, there is little reason to hope he will be able to resist putting on the show of shows—the televised apocalyptic violence of a full-blown war, complete with its guaranteed blockbuster ratings. Well before Trump, we had wars fought as televised entertainment. The 1990 Gulf War was dubbed the first video-game war, complete with its own logo and theme music on CNN. But that was nothing compared with the show put on during the 2003 Iraq invasion, based on a military strategy called "Shock and Awe." The attacks were designed as a spectacle for cable news consumers, but also for Iraqis, to maximize their sense of helplessness, to "teach them a lesson." Now, that fearsome technology is in the hands of the first reality TV president. We need to get ready, a subject I'll return to in Chapter 9.

Hollow Man

If there is one real aspect to the festival of fakery that is the Trump presidency, it's the hunger at the heart of it. The sheer insatiability. Trump likes to talk about how he doesn't need more money—he has more than enough. Yet he just can't help selling his products at every opportunity, can't stop working every angle. It's as if he suffers from some obscure modern illness—let's call it a brand personality disorder—that causes him to slip into brand promotion almost involuntarily. He'll be giving a political speech and then, suddenly, he's talking about how beautiful and expensive the marble is at a Trump hotel, or gratuitously telling his interviewer, when discussing how he ordered a lethal bombing of Syria, that the chocolate cake at Mar-a-Lago is "the most beautiful . . . you've ever seen."

That unquenchable hunger, that hollowness at the center, does speak to something real—to a profound emptiness at the heart of the very culture that spawned Donald Trump. And that hollowness is intimately connected to the rise of lifestyle brands, the shift that gave Trump an ever-expanding platform. The rise of the hollow brands—selling everything, owning next to nothing—happened over decades when the key institutions that used to provide individuals with a sense of community and shared identity were in sharp decline: tightly knit neighborhoods where people looked out for one another; large workplaces that held out the promise of a job for life; space and time for ordinary people to make their own art, not just consume it; organized religion; political movements and trade unions that were grounded in face-to-face relationships; public-interest media that strove to knit nations together in a common conversation.

All these institutions and traditions were and are imperfect, often deeply so. They left many people out, and very often enforced an unhealthy conformity. But they did offer something we humans need for our well-being, and for which we never cease to long: community, connection, a sense of mission larger than our immediate atomized desires. These two trends—the decline of communal institutions and the expansion of corporate brands in our culture—have had an inverse, seesaw-like relationship to one another over the decades: as the influence of those institutions that provided us with that essential sense of belonging went down, the power of commercial brands went up.

I've always taken solace from this dynamic. It means that, while our branded world can exploit the unmet need to be part of something larger than ourselves, it can't fill it in any sustained way: you make a purchase to be part of a tribe, a big idea, a revolution, and it feels good for a moment, but the satisfaction wears off almost before you've thrown out the packaging for that new pair of sneakers, that latest model iPhone, or whatever the surrogate is. Then you have to find a way to fill the void again. It's the perfect formula for endless consumption and perpetual self-commodification through social media, and it's a disaster for the planet, which cannot sustain these levels of consumption.

But it's always worth remembering: at the heart of this cycle is that very powerful force—the human longing for community and connection, which simply refuses to die. And that means there is still hope: if we rebuild our communities and begin to derive more meaning and a sense of the good life from them, many of us are going to be less susceptible to the siren song of mindless consumerism (and while we're at it, we might even spend less time producing and editing our personal brands on social media).

As we'll see in Part IV, many movements and theorists are working toward just this kind of shift in culture and values. Before we get to that, though, there are a few more important trails we need to follow to help us understand how we ended up here.

PART II

WHERE WE ARE NOW: CLIMATE OF INEQUALITY

I imagine that one of the reasons people cling to their hates so stubbornly is because they sense, once hate is gone, that they will be forced to deal with pain.

—JAMES BALDWIN
Notes of a Native Son, 1955

CHAPTER FOUR

THE CLIMATE CLOCK
STRIKES MIDNIGHT

Let's rewind a bit, to the week Trump won. At that moment, I was reeling from witnessing not one catastrophe, but two. And I don't think we can understand the true danger of the Trump disaster unless we grapple with both of them.

As I mentioned, I was in Australia for work, but I was also very conscious that, because of the carbon involved in that kind of travel, I might not be able to return for a long time. So I decided to visit, for the first time in my life, the Great Barrier Reef off the coast of Queensland, a World Heritage Site and the earth's largest natural structure made up of living creatures. It was simultaneously the most beautiful and the most frightening thing I had ever seen.

I spent a lot of time underwater as a kid. My father taught me to snorkel when I was six or seven, and those are some of my happiest memories. There was always something amazing to me about the intimacy of the interactions with ocean life. When you first swim up to a reef, the fish mostly scatter. But if you hang out for a few minutes, they stop seeing you as an intruder and you become part of the seascape to them—they'll swim right up to your mask, or nibble on your arm. As an anxious kid, I always found these experiences wonderfully dreamlike and peaceful.

As the Australian trip approached, I realized that my feelings about seeing the Reef were tied up in my being the mother of a four-year-old boy, Toma. As parents, we can sometimes make the mistake of exposing kids too early to all the threats and dangers facing the natural world. The first book about nature that a lot of children read is Dr. Seuss's *The Lorax*, which is all about pollution and beautiful places being turned into garbage and all the animals dying and disappearing and choking. It's really scary. I read it to Toma when he was two and watched the terror cross his face. And I thought, "No, this is completely wrong." Now we read stories about fast-talking squirrels and books that celebrate nature's beauty and wonder. Even if I know these books are about species that are on the brink of extinction, Toma doesn't need to worry about that yet. I figure that my job is to try to create as many positive experiences as possible that will attach him to the natural world. You need to love something first, before you can protect and defend it.

I also wanted to go to the Reef in my role as a journalist. Over the previous two years, something unprecedented in recorded history had happened. Because of record-breaking temperatures, more than 90 percent of the Great Barrier Reef had been impacted by what's known as a "mass bleaching event." It's hard to stress just how cataclysmic the bleaching has been. When coral is bleached, those beautiful, intensely colored creatures—an ecosystem as rich and teeming as the Amazon rain forest—turn ghostly and bone-white. Bleached coral can recover, if temperatures quickly go back down to normal levels. This time, they hadn't gone back down—so almost a quarter of the Reef has died.

It's worth underlining how little warming it took to bring about such a radical change. Ocean temperatures went up just one degree Celsius higher than the levels to which these incredible species are adapted, and that was enough for a massive die-off. Unlike many other climate change–related events, this wasn't some dramatic storm or wildfire—just silent, watery death.

When we got to the Reef, there was still an air of unreality about the whole thing: the Port Douglas boats packed with tourists were still going out, the surface of the water was blue and beautiful, there were stretches of spectacular turquoise. But the ocean has a way of hiding humanity's worst secrets, a lesson I first learned covering BP's Deepwater Horizon disaster, and seeing how quickly the spill disappeared from the headlines once the oil began to sink, though the damage below continued unabated.

We went out on the Reef with a team of extraordinarily dedicated marine biologists (all of whom were emotionally shattered by what they had been documenting) and a film crew from the *Guardian*. We started filming the parts of the Reef that are still alive and we managed to get Toma to put on a snorkel. To be honest, I wasn't sure he was going to be able to focus on the coral at all; he had just learned to swim and was wearing floaties. But the scientists were incredibly patient with him, and there were about five solid minutes when he really was able to pull it off and have a flash of true wonder—he "saw Nemo," he saw a sea cucumber. I think he even saw a sea turtle. These parts of the Reef, the ones that are neither bleached nor dead, are only a fraction of the whole, but they are still glorious—a riot of life, of electric-colored coral and fish, sea turtles and sharks swimming by.

We didn't take Toma on the boat when we filmed the dead and bleached parts of the Reef. And it was a graveyard. It was as if a cosmic switch had been flipped and suddenly one of the most beautiful places on earth had been turned into one of the ugliest. The coral bones were covered in a goo of decaying life—a brown goo. You just wanted to get away from there. Our wetsuits stank of death.

We chose to film the Reef in this state because, for many people, there is a sense that climate change is a distant crisis, that there's still a bit of time to procrastinate before we get serious. We wanted to show that radical changes to our planet, including parts we count on to be brimming with life, are not far off in the future—they are happening right now. And the impacts are enormous, including the fact that roughly one billion people around the world rely on the fish sustained by coral reefs for food and income.

And I wanted to try to show the disaster through Toma's eyes too. Because one of the most unjust aspects of climate disruption (and there are many) is that our actions as adults today will have their most severe impact on the lives of generations yet to come, as well as kids alive today who are too young to impact policy— kids like Toma and his friends, and their generation the world over. These children have done nothing to create the crisis, but they are the ones who will deal with the most extreme weather— the storms and droughts and fires and rising seas—and all the social and economic stresses that will flow as a result. They are the ones growing up amidst a mass extinction, robbed of so much beauty and so much of the companionship that comes from being surrounded by other life forms.

It is a form of theft, of violence—what the author and theorist Rob Nixon calls "slow violence." A clean, vibrant planet is the birthright of all living beings. That's why the Great Barrier Reef is classified as a World Heritage Site. It belongs to the world, and it is dying on our watch. I realized that the story I wanted to tell is about intergenerational theft and intergenerational justice. That's why I decided to put Toma on camera for the first time; I was reluctant, but I just couldn't tell that story without him.

By the end of the day, we were all completely wiped out. We had seen so much death, so much loss, but my son had also had this special experience. That night, tucking him into bed in our Port Douglas motel room, I said: "Toma, today is the day when you discovered there is a secret world under the sea." And he just looked up at me with an expression of pure bliss and said, "I saw it." I burst into tears, some mixture of joy and heartbreak at the knowledge that, just as he is becoming aware of this beauty in the world, all this magic, it is being drained away.

I have to admit, I was angry too. That whole day I had not been able to stop thinking about ExxonMobil—about how this company, it has now been documented, knew about climate change as far back as the seventies. According to a groundbreaking investigation by *InsideClimate News* (nominated for a Pulitzer Prize), Exxon did its own cutting-edge empirical research, taking CO_2 samples off its oil tankers and building state-of-the art climate models that predicted the coming changes such as sea-level rise. It also received warnings from its own senior scientists, including James Black who was categorical in his reports to his employer about the "general scientific agreement that the most likely manner in which mankind is influencing the global climate is through carbon dioxide release from the burning of fossil fuels." He also wrote that "man has a time window of five to 10 years before the need for hard decisions regarding changes in energy strategies might become critical." That was in 1978.

By the time Rex Tillerson took over the job of general manager of the central production division of Exxon USA, these facts had long been known in the company, including the uncomfortable one about how little time remained. Despite this, ExxonMobil has since then lavished more than $30 million on think tanks that systematically spread doubt through the press about the reality of climate science. Mobil (before its merger with Exxon) even took out its own full-page ads in the *New York Times* casting doubt on the science. ExxonMobil is currently under investigation by the attorneys general of New York, California, and Massachusetts for these alleged deceptions. Because of this campaign of misinformation, promoted by the entire fossil fuel sector, humanity lost key decades when we could have been taking the actions necessary to move to a clean economy—the same decades in which

ExxonMobil and others opened up vast frontiers for oil and gas. If we had not lost that time, the Great Barrier Reef might still be healthy today.

But my time at the Reef didn't leave me feeling entirely helpless. Because there are dogged communities and growing movements around the world determined to get their governments to wake up and stop drilling new oil and gas fields and digging new coal mines. We rushed like mad to turn the film around in four days so it could be out on the eve of the US elections, thinking it might play some tiny part in motivating people to vote, and then in fueling the pressure to get Hillary Clinton to do more on climate. And we made it—we posted the video on November 7.

The next day, Trump won. And then ExxonMobil's CEO was named secretary of state.

Truth Time

The stakes in the 2016 election were enormously high for a great many reasons, from the millions who stood to lose their health insurance to those targeted by racist attacks as Trump fanned the flames of rising white nationalism; from the families that stood to be torn apart by cruel immigration policies to the prospect of women losing the right to decide whether or not to become mothers, to the reality of sexual assault being normalized and trivialized at the highest reaches of power. With so many lives on the line, there is nothing to be gained by ranking issues by urgency and playing "my crisis is bigger than your crisis." If it's happening to you, if it's your family being torn apart or you who is being singled out for police harassment, or your grandmother who cannot afford a life-saving treatment, or your drinking water that's laced with lead—it's all a five-alarm fire.

Climate change isn't more important than any of these other issues, but it does have a different relationship to time. When the politics of climate change go wrong—and they are very, very wrong right now—we don't get to try again in four years. Because in four years the earth will have been radically changed by all the gases emitted in the interim, and our chances of averting an irreversible catastrophe will have shrunk.

This may sound alarmist, but I have interviewed the leading scientists in the world on this question, and their research shows that it's simply a neutral description of reality. The window during which there is time to lower emissions sufficiently to avoid truly catastrophic warming is closing rapidly. Lots of social movements have adopted Samuel Beckett's famous line "Try again. Fail again. Fail better" as a lighthearted motto. I've always liked the attitude; we can't be perfect, we won't always win, but we should strive to improve. The trouble is, Beckett's dictum doesn't work for climate—not at this stage in the game. If we keep failing to lower emissions, if we keep failing to kick-start the transition in earnest away from fossil fuels and to an economy based on renewables, if we keep dodging the question of wasteful consumption and the quest for more and more and bigger and bigger, there won't be more opportunities to fail better.

Nearly everything is moving faster than the climate change modeling projected, including Arctic sea-ice loss, ice-sheet collapse, ocean warming, sea-level rise, and coral bleaching. The next time voters in countries around the world go to the polls, more sea ice will have melted, more coastal land will have been lost, more species will have disappeared for good. The chance for us to keep temperatures below what it would take for island nations such as, say, Tuvalu or the Maldives to be saved from drowning becomes that much slimmer. These are irreversible changes—we don't get a do-over on a drowned country.

The latest peer-reviewed science tells us that if we want a good shot at protecting coastal cities in my son's lifetime—including metropolises like New York City and Mumbai—then we need to get off fossil fuels with superhuman speed. A paper from Oxford University that came out during the campaign, published in the *Applied Energy* journal, concluded that for humanity to have a fifty-fifty chance of meeting the temperature targets set in the climate accord negotiated in Paris at the end of 2015, every new power plant would have to be zero-carbon starting in 2018. That's the second year of the Trump presidency.

For most of us—including me—this is very hard information to wrap our heads around, because we are used to narratives that reassure us about the inevitability of eventual progress. Martin Luther King Jr. said, "The arc of the moral universe is long, but it bends toward justice." It's a powerful idea that sadly doesn't work for the climate crisis. The wealthy governments of the world have procrastinated for so long, and made the problem so much worse in the meantime, that the arc has to bend very, very fast now—or the shot at justice is gone for good. We are almost at midnight on the climate clock.

Not Just Another Election Cycle—Epic Bad Timing

During the Democratic primaries, I was really struck by the moment when a young woman confronted Hillary Clinton on the campaign trail and asked her if—given the scale of the global warming crisis—she would pledge not to take any more money from the fossil fuel interests that are supercharging it. Up to that point, Clinton's campaign had received large sums of money from employees and registered lobbyists of fossil fuel companies—about $1.7 million, according to Greenpeace's research. Clinton looked disgusted and snapped at the young woman, saying she was "so sick" of this issue coming up. A few days later, in an interview, Clinton said young people should "do their own research." The woman who had asked the question, Eva Resnick-Day, worked as a campaigner for Greenpeace. She had done her research, she insisted, "and that is why we are so terrified for the future. . . . What happens in the next four or eight years could determine the future of our planet and the human species."

For me, her words cut to the heart of why this was not just another election cycle. Why it was not only legitimate but necessary to question Hillary's web of corporate entanglements. Resnick-Day's comments also highlight one of the big reasons why Trump's presidency is harrowing: the most powerful man in the world is a person who says global warming is a hoax invented by the Chinese, and who is feverishly trashing the (already inadequate) restraints on fossil fuels that his country had put in place, encouraging other governments to do the same. And it's all happening at the worst possible time in human history.

We have so far warmed the planet by just one degree Celsius, and from that, we are already seeing dramatic results: the mass coral die-off, balmy Arctic weather leading to severe ice loss, the breaking apart of Antarctic ice sheets. If we continue on our current pollution trajectory, we are set to warm the planet by four to six degrees Celsius. The climate scientist and emissions expert Kevin Anderson says that four degrees of warming is "incompatible with any reasonable characterization of an organized, equitable and civilized global community." That is why governments came together in Paris and drew up an agreement to make their best efforts to get off this dangerous course, and try to limit warming to "well below" 2 degrees, pursuing efforts to keep it below 1.5 degrees. The high end of that temperature target represents double the warming we have already experienced, so it's by no means safe.

Which is why we have to try very hard to hit the lower end of that target. And that's tough. According to a September 2016 study by the Washington-based think tank Oil Change International, if governments want a solid chance of keeping temperature increases below two degrees Celsius, then all new and undeveloped fossil fuel reserves need to stay in the ground. The problem is, even before Trump, no major economy was doing what was required. They were all still trying to have it all ways—introducing some solid green policies but then approving expanded fossil fuel extraction and new pipelines. It's like eating lots of salad and a whole lot of junk food at the same time, and expecting to lose weight.

In the United States, Obama introduced the Clean Power Plan, which was set to accelerate the retirement of the country's aging coal plants and to require new ones to capture some of their carbon emissions, but he was simultaneously presiding over a boom in natural gas fracking and fracked oil in the Bakken. In Canada, the government has introduced national carbon pricing and a coal phaseout, but it is also allowing the tar sands to expand and approved a massive new liquid gas export terminal—pretty much guaranteeing that it won't hit its Paris goals.

Even so, the fact that so many governments signed the Paris accord to great fanfare, and at least paid lip service to the need to achieve its ambitious temperature targets, gave the climate movement a lot of leverage to push for policies that were in step with the stated goal. We were trying to hold them to their word in Paris, and we were making some progress.

But now Trump is saying: Leave all that money in the ground? Are you nuts?!

A Very Oily Administration

On the campaign trail, Trump's standard stump speech reliably hit all the crowd-pleasers: build the wall, bring back the jobs, law and order, Crooked Hillary. Climate change denial usually didn't make the list (though Trump would spout off if asked). But if the issue seemed peripheral during the campaign, that changed as soon as Trump began making appointments. And since his inauguration, taking aim at any and all climate protections has been a defining feature of the Trump administration. As if in a race against time, he and his team have set out to systematically tick off every single item on the fossil fuel industry's wish list. His top appointments, his plans to make severe budget cuts and gut environmental regulations, his conspiratorial denials of climate change, and even his entanglements with Russia—they all point in the same direction: a deep and abiding determination to kick off a no-holds-barred fossil fuel frenzy. There are many plots and intrigues swirling around Washington, most notoriously claims about the Trump team conspiring with Russia to influence the 2016 election outcome—and these are being investigated, as they should be. But make no mistake: Trump's collusion with the fossil fuel sector is the conspiracy hiding in plain sight.

Within days of taking office, he pushed through the Dakota Access pipeline, cutting off an environmental review and against the powerful opposition of the Standing Rock Sioux. He's cleared the way to approve the Keystone XL pipeline from Alberta, which Obama rejected in part because of the climate impacts. He has issued an executive order to roll back Obama's moratorium on new coal leases on federal lands, and has already announced plans to expand oil and gas drilling on the Gulf Coast. He's also killing Obama's Clean Power Plan. And as the administration rubber-stamps new fossil fuel projects, they're getting rid of all kinds of environmental regulations that made digging up and processing this carbon less profitable for companies like ExxonMobil. As a result, these projects, already disastrous from a climate perspective, are more likely to lead to industrial accidents like the Deepwater Horizon disaster—because that's what happens when regulators are missing in action.

As I write, it's not yet clear whether the US will officially withdraw from the Paris Accord; there is some disagreement about this within the administration. But whether the country stays or leaves it's undeniable that the Trump administration is shredding the commitments made under the accord.

In addition to Rex Tillerson, Trump has stacked his administration with fossil fuel executives and political figures with extensive ties to the industry—several of whom are opposed, or at best indifferent, to the mandates of the agencies they're now in charge of running. Scott Pruitt is Trump's head of the Environmental Protection Agency—but, as attorney general of Oklahoma, he sued the EPA multiple times and, perhaps not coincidentally, has received tens of thousands of dollars from fossil fuel companies. Trump's pick for energy secretary, Rick Perry, had myriad ties to the oil industry, including serving on the boards of two of the companies behind the Dakota Access pipeline. Back in 2011, while running for the GOP nomination, Perry campaigned on eliminating the energy department entirely.

Don't Ask, Don't Tell

Together, this group of men is doing favors for oil, gas, and coal companies on multiple fronts. For instance, Trump has killed a new program that required oil and gas companies to report how much methane—a very powerful greenhouse gas—their operations were releasing, including from leaks. Industry hated the program, which was only finalized in the last weeks of Obama's administration, in part because it was poised to blow the lid off the claim that natural gas is in any way a climate change solution. Trump is handing the industry a big gift by effectively saying: don't tell us, we don't want to know. From here on in, the rest of the world will have to guess the extent to which the US is a climate renegade, because a key piece of the data won't exist.

By far the biggest threat this industry faces is the demand for real action on climate change being voiced by people around the world, and the mounting consensus that taking the crisis seriously means a halt on new fossil fuel projects. That prospect strikes terror in the hearts of fossil fuel executives and in the governments of petro-states (like Russia), because it means that trillions of dollars' worth of proven reserves—currently propping up share prices—could become worthless overnight. This is sometimes referred to as "the carbon bubble," and by 2016 it was already beginning to deflate. Think of Trump as the guy running to the rescue with a bicycle pump, signaling to the industry that he's going to fill their bubble with a few more years' worth of toxic air. How? Easy. By making climate change disappear.

We can see it all playing out with a kind of absurd clarity. On day one, the White House website was cleansed of many of the references to climate change. There are plans to cut the NASA program that uses satellites to accumulate basic data on how the earth is changing—including disappearing glaciers and rising seas. The White House's budget director, Mick Mulvaney, was pretty blunt about all this: "Regarding the question as to climate change, I think the President was fairly straightforward—we're not spending money on that anymore. We consider that to be a waste of your money to go out and do that."

They are so determined to erase the reality of climate change that they are even aiming to wipe out programs that help communities cope with its impacts. Trump proposed cutting a National Oceanic and Atmospheric Association program that helps communities protect their coasts. He also wanted to slash the Federal Emergency Management Agency (FEMA), the agency charged with responding to large-scale natural disasters, and cut entirely its key program designed to help communities prepare for future crises. His plan to reduce the Environmental Protection Agency's (EPA) budget by over 30 percent would lay off thousands of people and eliminate the entire environmental justice program. The latter helps low-income communities—overwhelmingly African-American, Latino, and Indigenous—deal with some of the impacts of having the most toxic industries in their backyards. And it's worth noting that many of the measures—including cuts to programs dealing with lead poisoning from pipes—would disproportionately hurt children in marginalized communities. A Congressional budget deal has delayed the worst of the EPA cuts until 2018.

So Trump's rescue plan for the fossil fuel sector is multi-pronged: bury the evidence that climate change is happening by stopping research and gagging agencies; cut the programs that are tasked with coping with the real-world impacts of climate disruption; and remove all barriers to an acceleration of the very activities that are fueling the crisis—drilling for more oil and gas, mining and burning more coal.

Some of this backsliding can be balanced out by bold action in large states such as California and New York, which are pledging to rapidly roll out renewables regardless of Trump's pro–fossil fuel policies. But there is one other crucial factor that may determine whether the ExxonMobil subsidiary known as the Trump administration is able to unleash an irreversible catastrophe.

Price Is Everything

There is one thing above all that is currently restraining fossil fuel companies from launching large new extraction projects, and it's not a piece of legislation that Obama introduced and Trump can reverse. What's holding them back is the price of oil and gas. As I write this in 2017, the price is much lower than when Obama took office, because there's an oversupply—more oil and gas is available than consumers want.

The reason price is such an issue for new projects is that the cheap and easy-to-access fossil fuels have been steadily running out, particularly in the US. So what's left? Stuff that's hard and expensive to get to. It costs a lot of money to drill in the Arctic, or in very deep water, or to dig up and refine the semisolid oil found in Canada's Alberta tar sands. When the price of oil was soaring, as it was as recently as 2014, fossil fuel companies were making multi-billion dollar investments in order to go after those expensive fuel sources. With oil at $100 a barrel, they could still turn a hefty profit even with the high costs for extraction. And the development in this sector did spur economic growth, and it did create a lot of jobs. But the environmental costs were enormous: the Deepwater Horizon disaster in the Gulf of Mexico was intimately connected to the fact that these companies are drilling deeper than they ever have before. The reason the tar sands in Alberta are so controversial is that Indigenous lands and waterways have been badly contaminated by the invasive and carbon-intensive process of mining for that heavy crude.

Rex Tillerson's ExxonMobil went wild buying up high-cost heavy-oil reserves; it reached the point where fully one-third of the company's reserves were located in the Alberta tar sands. When the price of oil collapsed, it came as a major shock. Oil prices began to crash in 2014, with Brent crude—the global benchmark for oil—plummeting from $100 a barrel to $50 in just six months, and the price has hovered at around $55 a barrel ever since. As a result, we've seen a lot of companies pulling back from extreme energy projects. Fracking for oil and gas in the United States has cooled off, with devastating human costs: an estimated 170,000 oil and gas workers have lost their jobs after the 2014 price collapse. Investment in the Alberta tar sands dropped by an estimated 37 percent in the year following, and continues to fall. Shell pulled back from the Arctic and has sold most of its tar sands reserves. The French oil company Total has retreated from the tar sands as well. Even ExxonMobil has been forced to write off nearly 3.5 million barrels of tar sands oil because the market considered these reserves to be no longer worth extracting at current oil prices. Deepwater drilling is also in a lull.

For the big oil companies—particularly those that gambled on the price of oil staying high—all of this has been a disaster. And no oil major has suffered more than ExxonMobil. When prices were high, with Tillerson at the helm, the company broke the record for the highest corporate profits ever reported in the United States, earning $45 billion in 2012. Compare that to 2016, when Exxon's profits fell well shy of $8 billion. That's a more than 80 percent drop in profits in a span of just four years.

What does all this mean? It means that oil majors like ExxonMobil, and the banks that underwrote their bad bets, desperately want the price of oil to go back up—to get their super-profits back and to get the fossil fuel frenzy back on. So a very big question that needs answering is this: what is the Trump administration—aka Team ExxonMobil—going to do to achieve that?

We are already seeing some policies that appear designed to drive up oil prices. For instance, Trump moved to eliminate the Obama-era requirement that vehicles become more fuel-efficient—which means more trips to the gas station for consumers. Trump's budget plan, meanwhile, aimed to completely eliminate funding for new public transit projects, and kill funding for long-distance train services.

So far, though, the market isn't responding, at least not by much. The price of oil got a little bump after Trump was elected but has held pretty steady since. From a climate perspective, this is good news: cheap gas may encourage short-term consumption, but it discourages a lot of the long-term investments that lock us into a disastrous future. The concern—and it is a real one—is that Trump and Co. may well have more tricks up their sleeves to try to push up oil prices and realize their goal of setting off a fossil fuel frenzy.

The reason we need to have our eyes firmly fixed on this

dynamic is that nothing drives up the price of oil quite like war and other major shocks to the world market—a scenario we'll dig into in Chapter 9.

What Conservatives Understand about Global Warming—and Liberals Don't

For many years, I wondered why some people were so determined to deny global warming. It's strange at first glance. Why would you work so hard to deny the scientific facts that have been affirmed by 97 percent of climate scientists—facts whose effects we see all around us, with more confirmation in the news we consume every day? That question led me on a journey that informed my book *This Changes Everything*—and I think some of what I discovered when writing that book can help us make sense of the centrality of climate vandalism to the Trump administration.

What I found is that when hard-core conservatives deny climate change, they are not just protecting the trillions in wealth that are threatened by climate action. They are also defending something even more precious to them: an entire ideological project—neoliberalism—which holds that the market is always right, regulation is always wrong, private is good and public is bad, and taxes that support public services are the worst of all.

There is a lot of confusion around the word *neoliberalism*, and about who is a neoliberal. And understandably so. So let's break it down. Neoliberalism is an extreme form of capitalism that started to become dominant in the 1980s, under Ronald Reagan and Margaret Thatcher, but since the 1990s has been the reigning ideology of the world's elites, regardless of partisan affiliation. Still, its strictest and most dogmatic adherents remain where the movement started: on the US Right.

Neoliberalism is shorthand for an economic project that vilifies the public sphere and anything that's not either the workings of the market or the decisions of individual consumers. It is probably best summarized by another of Reagan's famous phrases, "The nine most terrifying words in the English language are: I'm from the government and I'm here to help." Under the neoliberal worldview, governments exist in order to create the optimal conditions for private interests to maximize their profits and wealth, based on the theory that the profits and economic growth that follow will benefit everyone in the trickle-down from the top—eventually. If it doesn't work, and stubborn inequalities remain or worsen (as they invariably do), then according to this worldview, that must be the personal failing of the individuals and communities that are suffering. They must have "a culture of crime," say, or lack a "work ethic," or perhaps it's absentee fathers, or some other racially tinged excuse for why government policy and public funds should never be used to reduce inequalities, improve lives, or address structural crises.

The primary tools of this project are all too familiar: privatization of the public sphere, deregulation of the corporate sphere, and low taxes paid for by cuts to public services, and all of this locked in under corporate-friendly trade deals. It's the same recipe everywhere, regardless of context, history, or the hopes and dreams of the people who live there. Larry Summers, when he was chief economist of the World Bank in 1991, summed up the ethos: "Spread the truth—the laws of economics are like the laws of engineering. One set of laws works everywhere." (Which is why I sometimes call neoliberalism "McGovernment.")

The 1989 collapse of the Berlin Wall was interpreted as the signal to take the campaign global. With socialism in decline, there was seemingly no longer any need to soften capitalism's edges anywhere. As Thatcher famously declared, "There is no alternative." (Another way of thinking about this is that neoliberalism is simply capitalism without competition, or capitalism lying on the couch in its undershirt saying, "What are you going to do, leave me?")

Neoliberalism is a very profitable set of ideas, which is why I am always a little hesitant to describe it as an ideology. What it really is, at its core, is a rationale for greed. That's what the American billionaire Warren Buffett meant when he made headlines a few years ago by telling CNN that "there's been class warfare going on for the last twenty years, and my class has won . . . the rich class." He was referring to the tremendous tax cuts the wealthy have enjoyed in this period, but you could extend that to the whole neoliberal policy package.

So what does this have to do with the widespread refusal by the Right to believe that climate change is happening, a refusal deeply embedded in the Trump administration? A lot. Because climate change, especially at this late date, can *only* be dealt with through collective action that sharply curtails the behavior of corporations such as ExxonMobil and Goldman Sachs. It demands investments in the public sphere—in new energy grids, public transit and light rail, and energy efficiency—on a scale not seen since the Second World War. And that can only happen by raising taxes on the wealthy and on corporations, the very people Trump is determined to shower with the most generous tax cuts, loopholes and regulatory breaks. Responding to climate change also means giving communities the freedom to prioritize local green industries—a process that often clashes directly with the corporate free trade deals that have been such an integral part of neoliberalism, and which bar "buy local" rules as protectionist. (Trump campaigned against those parts of free trade deals, but, as we will see in Chapter 6, he has no intention of rescinding those rules.)

In short, climate change detonates the ideological scaffolding on which contemporary conservatism rests. To admit that the climate crisis is real is to admit the end of the neoliberal project. That's why the Right is in a rebellion against the physical world, against science (which is what prompted hundreds of thousands of scientists around the world to participate in the March for

Science in April 2017, collectively defending a principle that really shouldn't need defending: that knowing as much as possible about our world is a good thing). But there is a reason why science has become such a battle zone—because it is revealing again and again that neoliberal business as usual leads to a species-threatening catastrophe.

What mainstream liberals have been saying for decades, by contrast, is that we simply need to tweak the existing system here and there and everything will be fine. You can have Goldman Sachs capitalism plus solar panels. But the challenge is much more fundamental than that. It requires throwing out the neoliberal rulebook, and confronting the centrality of ever-expanding consumption in how we measure economic progress. In one sense, then, the members of Trump's cabinet—with their desperate need to deny the reality of global warming, or belittle its implications—understand something that is fundamentally true: to avert climate chaos, we need to challenge the capitalist ideologies that have conquered the world since the 1980s. If you are the beneficiary of those ideologies, you are obviously going to be very unhappy about that. That's understandable. Global warming really does have radical progressive implications. If it's real—and it manifestly is—then the oligarch class cannot continue to run riot without rules. Stopping them is now a matter of humanity's collective survival.

If we fail, the death I saw at the Great Barrier Reef will spread to all corners of our collective home in ways we can scarcely imagine.

CHAPTER FIVE

THE GRABBER-IN-CHIEF

Since Trump took office, there's been a lot of talk about how we all need to stop "re-litigating the 2016 election"—that it's time to look forward, not backward.

To be honest, I'm tired of looking backward as well, because the tensions during the election, and in particular during the Democratic primary, were almost unbearable. For a long time, I couldn't look at social media because all I saw were people who used to like each other warring over "Bernie Bros" and "Hillary Bots." I lost friends over it, as others did on all sides—people who blame me and people like me for Hillary's defeat because we did not publicly endorse her or because we were so hard on her corporate entanglements during the primary. And I have trouble forgiving people like the liberal economist Paul Krugman, who has written so much of such great importance about economic inequality and bank fraud over the years, and yet used his influential platform in the *New York Times* to repeatedly attack the only candidate, Bernie Sanders, who was serious about battling income inequality and taking on the banks. It's perfectly understandable that people don't want to rehash those ugly battles—they were miserable.

We all cope with fear and uncertainty differently. A great many conservatives are dealing with their fears about a changing and destabilizing world by attempting to force back the clock. But if the Right specializes in turning backward, the Left specializes in turning inward and firing on each other in a circular hail of blame.

Still, I'm suspicious of the speed with which we are being told to move on. Because we do need to build as broad a coalition as possible against Trump and forces like him wherever we live—but we also need to avoid repeating the same mistakes that have created the conditions for the rise of Trumpism and its counterparts around the world. And unfortunately, there's some evidence that the only lesson a lot of establishment Democrats are learning is: don't let Russians hack your e-mail.

So I think we should take a deep breath and dare to look back, if only briefly—not to reopen old wounds, but just to see what there is to learn. Because we can't get off the road we are on if we aren't honest about the factors that landed us here.

Foul Mood Rising

If there is a single, overarching lesson to be drawn from the foul mood rising around the world, it may be this: we should never, ever underestimate the power of hate. Never underestimate the appeal of wielding power over "the other," be they migrants, Muslims, Blacks, Mexicans, women, the other in any form. Especially during times of economic hardship, when a great many people have good reason to fear that the jobs that can support a decent life are disappearing for good.

Trump speaks directly to that economic panic, and, simultaneously, to the resentment felt by a large segment of white America about the changing face of their country, about positions of power and privilege increasingly being held by people who do not look like them. The intensity and irrationality of the rage Trump and his strongest supporters reserved for Barack Obama, the years of feverish desire to strip him of his Americanness by "proving" he was Kenyan, thereby rendering him "other," cannot be explained by anything but race hatred. This is the "whitelash" that CNN commentator Van Jones named on election night, and there is no doubt that for a considerable segment of Trump's voters it is a ferocious force.

Much of the rage directed at Hillary Clinton during the campaign came from a similarly primal place. Here was not just a female candidate, but a woman who identifies with and is a product of the movement for women's liberation, and who did not package her quest for power in either cuteness or coyness. As the maniacal chants of "Lock her up!" made clear, for many in America, it was, quite simply, unbearable.

I am no fan of many of Clinton's policies. But her policies are not what provoked the seething hatred she encountered—that came from a deeper place. It is not insignificant, I think, that one of the first big controversies of the campaign was Trump's comment that then Fox News anchor Megyn Kelly, who had dared to ask him a tough question about previous sexist comments, had "blood coming out of her wherever." This basest of insults—invoking the ancient idea that women's menstruation makes them unfit for public life—was an early clue that the blind rage at women overstepping their allotted boundaries would become a driving force of the campaign. It was a hint, too, about the glue that connects a proud playboy like Donald Trump with a sexual scold like Mike Pence (who apparently won't have a meal alone with a female coworker): a shared belief that women's bodies exist to serve men, whether as objects of sexual gratification or as baby-making machines. And it was a preview of the rooms packed with white men who would soon be making fateful decisions about women's health and reproductive freedoms.

The Ranking of Human Life

In the 2016 US presidential elections, we heard the roar of men who believe they and they alone have the right to rule—in public, and in private behind closed doors. One of the most chilling details about the men who surround Trump, and who support him most publicly in the media, is the number of them who have been accused of beating, harassing, or sexually abusing women. The list includes Steve Bannon (whose ex-wife told police that he physically and verbally abused her—the case was dismissed when his ex-wife couldn't be found by prosecutors to act as a witness); Trump's original pick for labor secretary, Andrew Puzder (whose ex-wife claimed in court documents that he caused permanent injuries after "striking her violently about the face, chest, back, shoulders, and neck, without provocation or cause"—though she later recanted); Bill O'Reilly, of course, one of Trump's most powerful champions in the media; and Roger Ailes (who worked as an adviser to the Trump campaign after being forced to leave Fox News following allegations of sexual harassment by more than two dozen women, many at his own network, and who, like O'Reilly, denied the allegations). And the list would be incomplete without Trump himself, who has been accused by multiple women, including in lawsuits, of sexual assault and harassment (he denies all allegations), and whose first wife, Ivana, reportedly swore in a deposition that her husband raped her in 1989 (like Andrew Puzder's ex-wife, she recanted).

There is no shortage of sexual predators on the liberal side of the political spectrum, but the litany of allegations, accusations, and hush money that swirls around Trump's inner circle is unlike anything we have seen before. No matter the allegation, it is met with a wall of denial, of powerful men vouching for other powerful men, sending a message to the world that women are not to be believed. Perhaps this shouldn't come as a surprise, given

Trump's brand: he's the boss who does what he wants—grabs what and whomever he wants; mocks, shames, and humiliates whomever he wants whenever he wants. That is what the Grabber-in-Chief is selling. And there is clearly a rather large market for it.

The Problem with "Jobs Voters"

Many of Trump's voters were not primarily driven by "whitelash" or "malelash" sentiments. Plenty of them said they voted for Trump because they liked what he said about trade and jobs, or because they wanted to stick it to the "swamp" of DC elites.

But there's a problem with these stories. You cannot cast a ballot for a person who is openly riling up hatred based on race, gender, or physical ability unless, on some level, you think those issues aren't important. That the lives of the people being put in tangible danger by this rhetoric (and the policies that flow from it) matter less than your life and the lives of people who look more like you. You just can't do it unless you are willing to sacrifice those other categories of people for your (hoped-for) gain. To put it bluntly, a vote for Trump might not reflect active hatred, but there is still, at best, a troubling indifference behind the act.

The racial and gender resentments that did so much to bring Trump to power are not new. They have been omnipresent through history, rising and falling with additional stresses and provocations. There are, however, deep structural reasons why Trump's version of a very old tactic is resonating so powerfully now, at this particular moment. Some of them have to do with those changes in white male status, but that tells only part of the story. What really won it for Trump was how those losses in social status were layered on top of losses in basic economic security.

The people who have been hit hardest by neoliberal policies such as slashed social services and banking deregulation are not

Trump's white voters—not by a long shot. These policies have done far more to compromise the financial status of Black and Latino families, and it is within communities of color that the deepest service cuts have been inflicted.

Moreover, the flip side of neoliberal economic policies that exile whole segments of the population from the formal economy has been an explosion of the state apparatus aimed at control and containment: militarized police, fortressed borders, immigration detention, and mass incarceration. The forty years since the neoliberal revolution began have seen the number of people behind bars in the United States increase by approximately 500 percent—a phenomenon, once again, that disproportionately affects Black and brown people, though whites are most certainly swept up in the system as well.

It's also important to note that Trump's base wasn't mostly poor; it was solidly middle-income, with most of his voters earning between $50,000 and $200,000 a year (with a concentration at the lower end of that range). Since so many Trump voters are not destitute, some argue that their vote can't be motivated by economic stress.

But that misses an important factor. A CNN analysis of exit polls found that Trump won 77 percent of the vote among those who said that their financial situation was "worse today" than it had been four years earlier. In other words, they may have been doing well compared with the country's average, but many had lost ground. And indeed the losses began long before that.

Insecure on Every Front

Over the past three decades, but accelerating since the 2008 financial crisis, pretty much everyone apart from the one percent has been losing job security as well as whatever feeble safety net used to exist. That means a lost job has greater implications now for one's ability to pay for health care or hold on to a home. This state of affairs hurts Trump's working-class white male voters just as it does so many others. On the other hand, because many of Trump's blue-collar voters had a notably better deal until fairly recently—able to access well-paid, unionized manufacturing jobs that supported middle-class lives—these losses appear to come as more of a shock.

This is reflected in a marked rise in deaths among white, middle-aged Americans without college degrees, mainly from suicide, prescription drug overdoses, and alcohol-related illnesses. And this is particular to whites: mortality rates for Black and Hispanic Americans in similar demographic brackets are falling. Anne Case and Angus Deaton, the Princeton economists who noticed this trend dating back to 1999 and authored a landmark paper on what they term "deaths of despair," explain the discrepancy as coming down to different prior experiences and expectations, or "the failure of life to turn out as expected." Another way of thinking about it is: when a building starts to collapse, it's the people on the higher floors who have further to fall—that's just physics.

On top of those losses, there are also the ground-shifting uncertainties associated with living in a changing country, a nation rapidly becoming more ethnically diverse, and where women are gaining more access to power. That's part of progress toward equality, the result of hard-fought battles, but it does mean that white men are losing economic security (which everyone has a right to) *and* their sense of a superior status (which they never had a right to) at the same time. In the rush to condemn the latter form of entitlement, we shouldn't lose sight of something important: not all forms of entitlement are illegitimate. All people are entitled to a dignified life. In wealthy countries, it is not greedy or an expression of unearned privilege to expect some basic security in your job when you work hard for decades, some certainty that you will be taken care of in old age, that you won't be bankrupted by illness, and that your kids will have access to the tools they need to excel. In a decent society, people should feel entitled to those things. That's human privilege. And yet those sorts of entitlements have been under vicious attack by the Right for four decades, to the extent that the word *entitlements*—referring to pensions and health care—is a slur in Washington, DC.

It is this complex mix of factors that allowed Trump to come along and say: I will champion the beleaguered working man. I will get you those manufacturing jobs back. I'll get rid of these free trade agreements. I'll return your power to you. I'll make you a real man again. Free to grab women without asking all those boring questions. Oh, and the most potent part of Trump's promise to his base: I will take away the competition from brown people, who will be deported or banned, and Black people, who will be locked up if they fight for their rights. In other words, he would put white men safely back on top once again.

The power of that promise is part of why Trump's election win was like a Bat-Signal for hatemongers of all kinds. The Southern Poverty Law Center reported close to a tripling of anti-Muslim hate groups in 2016 alone. In the month after Trump's election, there were more than a thousand reported incidents of hate targeting people of color. Thirty-two-year-old Srinivas Kuchibhotla, an immigrant engineer from India, was shot dead at a bar in Olathe, Kansas, by a white man who reportedly yelled, "Get out of my country!" before opening fire. In the first two months of 2017, seven transgender people were murdered, prompting calls for a federal hate crimes investigation.

To a terrifying degree, skin color and gender conformity are determining who is physically safe in the hands of the state, who is at risk from vigilante violence, who can express themselves without constant harassment, who can cross a border without terror, and who can worship without fear.

The Identity Blame Game

Which is why it's short-sighted, not to mention dangerous, to call for liberals and progressives to abandon their focus on "identity politics" and concentrate instead on economics and class—as if these factors could in any way be pried apart.

Railing against so-called identity politics and political correctness is standard fare on Fox News and Breitbart News, but those aren't the only places it's coming from, and the critics have only become more vocal since the election. The lesson a great many liberal Democrats seem to have taken away from Hillary Clinton's defeat is that her direct appeals to women and minorities on the campaign trail made white working-class men feel left out, driving them to Trump. Columbia University professor Mark Lilla expressed this most prominently in a post-election essay in the *New York Times*. He chided Clinton for "calling out explicitly to African-American, Latino, LGBT and women voters at every stop. This was a strategic mistake." This focus on the traditionally marginalized groups, and the "moral panic about racial, gender and sexual identity . . . has distorted liberalism's message and prevented it from becoming a unifying force capable of governing." Unity, apparently, requires that all those noisy minorities (combined, an overwhelming majority, actually) need to pipe down about their individual grievances so Democrats can get back to "It's the economy, stupid," the mantra of Bill Clinton's 1992 winning presidential campaign.

Except this is exactly the wrong conclusion to draw from the 2016 elections. Clinton's failure was not one of messaging but of track record. Specifically, it was the stupid economics of neoliberalism, fully embraced by her, her husband, and her party's establishment, that left Clinton without a credible offer to make to those white workers who had voted for Obama (twice) and decided, this time, to vote Trump. True, Trump's plans weren't credible, but at least they were different.

Similarly, if there was a problem with her focus on gender, sexuality, and racial identity, it was that Clinton's brand of identity politics does not challenge the system that produced and entrenched these inequalities, but seeks only to make that system more "inclusive." So, yes to marriage equality and abortion access and transgender bathrooms, but forget about the right to housing, the right to a wage that supports a family (Clinton resisted the calls for a $15 minimum wage), the universal right to free health care, or anything else that requires serious redistribution of wealth from top to bottom and would mean challenging the neoliberal playbook. On the campaign trail, Clinton mocked her opponent's "Trumped-up trickle-down economics," but her own philosophy is what we might call "trickle-down identity politics": tweak the system just enough to change the genders, colors, and sexual orientation of some of the people at the top, and wait for the justice to trickle down to everyone else. And it turns out that trickle-down works about as well in the identity sphere as it does in the economic one.

We know this because it's been tried. There have been historic symbolic victories for diversity in recent years—an African-American first family, two Black attorneys general, Hollywood pushed into recognizing Black directors and actors, out gays and lesbians working as news anchors and heading Fortune 500 companies, hit TV shows built around transgender characters, an overall increase in the number of women in management positions, to name just a few. These victories for diversity and inclusion matter, they change lives and bring in viewpoints that would otherwise be absent. It was immensely important that a generation of kids grew up seeing Obama in the most powerful office in the world. And yet this top-down approach to change, if it is not accompanied by bottom-up policies that address systemic issues such as crumbling schools and lack of access to decent housing, is not going to lead to real equality. Not even close.

In the United States, the significant gains made for greater diversity and inclusion at the top in recent years have occurred at a time of mass deportations of immigrants, and as the wealth gap between Black and white Americans actually increased. According to the Urban Institute, between 2007 and 2010 the average wealth of white families fell by 11 percent (a huge amount), but Black families saw their wealth fall by 31 percent. In other words, Blacks and whites became *more* unequal during a period of tremendous symbolic advancements, not less. Part of this is because Black families were disproportionately targeted for subprime loans, so they were hit the hardest when the market collapsed in 2008.

During this same period, young Black men continued to be shot and killed by police at an obscene rate (five times higher than white men of the same age bracket, according to a study by the *Guardian*), their murders often captured on video and seared into the imaginations of still-developing young minds. It is against this backdrop that Black Lives Matter has become this generation's civil rights movement. As Keeanga-Yamahtta Taylor, author of *From #BlackLivesMatter to Black Liberation*, writes: "The Black political establishment, led by President Barack Obama, had shown over and over again that it was not capable of the most basic task: keeping Black children alive. The young people would have to do it themselves." Similarly, while there are a great many women in positions of power—not enough, but substantially more than a generation ago—low-income women are working longer hours, often at multiple jobs, without security, just to pay the bills. (Two-thirds of minimum-wage workers in the States are women.) In the World Economic Forum's annual global rankings on the economic gender gap, the US fell from the 28th spot in 2015 all the way down to 45th place in 2016.

While white Trump voters responded to their precariousness by raging at the world, many traditional liberals seem to have responded by tuning out. When Hillary Clinton called out identifiable groups at every rally, declaring that she would "stand up" for each of them, it was too tepid an offering to build the groundswell of support she needed. So while white identity politics pumped up Trump's base, trickle-down identity politics fell flat for his opponent. In crucial states such as Iowa, Ohio, and Wisconsin, Clinton drew 15 to 20 percent fewer Democratic voters than Barack Obama had in 2012. And that depressed progressive turnout is a big part of how Trump managed to eke out an electoral win (despite losing the popular vote).

So perhaps this is another lesson to draw from 2016. Fear of "the other" may be an animating force for many supporters of far-right parties, but "inclusion" of the other within an inherently unjust system will not be powerful enough to defeat those forces. It wasn't inspiring enough to galvanize the demoralized Democratic base in 2016, or to defeat Brexit, and there is no reason to believe that dynamic will change anytime soon.

Instead, the overarching task before us is not to rank our various issues—identity versus economics, race versus gender— and for one to vanquish all the others in some sort of oppression cage match. It is to understand in our bones how these forms of oppression intersect and prop each other up, creating the complex scaffolding that allowed a kleptocratic thug to grab the world's most powerful job as if it were a hostess at a strip club.

"Racial Capitalism"

This is a good time to remember that manufacturing false hierarchies based on race and gender in order to enforce a brutal class system is a very long story. Our modern capitalist economy was born thanks to two very large subsidies: stolen Indigenous land

and stolen African people. Both required the creation of intellectual theories that ranked the relative value of human lives and
labor, placing white men at the top. These church and state–
sanctioned theories of white (and Christian) supremacy are what
allowed Indigenous civilizations to be actively "unseen" by
European explorers—visually perceived and yet not acknowledged to have preexisting rights to the land—and entire richly
populated continents to be legally classified as unoccupied and
therefore fair game on an absurd "finders keepers" basis.

It was these same systems of human ranking that were
deployed to justify the mass kidnapping, shackling, and torturing
of other humans in order to force them to work that stolen
land—which led the late political theorist Cedric Robinson to
describe the market economy that gave birth to the United States
not simply as capitalism but as "racial capitalism." The cotton
and sugar picked by enslaved Africans was the fuel that kick-
started the Industrial Revolution. The ability to discount darker
people and darker nations in order to justify stealing their land
and labor was foundational, and none of it would have been
possible without those theories of racial supremacy that gave the
whole morally bankrupt system a patina of legal respectability. In
other words, economics was never separable from "identity politics," certainly not in colonial nations like the United States—so
why would it suddenly be today?

As the civil rights lawyer Michelle Alexander wrote in her book
The New Jim Crow, the politics of racial hierarchy have been the
ever-present accomplices to the market system as it evolved
through the centuries. Elites in the United States have used race
as a wedge, she writes, "to decimate a multiracial alliance of poor
people"—first in the face of slave rebellions supported by white
workers, then with Jim Crow laws, and later during the so-called
war on drugs. Every time these multiethnic coalitions have become
powerful enough to threaten corporate power, white workers have

When corporate power threatened—

been convinced that their real enemies are darker-skinned people stealing "their" jobs or threatening their neighborhoods. And there has been no more effective way to convince white voters to support the defunding of schools, bus systems, and welfare than by telling them (however wrongly) that most of the beneficiaries of those services are darker-skinned people, many of them "illegal," out to scam the system. In Europe, fearmongering about how migrants are stealing jobs, exploiting social services, and eroding the culture has played a similarly enabling role.

Ronald Reagan kicked this into high gear in the United States with the myth that food stamps were being collected by fur-wearing, Cadillac-driving "welfare queens" and used to subsidize a culture of crime. And Trump was no small player in this hysteria. In 1989, after five Black and Latino teenagers were accused of raping a white woman in Central Park, he bought full-page ads in several New York daily papers calling for the return of the death penalty. The Central Park Five were later exonerated by DNA evidence, and their sentences were vacated. Trump refused to apologize or retract his claims. No wonder, then, that his Justice Department, under the direction of Attorney General Jeff Sessions, is arguing that social services and infrastructure in cities such as New York and Chicago are "crumbling under the weight of illegal immigration and violent crime"—conveniently moving the subject away from years of neoliberal neglect toward the supposed need to crack down on crime, and to bar these cities from declaring themselves "sanctuaries" for immigrants.

Divide and Conquer

In truth, nothing has done more to help build our present corporate dystopia than the persistent and systematic pitting of working-class whites against Blacks, citizens against migrants, and men against women. White supremacy, misogyny, homophobia, and transphobia have been the elite's most potent defenses against genuine democracy. A divide-and-terrorize strategy, alongside ever more creative regulations that make it harder for many minorities to vote, is the only way to carry out a political and economic agenda that benefits such a narrow portion of the population.

We also know from history that white supremacist and fascist movements—though they may always burn in the background—are far more likely to turn into wildfires during periods of sustained economic hardship and national decline. That is the lesson of Weimar Germany, which—ravaged by war and humiliated by punishing economic sanctions—became ripe for Nazism. That warning was supposed to have echoed through the ages.

After the Holocaust, the world came together to try to create conditions that would prevent genocidal logic from ever again taking hold. It was this, combined with significant pressure from below, that formed the rationale for generous social programs throughout Europe. Western powers embraced the principle that market economies needed to guarantee enough basic dignity that disillusioned citizens would not go looking for scapegoats or extreme ideologies.

But all that has been discarded, and we are allowing conditions eerily similar to those in the 1930s to be re-created today. Since the 2008 financial crisis, the International Monetary Fund (IMF), the European Commission, and the European Central Bank (known as the "troika") have forced country after country to accept "shock therapy"–style reforms in exchange for desperately needed bailout funds. To countries such as Greece, Italy, Portugal, and even France, they said: "Sure, we'll bail you out, but only in exchange for your abject humiliation. Only in exchange for you giving up control over your economic affairs, only if you delegate all key decisions to us, only if you privatize large parts of your economy, including parts of your economy that are seen as central to your identity, like your mineral wealth. Only if you accept

Economic
humiliation

cuts to salaries and pensions and health care." There is a bitter irony here, because the IMF was created after World War II with the express mandate of preventing the kinds of economic punishment that fueled so much resentment in Germany after World War I. And yet it was an active part of the process that helped create the conditions for neo-fascist parties to gain ground in Greece, Belgium, France, Hungary, Slovakia, and so many other countries. Our current financial system is spreading economic humiliation all over the world—and it's having the precise effects that the economist and diplomat John Maynard Keynes warned of a century ago, when he wrote that if the world imposed punishing economic sanctions on Germany, "vengeance, I dare predict, will not limp."

I understand the urge to boil Trump's election down to just one or two causes. To say it is all simply an expression of the ugliest forces in the United States, which never went away and roared to the foreground when a demagogue emerged who tore off the mask. To say it is all about race, a blind rage at the loss of white privilege. Or to say that it's all attributable to women-hatred, since the very fact that Hillary Clinton could have been defeated by so vile and ignorant a figure as Trump is a wound that, for a great many women, refuses to heal.

But the reduction of the current crisis to just one or two factors at the exclusion of all else won't get us any closer to understanding how to defeat these forces now or the next time out. If we cannot become just a little bit curious about how all these elements—race, gender, class, economics, history, culture—have intersected with one another to produce the current crisis, we will, at best, be stuck where we were before Trump won. And that was not a safe place.

Because already, before Trump, we had a culture that treats both people and planet like so much garbage. A system that extracts lifetimes of labor from workers and then discards them without protection. That treats millions of people, excluded from economic opportunity, as refuse to be thrown away inside prisons. That treats government as a resource to be mined for private wealth, leaving wreckage behind. That treats the land, water, and air that sustain all of life as little more than a bottomless sewer.

Lovelessness as Policy

The author and intellectual Cornel West has said that "justice is what love looks like in public." I often think that neoliberalism is what lovelessness looks like as policy. It looks like generations of children, overwhelmingly Black and brown, raised amidst an uncaring landscape. It looks like the rat-infested schools of Detroit. It looks like water pipes leaking lead and poisoning young minds in Flint. It looks like foreclosed mortgages on homes that were built to collapse. It looks like famished hospitals that feel more like jails—and overstuffed jails that are humanity's best approximation of hell. It looks like trashing the beauty of the planet as if it had no value at all. It is, much like Trump himself, greed and carelessness incarnate.

While our global economic model is failing the vast majority of people on the planet, it is not failing all of us equally. The hatred that Trump and his team are helping to direct at the most vulnerable is not a separate project from their economic pillage on behalf of the ultra rich, their corporate coup—the former enables the latter. Trump's ugliness on race and gender serves a specific set of wildly profitable goals, as identity-based hatreds always have.

Fortunately, the fastest-growing grassroots political formations of our era—from the movement to end violence against women to the Movement for Black Lives, from workers calling for a living wage to Indigenous rights and climate justice movements—are rejecting a single-issue approach. They have embraced the "intersectionality" framework articulated by feminist and civil rights

Need to reject single-issue approach

advocate Kimberlé Williams Crenshaw. That means identifying how multiple issues—race, gender, income, sexuality, physical ability, immigration status, language—intersect and overlap within an individual's life experience, and also within structures of power.

The Trump administration does not choose between amping up law and order, attacking women's reproductive rights, escalating foreign conflicts, scapegoating immigrants, setting off a fossil fuel frenzy, and otherwise deregulating the economy in the interests of the super-rich. They are proceeding on all these fronts (and others) simultaneously, knowing them to be component parts of the singular project of "making America great again."

Which is why any opposition that is serious about taking on Trump, or other far-right forces like him around the world, must embrace the task of telling a new history of how we ended up here, in this perilous moment. A history that compellingly shows the role played by the politics of division and separation. Racial divisions. Class divisions. Gender divisions. Citizenship divisions.

And a false division between humans and the natural world.

Only then will it become possible to truly come together to win the world we need.

CHAPTER SIX

POLITICS HATES A VACUUM

There have been a lot of lowlights in Trump's short presidency so far, from candlelit ballistic missile summits at Mar-a-Lago to unfiltered, angry tweets about department stores. But from a resistance perspective, it's still hard to beat the low reached on Trump's first full day at the office, on the Monday after inauguration. That's when a group of smiling US union leaders strolled out of the White House and up to a bank of waiting cameras and declared their allegiance to Donald Trump.

Sean McGarvey, president of North America's Building Trades Unions, reported that Trump had taken the delegation representing more than half a dozen unions on a tour of the Oval Office, showing a level of respect that was "nothing short of incredible." More praise came from Doug McCarron, president of the United Brotherhood of Carpenters. He described Trump's inaugural address—judged by most to have been a belligerent spoken-tweet storm—as "a great moment for working men and women."

It was hard to watch. Trump was already waging war on the most vulnerable workers in the economy, and there was talk of budget cuts so draconian they would mean mass layoffs for public sector workers like bus drivers. So why were these labor leaders, representing around a quarter of all unionized workers in the United States, breaking the most sacred principle of the union movement—solidarity with other workers? Most of the unions whose leaders toured the White House had been loyal to the Democrats for decades. Why choose this moment, when so many were in pain, to heap praise on Donald Trump?

Well, they explained that part of their deal with the devil had to do with Trump's energy plans—all those pipelines. And some of it had to do with Trump's pledge to spend on infrastructure (though it went unsaid, they may even have been buoyed by talk of spending $21 billion on the border wall with Mexico). But the clincher, the union heads were clear, was that here, finally, was a president who had their backs on free trade.

Indeed, Trump had wasted no time on that front. That same day, shortly before meeting with the union delegation, he signed an executive order withdrawing the United States from the Trans-Pacific Partnership, the eleven-country trade deal that he'd railed against on the campaign trail as the "rape of our country." At the signing ceremony where the US officially left the TPP, Trump announced, "It's a great thing for the American worker."

Subsequently, a few people wrote to me to ask if this might be the silver lining in Trump's presidency. Wasn't it a good thing that trade deals that many progressives had been criticizing for decades were now on the chopping block or, like the North American Free Trade Agreement, set to be reopened and renegotiated to "bring the jobs back"? I understand the desire to find bright sides to the daily chaos unfolding in the White House. But Trump's trade plans are not one of them.

The whole thing reminds me of all the liberal hawks who backed George W. Bush's invasion of Iraq because the war coincided with their desire to liberate Iraqis from Saddam Hussein—the "humanitarian intervention" argument. There was nothing in the Bush–Cheney track record or worldview to suggest there would be anything democratic or humanitarian about their invasion and occupation of Iraq—and, sure enough, the occupation rapidly became the site of killing fields and torture committed by the US military and its contractors, as well as out-of-control war profiteering. So what is there in Trump's track record, in his treatment of his own workers, in the appointments he has made, in the pro-corporate policies he has already pushed through, that should cause anyone to believe that the way he will renegotiate trade deals, or "bring back the jobs," will in any way be in the interests of workers or the environment?

Rather than hope that Trump is going to magically transform into Bernie Sanders, and choose this one arena in which to be a genuine advocate for anyone who isn't related to him, we would do far better to ask some tough questions about how it's been possible for a gang of unapologetic plutocrats, with open disdain for democratic norms, to hijack an issue like corporate free trade in the first place.

The Race to the Bottom

Trump has made trade deals a signature issue for two reasons. The first, on full display that day at the White House, is that it's a great way to steal votes from the Democrats. The right-wing pundit Charles Krauthammer—no fan of unions—declared on Fox News that Trump's cozy union summit was a "great act of political larceny."

The second reason is that Trump—who we know believes his own super-negotiator PR—has said he can negotiate better deals than his predecessors. But here's the catch: by "better," he doesn't mean better for unionized workers, and certainly not better for the environment. He means better in the same way he always means better—better for him and his corporate empire, better for the bankers and oil executives who make up his administration. In other words, trade rules, if Trump gets his way, are about to get a lot worse for regular people—not just in the United States, but around the world.

You only have to look at what Trump has done since taking office. On the same day he flattered the union leaders by giving them a private tour, he also met with business leaders and announced plans to cut regulations by 75 percent and cut taxes for corporations to 15 percent. It's workers who pay the price for policies like this. Without regulations, their jobs become more unsafe, with more on-the-job injuries, and it's workers who use the services that are getting slashed to pay for tax cuts to the wealthy. Trump has already reneged on his promise to make sure the Keystone XL pipeline would be built with American steel, an early indication of the depth of his commitment to "Buy American, Hire American."

There is also every reason to suspect that the administration's plans to attract manufacturing back to the States will rely on rolling back many of the protections that unions have won over the last century—including the remaining protections for the right to bargain collectively. Many around Trump have pushed hard to make it more difficult for unions to organize, particularly with so-called right-to-work legislation, and with Republicans in control of the House and Senate, that priority will remain on the agenda.

The long list of gifts the Trump administration has already handed out to corporate America makes it clear that Trump's strategy for "making America great again" by reviving manufacturing is to make American manufacturing *cheap* again. Without all those pesky regulations, with far lower corporate tax rates, with Trump's all-out assault on environmental protections, American workers will indeed be closer to competing on cost with workers in low-wage countries like Mexico.

Trump told us all we needed to know about his attitude toward workers with his first pick for labor secretary, the cabinet post that is supposed to protect the US workforce. He chose Andrew

Puzder—a nomination that ultimately failed, but one so egregious that it's worth recalling as a marker of Trump's intentions. Puzder is the CEO of a restaurant empire that includes the fast-food chains Hardee's and Carl's Jr., and he is widely considered to be among the most abusive employers in the country. Dozens of lawsuits have alleged that his company and its franchises have failed to pay workers for overtime and other work, leading to millions in settlements. The correct term for this is *wage theft*. He has also mused publicly about the benefits of working with machines instead of workers: "They never take a vacation, they never show up late, there's never a slip-and-fall, or an age, sex, or race discrimination case," he told *Business Insider*. Senate Minority Leader Charles Schumer called Puzder, worth an estimated $45 million, "probably the most anti-worker" choice ever. What Trump's admiration for Puzder suggests is that his real plan for luring back manufacturing is to suppress rights, wages, and protections to such a degree that working in a factory will be a lot like working at Hardee's under Andrew Puzder. In other words, it's yet another plan to take from the vulnerable to benefit the already outrageously rich.

What we are witnessing is not a silver lining of any sort. It's the push to the finish line in the "race to the bottom" that opponents of these corporate trade deals always feared.

Yes, It's Possible to Make Bad Trade Deals Worse

Trump is not planning to remove the parts of trade deals that are most damaging to workers—the parts, for instance, that prohibit policies which are designed to favor local, over foreign, production. Or the parts that allow corporations to sue national governments if they introduce laws—including laws designed to create jobs and protect workers—that businesses deem to be unfairly cutting into their profits.

Contrary to campaign pledges to penalize companies that move production outside the United States, the actual plan seems to be to *expand* protections for corporations that move production offshore. This is not speculation. Just two months into the new presidency, a draft letter was leaked of the administration's notice to Congress stating its intent to renegotiate the North American Free Trade Agreement (NAFTA). According to Public Citizen's Global Trade Watch's analysis, the administration plans to take the worst elements of the Trans-Pacific Partnership and add them to, or strengthen them in, NAFTA—while not even scrapping the language that denies the US the right to implement "Buy American" rules. As Lori Wallach, director of Global Trade Watch, put it, "for those who trusted Trump's pledge to make NAFTA 'much better' for working people, it's a punch in the face."

One of the most insidious parts of many trade deals is the aggressive protection they provide for patents and trademarks, which often puts lifesaving drugs and critical technologies out of reach for the poor. The Trumps have built a global empire that relies, above all else, on being granted trademarks and licenses and having them fiercely protected—so we can expect the parts of deals concerning intellectual property to become more harmful, not less.

The strongest evidence of Trump's plans is the person he has chosen to oversee his trade negotiations. His commerce secretary is Wilbur Ross, a former banker and billionaire venture capitalist who made a fortune taking over firms and restructuring them to make them more profitable—a feat almost invariably accomplished by laying off workers and moving production to cheaper locations. In 2004, for example, he bought Cone Mills, an American textile company. After less than a decade of restructuring, corporate mergers, and outsourcing, the US workforce in one North Carolina factory dropped from over 1,000 to just 300 while Ross expanded production in China and Mexico.

Putting a CEO like Ross in charge of trade is just one more example of the corporate coup—cutting out any pretense of a neutral government mediator and instead placing corporations directly in charge of the final stage of the decimation of the public sphere and the public interest.

If this agenda is fully realized, workers in the United States will find themselves with fewer protections than they have had at any point since the Dickensian nightmares of the Gilded Age.

But resistance is rising. Andrew Puzder was forced to withdraw his nomination for labor secretary, in part because of organizing by restaurant workers across the country. And when Trump was invited to address a convention of two thousand members of North America's Building Trades Unions, the organization that had sung his praises at the White House, a group of workers decided they were fed up with their union's decision to cozy up to the "billionaire-in-chief." When Trump spoke to the room packed with union members, they stood up, turned their backs on him, and held up signs that said #RESIST—until they were removed by security.

Not all trade unions have fallen for Trump's trade swindle. Most labor leaders, particularly those representing multiracial workforces—including National Nurses United, unions representing public transit workers, and the Service Employees International Union—understand that Trump represents an existential threat to their movement and are organizing accordingly. And yet the earlier question remains: how could Trump's transparently absurd posture as a champion of the working man find a ready audience with a not-insubstantial part of the US labor movement in the first place?

A large part of the answer has to do with the fact that much of this political battleground has been ceded by liberals to the Right.

Remembering a Powerful Global Movement

Beginning in the 1990s, I was part of a global movement warning that corporate free trade agreements, and the model of global commerce they accelerated, were leading to a level of human dispossession and environmental destruction that would rapidly be untenable. It was a multigenerational movement that spanned dozens of countries and sectors, bringing together nonprofit organizations, radical anarchists, Indigenous communities, churches, trade unions, and more. It was messy, ideologically inchoate, imperfect—but it was also large and, for a time, powerful enough to clock some major wins.

Indeed, it came close to being, in some important ways, the kind of broad-based coalition that is needed at the present moment to take on the pseudo-populist Right. So now seems like a good time to look at the lessons of our movement's rise—and fall. Because if that movement had been able to translate its street power into more policy victories, it would have been unthinkable for Trump and his corporate cabinet to tap into the rage at unfair global trade rules and wrap themselves in the cloak of "fair trade."

In the late 1990s through to the early 2000s, from London to Genoa, to Mumbai, to Buenos Aires, Quebec City and Miami, there could not be a high-level gathering to advance the neoliberal economic agenda without counterdemonstrations. That's what happened in Seattle during a summit of the World Trade Organization, where the city was completely shut down by protesters, derailing the meetings. It happened a few months later at the annual meetings of the International Monetary Fund and World Bank in Washington, and at summits to push the Free Trade Area of the Americas, a deal that would have stretched from Alaska to Tierra del Fuego. And this movement was no small thing: by July 2001, roughly 300,000 people were on the streets of Genoa during a G8 meeting.

Unlike today's hypernationalist right-wing movements that rail against "globalism," our movement was proudly international and internationalist, using the novelty of a still-young Internet to organize easily across national borders, online and face to face. Finding common ground in how those deals were increasing inequality and looting the public sphere in all our countries, we called for open borders for people, the liberation of medicines, seeds, and crucial technologies from restrictive patent protections, and far more controls over corporations.

At its core, the movement was about deep democracy, from local to global, and it stood in opposition to what we used to call "corporate rule"—a frame more relevant today than ever. Our objection was obviously not to trade; cultures have always traded goods across borders, and always will. We objected to the way transnational institutions were using trade deals to globalize pro-corporate policies that were extremely profitable for a small group of players but which were steadily devouring so much of what used to be public and commonly held: seeds, water rights, public health care, and much more.

One of the early fights that typified what was at stake involved the Bolivian city of Cochabamba and the American corporation Bechtel. As part of the push to privatize the city's services, Bechtel won a contract to run the local water system. As a result, prices for this most essential of services soared, and it was even deemed illegal to collect rainwater without special permission. Residents of Cochabamba rose up in what became known as "the Water War" and threw Bechtel out of the country. But then Bechtel turned around and sued Bolivia for $50 million in damages and lost revenue. So even when the people reclaimed their democratic rights over this corporation, they were still vulnerable to brutal claims in trade court. Which is why we saw trade policy as such a core fight between democracy and oligarchy.

Anyone who has paid attention during Trump's first months in office, or seen who he has surrounded himself with, knows that he is not going to reverse these trends, but accelerate them.

Teamsters and Turtles—Together at Last!

One area of concern was how these deals were leading to devastating job losses, leaving behind rust belts from Detroit to Buenos Aires, while companies such as Ford and Toyota looked for ever-cheaper places to produce. But for the most part, our opposition was not grounded in Trump-style protectionism; it was trying to stem the beginning of what already looked like a race to the bottom, a new world order that was negatively impacting workers and the environment in every country. We were arguing for a model of trade that would start with the imperative to protect people and the planet. That was crucial then—it's urgent now.

The movement was even starting to win. We defeated the proposed Free Trade Area of the Americas. We brought World Trade Organization negotiations to a standstill. And the World Bank and the International Monetary Fund could no longer speak of "structural adjustment"—meaning forcing neoliberalism on poor countries—in the open.

Looking back, one of the reasons we succeeded was that we stopped fixating on our differences, and came together across sectors and national borders to fight for a common goal. There were plenty of conflicts over tactics, and environmentalists and trade unionists still had large areas of disagreement. In spite of that, however, on the streets of Seattle you had trade unions like the Teamsters marching alongside environmentalists under the banner *Teamsters and Turtles: Together at last!*

That's a long way from those trade union leaders outside the White House, cheering on Trump.

Shocked Out of the Way

So what the hell happened?

The short answer is: shock happened. The September 11 attacks, and the whole era of the so-called War on Terror, pretty much wiped our movement off the map in North America and Europe—an experience that started me off on an exploration of the political uses (and misuses) of crisis that has gripped me ever since.

Of course, the movement never disappeared completely, and many organizations and good people continued to work diligently to raise the alarm about new unfair trade deals. In Latin America, opposition forces came into government in such countries as Bolivia and Ecuador and set up their own "fair trade" networks. But in the Global North, we rapidly ceased to be an unignorable mass movement that changed the conversation in dozens of countries. After September 11, 2001, we suddenly found ourselves under attack from politicians and media commentators equating rowdy anticorporate street demonstrations (and yes, there had been battles with the police and broken store windows) with the deranged forces that had staged the attacks on the World Trade Center. It was a vile comparison, entirely without basis. But it didn't matter.

Our movement had always been a very big tent—a "movement of movements," as we called it (a phrase that has come back into the lexicon). But after September 11, large parts of the coalition got spooked by the "with us or with the terrorists" rhetoric. The nonprofits who rely on large foundations feared losing their funding and withdrew, as did some key unions. Almost overnight, people went back to their single-issue silos, and this remarkable (if imperfect) cross-sectoral alliance, which had brought together such a diversity of people under a pro-democracy umbrella, virtually disappeared. This left a vacuum for Trump and far-right parties in Europe to step in, exploit the justified rage at loss of control to unaccountable transnational institutions, direct it toward immigrants and Muslims and anyone else who makes an easy target, and take the project of corporate rule into new and uncharted waters.

Many stayed active in this period and joined other broad coalitions, but by comparison these were thin and tactical: "Defeat Bush," "Stop the War." The deeper analysis of the global economic forces we were all up against regardless of which party was in power was largely lost.

Vacuum, Meet Trump

This is important to remember because there's a real risk today of repeating those mistakes—of coming together around lowest-common-denominator demands such as "Impeach Trump" or "Elect Democrats" and, in the process, losing our focus on the conditions and politics that allowed Trump's rise and are fueling the growth of far-right parties around the world. One thing we know for certain from the Bush years is that saying no is not enough.

I'll never forget that, just a few days after the September 11 attacks, the *National Post*—a right-wing paper in Canada—ran a story headlined ANTI-GLOBALIZATION IS SO YESTERDAY. They couldn't wait to bury our movement. But they were spectacularly wrong—there is nothing "yesterday" about the alarm we raised. The pain and dislocation didn't go away just because the media decided it was time to talk about terrorism 24/7.

On the contrary, the crises deepened, forcing millions to leave their homes in search of a better life. A 2017 study from the Center for Economic and Policy Research found that Mexico's poverty rate has risen since the 1994 implementation of NAFTA, with 20 million additional people now living in poverty—a major factor pushing Mexican migration to the United States. Meanwhile, in North America and Europe, white workers grew progressively more pissed off at having their voices ignored. This opened the space for demagogues like Trump to step in and direct workers' rage away from plutocrats like him, who had profited so lavishly from the outsourcing opportunities enabled by these deals, and at Mexican migrants instead, victims of the same policies that were hollowing out their communities, the very same bad deals.

This is the space the Brexit campaign usurped, under its slogan "Take back control!" And it is the same rage that France's Marine Le Pen of the far-right Front National speaks to when she tells crowds that globalization has meant "manufacturing by slaves for selling to the unemployed." Around the world, far-right forces are gaining ground by harnessing the power of nostalgic nationalism and anger directed at remote economic bureaucracies—whether Washington, NAFTA, the WTO, or the EU—and mixing it with racism and xenophobia, offering an illusion of control through bashing immigrants, vilifying Muslims, and degrading women.

It's a toxic combination, and it was an avoidable one. Confronting the cruelties of a system designed by and for the wealthiest interests on earth is terrain that rightly belongs to the Left. But the hard truth is that after September 11, large parts of the progressive side of the political spectrum got spooked, and that left the economic-populist space open to abuse. Politics hates a vacuum; if it isn't filled with hope, someone will fill it with fear.

The good news is that the progressive anti-free-trade coalition has finally started to revive in the past couple of years. In Europe— particularly in Germany, France, and Belgium—there has been a big recent surge of unions and environmentalists coming together to oppose corporate trade deals with the United States and Canada. Bernie Sanders, meanwhile, came out powerfully against the Trans-Pacific Partnership, slamming it as "part of a global race to the bottom to boost the profits of large corporations and Wall Street by outsourcing jobs; undercutting worker rights;

dismantling labor, environmental, health, food safety and financial laws; and allowing corporations to challenge our laws in
international tribunals rather than our own court system."

If Sanders had run against Trump on that message, he might
well have peeled away some of the white and Latino workers
who ended up voting Republican in 2016. But Sanders didn't
run against Trump—Hillary Clinton did. And with her long history of both backing and personally negotiating precisely these
sorts of deals, she had no credibility when she criticized them on
the campaign trail. Whenever she tried, it became one more
opportunity to paint her as a typical shifty politician.

The Perils of Ceding the Populist Ground

Tired of the betrayals, some gave up on centrist parties and voted
for self-styled "outsiders" and "insurgents" like Trump. Many
more around the world have just given up, period—staying home
during elections, disengaging from electoral politics, convinced
that the whole system is rigged and is never going to help improve
their lives. This phenomenon was most evident in the United
States, in the 2016 elections, when despite unprecedented wall-
to-wall coverage, despite the presence of a flamboyant and dangerous demagogue in the race, and despite the chance to make
history by voting in the first woman president, approximately 90
million eligible voting-age Americans shrugged and decided to
stay home instead. Far more would-be voters chose not to vote—
roughly 40 percent—than chose to cast a ballot for either Hillary
Clinton or Donald Trump, who each got roughly 25 percent of
total eligible voters. That is a staggering level of disengagement
in a democracy.

Which brings us back to those labor leaders at the White
House. Yes, it was a deal with the devil. But the mere fact that
these union heads were willing to align themselves with an

administration as regressive as Trump's reflects the systemic neglect of and disdain for workers that has characterized both the Democratic and Republican parties for decades.

No, Oprah and Zuckerberg Will Not Save Us

Billionaire as Savior (handwritten annotation)

Trump's path to the White House was partially paved by two men who are beloved by many US liberals—Bill Clinton and Bill Gates. That may seem counterintuitive, but bear with me.

Donald Trump stood before the world and proclaimed he had one qualification to be president: *I'm rich.* To be more specific, he said, "Part of the beauty of me is that I'm very rich." He presented his wealth as evidence that he was "very smart," and indeed superior in every respect. So magical were the powers that flowed from the mere fact of having accumulated this much cash (how much, we don't know) that it would surely compensate for complete political inexperience or lack of the most basic administrative or historical knowledge. Once in office, he extended this logic to other members of the super-rich club, filling his government with individuals whose sole qualification for public office was their enormous, often inherited wealth.

Above all, Trump extended the equation of wealth with magical powers to members of his own dynastic family, bestowing on son-in-law Jared Kushner (a real estate developer born a multimillionaire) a portfolio so overstuffed with weighty responsibilities it rapidly became a media joke. Tallying up the duties so far—brokering Middle East peace, planning the Mar-a-Lago summit with China, monitoring US activities in Iraq, ordering drone strikes on Yemen, making government run more like a business—*New York Times* columnist Frank Bruni wondered, "Why don't we just stitch him a red cape, put him in spandex, affix a stylized 'S' to his chest and be done with it? SuperJared has taken flight."

It would be reassuring if we could pin this billionaire-as-savior complex on Trump's Twitter-addled brain, or on his advisers at the Heritage Foundation, with their Ayn Randian worship of "free enterprise" and men who build tall things. But the fact is, Trump and Kushner are not the first to imagine that their great wealth endows them with Marvel Comic-like superpowers, nor the first to be encouraged in their delusions.

For two decades now, elite liberals have been looking to the billionaire class to solve the problems we used to address with collective action and a strong public sector—a phenomenon sometimes called "philanthrocapitalism." Billionaire CEOs and celebrities—Bill Gates, Richard Branson, Michael Bloomberg, Mark Zuckerberg, Oprah, and always, for some reason, Bono— are treated less like normal people who are gifted in their fields and happen to be good at making a great deal of money, and more like demigods. *Business Insider* ran a listicle in 2011 headlined "10 Ways Bill Gates Is Saving the World"—a perfect distillation of the enormous powers and responsibilities being delegated to, and projected upon, this tiny clique and their charitable foundations.

The Gates Foundation alone is worth $40 billion, making it the largest charitable organization in the world. In key sectors including agriculture in Africa, infectious diseases, and the US education system, the foundation's power rivals that of major United Nations and US government agencies. And yet, despite this unprecedented influence, the foundation's inner workings are notoriously secretive, with key decisions made by Bill, his wife Melinda, his father William Gates, and fellow multi- billionaire Warren Buffett (a nepotistic hiring policy worthy of the Trumps). And it's worth remembering that Gates was not always seen as a world savior. Indeed, in the 1990s, Gates was widely regarded as a corporate villain, known for exploitative employment practices and for building what looked like a predatory software monopoly. Then, with Flash-like speed, he reinvented himself as a global superhero, one who could single-handedly fix the most intractable of social crises. Never mind whether Gates has any specific expertise in the areas in question, or that many of the Gates Foundation's silver-bullet fixes have backfired badly.

Gates and his fellow world-saving billionaires are part of what has come to be known as "the Davos class," named for the annual World Economic Summit held at the top of a mountain in Davos, Switzerland. This is the hyper-connected network of banking and tech billionaires, elected leaders who are cozy with those interests, and Hollywood celebrities who make the whole thing seem unbearably glamorous. At Davos's 2017 summit, for example, Shakira spoke about her charitable work on education in Colombia, and celebrity chef Jamie Oliver discussed his plan to fight diabetes and obesity. Gates featured prominently, as always, announcing with other partners a new $460-million fund to fight the spread of infectious disease.

The power of the Davos class exploded in the 1990s, with US president Bill Clinton and UK prime minister Tony Blair as charter members. Once out of office, both Blair and Clinton continued their involvement. The Clinton Foundation established the annual Clinton Global Initiative, a kind of "Davos on the Hudson" featuring a continuous parade of oligarchs who, rather than pay their taxes at a fair rate, publicly shared their plans to fix the world out of the goodness of their hearts.

For many, the Clinton Foundation was the embodiment of the public merger of the Democratic Party—the traditional party of workers and unions—with the wealthiest interests in the world. Its mission can be summarized like this: there is now so much private wealth sloshing around our planet that every single problem on earth, no matter how large, can be solved by convincing the ultrarich to do the right things with their loose change.

Naturally, the people to convince them to do these fine things were the Clintons, the ultimate relationship brokers and deal makers, with the help of an entourage of A-list celebrities.

For those involved, it no doubt seemed righteous. And yet for multitudes around the world, the whole Davos class came to symbolize the idea that success was a party to which they were not invited, and they knew in their hearts that this rising wealth and power was somehow connected to their growing debts and powerlessness, and the increasing precariousness of their children's futures. The fact that politicians who promised to protect working people's interests were so entangled with the Davos class only increased the rage. The debate over Barack Obama accepting $400,000 for a speech to a Wall Street audience needs to be understood in this context.

Trump didn't run with the Davos crowd (indeed, he tapped into the rage against it). And many from that glamorous, liberal-leaning world are horrified by the Trump presidency. Yet the precedents set by mountaintop do-gooderism are part of the reason it became fathomable for Trump to run in the first place, and for millions of Americans to vote to hand over their government directly to a man whose sole qualification for the job was his wealth. This is not just about those who cast ballots for Trump. A great many of us who would never have voted for him have grown numbly accustomed to the notion that the mere fact of an individual having a large bank account (or many bank accounts, lots of them hidden offshore) somehow means they have bottomless expertise. Indeed, governments of all stripes have been happy to hand over more and more of what used to be seen as public policy challenges to a tiny group of very high-net-worth individuals.

Trump's assertion that he knows how to fix America because he's rich is nothing more than an uncouth, vulgar echo of a dangerous idea we have been hearing for years: that Bill Gates can fix Africa. Or that Richard Branson and Michael Bloomberg can solve climate change.

The Breaking Point: Bailing Out the Banks

The divide between the Davos class and everyone else has been widening since the 1980s. But for a lot of people, the breaking point came with the 2008 financial crisis.

After forcing decades of grinding austerity on people, Treasury secretaries and finance ministers and chancellors of the exchequer suddenly found trillions of dollars to rescue the banks; people witnessed their governments printing vast sums of money. They had given up so much—pensions, wages, decent schools—when in fact, contrary to what Margaret Thatcher claimed, there were alternatives. All of a sudden it turned out that governments can do all kinds of things to interfere in the market, and have seemingly unlimited resources with which to help you out if only you are rich enough. At that moment, everyone on earth saw that they had been lied to.

The implications of this unmasking are still reverberating. The anger that is roiling electorates, on both the right and left sides of the political spectrum, is not only about what's been lost. It's also about the injustice of it all, knowing that the wrenching losses of our era are not being shared, that the Davos class were never really looking after those at the bottom of the mountain.

Which means that defeating the rising pseudo-populist Right is not just a matter of electoral strategy, not just about finding the right candidates. It's about being willing to engage in a battle of ideas—during and, more importantly, between elections—that will take on the corrosive, and deeply bipartisan, wealth-worshiping worldview that created the backlash in the first place.

Unless progressives learn to speak to the legitimate rage at the grotesque levels of inequality that exist right now, the Right is going to keep winning. There is no superhero enlightened billionaire coming to save us from the villains in power. Not Oprah, not Zuckerberg, and not Elon Musk.

We're going to have to save ourselves, by coming together as never before. And in 2016 we caught a glimpse of that potential.

CHAPTER SEVEN

LEARN TO LOVE ECONOMIC POPULISM

Bernie Sanders is the only candidate for US president I have ever openly backed. I've never felt entirely comfortable with candidate endorsements. I made an exception in 2016 because, for the first time in my voting life, there was a candidate inside the Democratic Party primaries who was speaking directly to the triple crises of neoliberalism, economic inequality, and climate change. The fact that his campaign caught fire in that context, where he could not be smeared as a spoiler or vote-splitter (though many tried anyway), is what made his campaign different. Bernie was not a protest candidate; once he pulled off an early upset by winning New Hampshire, the game was on. It was suddenly clear that, contrary to all received wisdom (including my own), Sanders had a shot at beating Hillary Clinton and becoming the presidential candidate for the Democratic Party. In the end, he carried more than twenty states, with 13 million votes. For a self-described democratic socialist, that represents a seismic shift in the political map.

Many national polls showed that Sanders had a better chance of beating Trump than Clinton did (though that might have changed had he won the primary and faced a full right-wing onslaught). Bernie was incredibly well suited to this moment of popular outrage and rejection of establishment politics. He was able to speak directly to the indignation over legalized political corruption, but from a progressive perspective—with genuine warmth and without personal malice. That's rare. He championed policies that would have reined in the banks and made education affordable again. He railed against the injustice that the bankers had never been held accountable. And, after a lifetime in politics, he was untainted by corruption scandals. That's even more rare. Precisely because Bernie is about as far as you can get from the polished world of celebrity reality TV, it would have been hard to find a better foil for Trump and the excesses of the Mar-a-Lago set.

During the campaign, one of the early images that went viral was of Sanders on a plane, white hair disheveled, crammed into an economy-class middle seat. Running that kind of candidate against a man in a private jet with big gold letters on the side would have been the campaign of the century. And it's clear that people are still drawn to the contrast: two months into Trump's term, a Fox News poll found that Sanders had the highest net favorability rating of any politician in the country.

The reason it's worth going over these facts is that when a candidate like that presents him or herself, and when that candidate proves that, with the right backing and support, they could conceivably win, it's worth understanding what stood in the way—so that the mistakes aren't repeated. Because in 2016, there was—almost—a transformative option on the ballot, and there could actually be one next time.

Fear of the Unruly Masses (and Unruly Tresses?)

This is not an argument about whether or not people should have voted for Hillary against Trump. This is about whether there could have been a candidate on the ballot not just more capable of beating Trump but more capable at getting at some of the underlying forces that supercharged Trump's rise. For me, the tragedy of Trump is not only that the United States is now led by a man who represents the worst of all that the culture is capable of, all of it bundled into one human being. It's that the country was within reach of the best and most hopeful political possibility to emerge in my lifetime, imperfect as Sanders is, and just as the climate clock was about to strike midnight.

So why couldn't he connect with enough voters to go over the top?

I get that staunch neoliberals in the Democratic Party didn't want Sanders. He's a threat to that whole model, and his economic populism caused deep discomfort in many high places. So I won't spend time here rehashing how the Democratic National Committee sabotaged Bernie's campaign, exchanging information and strategy with the Clinton camp to serve that purpose. But his campaign was also forcefully attacked by people who are progressive. Some looked in the eye of a candidate who was promising to materially and seriously improve the lives of working people across the country, and turn climate change into a generational mission, and chose to back Clinton, the candidate of an untenable status quo, instead.

The hostility of so many powerful US liberals to Bernie Sanders—and the determination to hold him back when he was on a winning streak—was both troubling and revealing. Because we so often hear that while they personally support bolder policies to fight inequality, those policies aren't worth championing because the American public is too conservative, too pro-capitalist, and would never support them. So they back establishment candidates in the name of pragmatism—choosing the person with the best chance of winning against Republicans.

Yet Bernie showed that positions previously dismissed as too radical for anything but the fringe Left—such as universal public health care and breaking up the banks and forgiving student debt and free college tuition and keeping fossil fuels in the ground and getting to 100 percent renewable energy—were wildly popular in the most capitalist country on earth, supported by millions of people. He showed that transformational change was not a pipe dream after all. On the other hand, what was considered the "safe" choice—Hillary Clinton—turned out to be a very dangerous choice.

Whose Revolution?

It's urgent that we figure out why Sanders failed to galvanize significant numbers of progressive intellectuals and important social movements that were far from thrilled with Clinton and establishment Democrats. Some backed Sanders tepidly, or chose not to back any candidate in the race, convinced that no one had earned their vote, and that Bernie's "political revolution" didn't truly include them.

Though I did endorse Bernie, I recognize that there were legitimate reasons why many people of color and women made a different choice. Though Clinton thought her nods to identity politics could substitute for substantial economic change, it often appeared as if Bernie thought that economics could paper over the unique needs and histories of Black people, women, and other traditionally marginalized groups. Yes, he faced unfair smears in this regard. But the more important lesson is that without Bernie's weaknesses on race and gender, he could have won, no matter how hard the Democratic Party establishment tried to hold him back. He would have won if he had persuaded more middle-aged and older women that he understood how important and precarious reproductive rights still are, and that he fully grasped the urgency of the epidemic of violence against women. In key states such as Pennsylvania and New York, he could have won if he had been able to win the support of just half of Black voters. But to do that, he would have needed to clearly and compellingly connect the dots between the country's deepest economic inequalities and the persistent legacy of slavery, Jim Crow laws, and housing and financial discrimination.

Ta-Nehisi Coates, writing in the *Atlantic*, pointed out that when it came to confronting that legacy, the boldness and radicalism Sanders displayed when taking on Wall Street suddenly petered out. Asked whether he supported some form of reparations for slavery, he dismissed the idea as politically impractical and unnecessarily "divisive," saying that big investments in communities of color would have the same effect. But as Coates rightly pointed out, the whole point of Sanders's candidacy was to push the envelope of what is considered politically possible—so where was that same boldness when it came to racial equality? "The spectacle of a socialist candidate opposing reparations as 'divisive' (there are few political labels more divisive in the minds of Americans than socialist) is only rivalled by the implausibility of Sanders posing as a pragmatist," Coates wrote. (Despite his strong critique, Coates publicly said he would be voting for Sanders in the primary as "the best option that we have in the race.")

Michelle Alexander, author of *The New Jim Crow*, came out strongly against Clinton during the primaries, arguing that her track record on criminal justice and welfare meant she did not deserve the Black vote. But she also chose not to publicly endorse Sanders. The most urgent message of the 2016 election, she told me, is: "If progressives think they can win in the long run without engaging meaningfully with Black folks and taking racial history more seriously, they better get Elon Musk on speed dial and start planning their future home on Mars, because this planet will be going up in smoke."

It's a message we need to learn fast. Because if Left populist candidates keep missing the mark, and Democrats keep putting up establishment candidates in their place, there is every reason to expect an increasingly belligerent Right to keep on winning.

A Toxic Cocktail Around the World

Trump thundered: All is hell. And Clinton answered: All is well—we just need a few minor tweaks here and there to make it more inclusive. "Love trumps Hate" was Clinton's final slogan. But love alone wasn't up to the job; it needed something stronger to help it out, something like justice.

As a candidate, Hillary Clinton was in no position to speak to the mounting popular rage that defines our times. She had helped negotiate trade deals like the TPP that so many see as a threat; the first Clinton administration had deregulated the banks and derivatives market, laying the groundwork for the financial crash (she never came out against the move and had taken not-insignificant speaking fees from those banks herself). So she tried to paper over the popular distress . . . with the results we know.

In the absence of a progressive alternative, Trump had a free hand to connect with skeptical voters by saying: I feel your pain. You *have* been screwed. On the campaign trail, he directed some of the rage at the corporations who had pushed for these policies—but that's mostly forgotten now. Most of his wrath was saved for the various racist bogeymen he conjured up: the immigrants coming to rape you, the Muslims coming to blow you up, the Black activists who don't respect our men in uniform, and the Black president who messed everything up.

The Brexit campaign spoke to that same toxic cocktail of real economic pain and genuinely eroded democracy combined with identity-based entitlement. And just as Hillary Clinton had no compelling answer to Trump's fake economic populism, the Remain campaign had no answer to Nigel Farage and UKIP, when they said that people's lives were out of control and public services were underfunded (even as their proposed solution was poised to make things even worse).

The crucial lesson of Brexit and of Trump's victory, is that leaders who are seen as representing the failed neoliberal status quo are no match for the demagogues and neo-fascists. Only a bold and genuinely redistributive progressive agenda can offer real answers to inequality and the crises in democracy, while directing popular rage where it belongs: at those who have benefited so extravagantly from the auctioning off of public wealth; the polluting of land, air, and water; and the deregulation of the financial sphere.

We need to remember this the next time we're asked to back a party or candidate in an election. In this destabilized era, status-quo politicians often cannot get the job done. On the other hand, the choice that may at first seem radical, maybe even a little risky, may well be the more pragmatic one in this volatile era.

And from the perspective of our warming planet, it's worth remembering that radical political and economic change is our only hope of avoiding radical change to our physical world.

Whatever happens, the next few years are going to be rocky. So before we focus on how to win the world we want and need, we first have to get ready for the next wave of crises coming from the Trump White House, shocks that could well reverberate the world over.

PART III

HOW IT COULD GET WORSE: THE SHOCKS TO COME

*History is important. If you don't know history it's as if
you were born yesterday. And if you were born yesterday,
anybody up there in a position of power can tell you anything,
and you have no way of checking up on it.*

— HOWARD ZINN
You Can't Be Neutral on a Moving Train, 2004 documentary

CHAPTER EIGHT

MASTERS OF DISASTER
DOING AN END RUN AROUND DEMOCRACY

There have been times in my reporting from disaster zones when I have had the unsettling feeling that I was seeing not just a crisis in the here and now, but a glimpse of our collective future — a preview of where the road we are all on is headed unless we somehow grab the wheel and swerve. When I listen to Trump speak, with his obvious relish in creating an atmosphere of chaos and destabilization, I often think: I've seen this before, I've seen it in those strange moments when portals seemed to open up into our collective future.

One of those moments arrived in New Orleans after Hurricane Katrina, as I watched hordes of private military contractors descend on the flooded city to find ways to profit from the disaster, even as thousands of the city's residents, abandoned by their government, were treated like dangerous criminals just for trying to survive.

I watched another such dystopian window open in 2003 in Baghdad, shortly after the invasion. At that time, the US occupation had carved the city in two. At its heart, behind enormous concrete walls and bomb detectors, there was the Green Zone — a little chunk of the United States rebuilt in Iraq, with bars serving hard liquor, fast-food joints, gyms, and a pool where there seemed to be a party 24/7. And then—beyond those walls—there was a city bombed to rubble, where there was often no electricity for hospitals, and where violence, between Iraqi factions and US occupation forces, was spiraling out of control. That was the Red Zone.

The Green Zone at the time was the fiefdom of Paul Bremer, former assistant to Henry Kissinger and director of Kissinger's consulting firm, whom George W. Bush had named as the chief US envoy to Iraq. Since there was no functioning national government, that essentially made him Iraq's supreme leader. Bremer's was an entirely privatized empire. Dressed in combat boots and a sharp business suit, Bremer was always protected by a phalanx of black-clad mercenaries working for the now-defunct company Blackwater, and the Green Zone itself was run by Halliburton—one of the largest oil field companies in the world, previously headed by then vice president Dick Cheney—along with a network of other private contractors.

When US officials made forays outside the Green Zone (or the "emerald city," as some journalists called it), they did so in heavily armored convoys, with soldiers and mercenaries pointing machine guns outward in all directions, guided by an ethic of "shoot first, ask questions later." Regular Iraqis supposedly being liberated by all this weaponry had no protection, except for the kind provided by religious militias in exchange for loyalty. The message broadcast by the convoys was loud and clear: some lives count a hell of a lot more than others.

From deep inside his Green Zone fortress, Bremer issued decree after decree about how Iraq should be remade into a model free-market economy. Come to think of it, it was a lot like Donald Trump's White House. And the edicts were pretty similar too. Bremer ordered, for instance, that Iraq should have a 15 percent flat tax (quite similar to what Trump has proposed), that its state-owned assets should be rapidly auctioned off (under consideration by Trump), and that government should be dramatically down-sized (Trump again). The pace was frantic. Bremer, with an eye on the fossil fuel fields of Iraq and beyond, was determined to get his country makeover done before Iraqis went to the polls and had any kind of say in what their "liberated" future would look like.

In one particularly surreal chapter, Bremer and the State Department brought in advisers from Russia who had led that country's disastrous experiment with "economic shock therapy," the corruption-laden deregulation and privatization frenzy which produced that country's notorious class of oligarchs. Inside the Green Zone, the visitors—including Yegor Gaidar, known as Russia's "Dr. Shock"—lectured the US-appointed Iraqi politicians about how important it was to radically remake the economy all at once and without hesitating, before Iraq's population recovered from the war. Iraqis would never have accepted these policies if they'd had a say (and they did in fact reject many of them later). It was only the extreme crisis that made Bremer's plan conceivable.

In fact, Bremer's open determination to auction off Iraq's state-owned assets under cover of crisis did a lot to confirm the widespread perception that the invasion was more about liberating Iraq's wealth for foreign companies than about liberating its people from despotism. The country spiraled into violence. The US military and its private contractors responded with more violence, more shocks. Unfathomable sums of money disappeared into the black hole of the contractor economy—money that came to be known as "Iraq's missing billions."

It wasn't just the seamless merger of corporate power and open warfare that felt like a glimpse into the dystopian future imagined so many times in science fiction and Hollywood films. It was also the clear mechanism of using crisis to ram through policies that would never have been feasible in normal times. It was in Iraq that I developed the thesis for *The Shock Doctrine.*

Originally, the book was going to focus exclusively on Bush's war, but then I started to notice the same tactics (and the same contractors, such as Halliburton, Blackwater, Bechtel . . .) in disaster zones around the world. First came an intense crisis—natural disaster, terrorist attack—then came the blitzkrieg of pro-corporate policies. Often the strategy of crisis exploitation was discussed right out in the open—no dark conspiracy theories required.

As I delved deeper, I realized that this strategy had been a silent partner to the imposition of neoliberalism for more than forty years. That "shock tactics" follow a clear pattern: wait for a crisis (or even, in some instances, as in Chile or Russia, help foment one), declare a moment of what is sometimes called "extraordinary politics," suspend some or all democratic norms—and then ram the corporate wish list through as quickly as possible. The research showed that virtually any tumultuous situation, if framed with sufficient hysteria by political leaders, could serve this softening-up function. It could be an event as radical as a military coup, but the economic shock of a market or budget crisis would also do the trick. In the midst of hyperinflation or a banking collapse, for instance, the country's governing elites were frequently able to sell a panicked population on the necessity for attacks on social protections, or enormous bailouts to prop up the financial private sector—because the alternative, they claimed, was outright economic apocalypse.

The Shock Doctor's Handbook

Shock tactics were first deployed in the service of neoliberalism in the early 1970s, in Latin America, and they are still being used today to extract "free-market" concessions against the popular will.

We've seen it happen recently, before Trump, in US cities including Detroit and Flint, where looming municipal bankruptcy became the pretext for dissolving local democracy and appointing "emergency managers." It is unfolding in Puerto Rico, where the ongoing debt crisis has been used to install the unaccountable "Financial Oversight and Management Board," an enforcement mechanism for harsh austerity measures, including cuts to pensions and waves of school closures. It is being deployed in Brazil, where the highly questionable impeachment of President Dilma Rousseff in 2016 was followed by the installation of an unelected, zealously pro-business regime that has frozen public spending for the next twenty years, imposed punishing austerity, and begun selling off airports, power stations, and other public assets in a frenzy of privatization.

And it is happening in blatant form under the presidency of Donald Trump. On the campaign trail, he did not tell his adoring crowds that he would cut funds for meals-on-wheels, a vital source of nutrition for the elderly and disabled, or admit that he was going to try to take health insurance away from millions of Americans. He said the very opposite, as on so many other issues.

Since taking office, he's never allowed the atmosphere of chaos and crisis to let up. The outrages come so fast and furious that many are understandably struggling to find their footing. Experiencing Trump's tsunami of Oval Office decrees—seven executive orders in his first eleven full days, plus eleven presidential memoranda issued in that same period—has felt a little like standing in front of one of those tennis ball machines. Opponents might swat back a ball or two, but we're all still getting hit in the face over and over again. Even the widespread belief among many (or is it hope?) that Trump will not last his full term contributes to the collective vertigo: nothing about the current situation is stable or static, which is a very difficult position from which to strategize or organize.

Democracy, Suspended until Further Notice

The last half century shows how deliberately—and effectively—the shock doctrine strategy has been deployed by governments to overcome democratic resistance to profoundly damaging policies. And some kind of democracy-avoidance strategy is needed, because many neoliberal policies are so unpopular that people reliably reject them both at the polls and in the streets. With good reason: as the tremendous hoarding (and hiding) of vast sums of wealth by a small and unaccountable global class of virtual oligarchs makes clear, those who benefit most from these radical social restructurings are a small minority, while the majority see their standard of living stagnate or slip, even in periods of rapid economic growth. Which is why, for those who are determined to push through these policies, majority rule and democratic freedoms aren't a friend—they are a hindrance and a threat.

Not every neoliberal policy is unpopular, of course. People do like tax cuts (for the middle class and working poor, if not for the super-rich), as well as the idea of cutting "red tape" (at least in theory). But they also, on the whole, like their taxes to pay for state-funded health care, clean water, good public schools, safe workplaces, pensions, and other programs to care for the elderly and disadvantaged. Politicians planning to slash these kinds of essential protections and services, or to privatize them, are rightly wary of putting those plans at the center of their electoral platforms. Far more common is for neoliberal politicians to campaign on promises of cutting taxes and government waste while protecting essential services, and then, under cover of some sort of crisis (real or exaggerated), claim, with apparent reluctance and wringing of hands, that, sorry, we have no choice but to go after your health care.

Doing It Fast and All at Once

The bottom line is that hard-core free marketers or "libertarians" (as the billionaire Koch brothers describe themselves) are attracted to moments of cataclysm because non-apocalyptic reality is actually inhospitable to their antidemocratic ambitions.

Speed is of the essence in all this, since periods of shock are temporary by nature. Like Bremer, shock-drunk leaders and their funders usually try to follow Machiavelli's advice in *The Prince*: "For injuries ought to be done all at one time, so that, being tasted less, they offend less." The logic is straightforward enough: People can develop responses to sequential or gradual change. But if dozens of changes come from all directions at once, the hope is that populations will rapidly become exhausted and overwhelmed, and will ultimately swallow their bitter medicine. (Recall the description of Poland's shock therapy as unfolding in "dog years.")

The Shock Doctrine was controversial when it came out in 2007. I was challenging a rosy version of history that many of us have grown up with—the version which tells us that deregulated markets and democracy advanced together, hand in hand, over the second half of the twentieth century. The truth, it turns out, is much uglier. The extreme form of capitalism that has been remaking our world in this period—which Nobel Prize–winning economist Joseph Stiglitz has termed "market fundamentalism"—very often could advance only in contexts where democracy was suspended and people's freedoms were sharply curtailed. In some cases, ferocious violence, including torture, was used to keep rebellious populations under control.

The late economist Milton Friedman called his most famous book *Capitalism and Freedom*, presenting human liberation and market liberation as flip sides of the same coin. And yet the first country to put Friedman's ideas into practice in unadulterated form was not a democracy—it was Chile, in the immediate after-math of the CIA-supported coup that overthrew a democrati-cally elected socialist president, Salvador Allende, and installed a far-right dictator, General Augusto Pinochet.

This was not an accident—the ideas were just too unpopular to be introduced without the help of a strong-arm despot. Richard Nixon had famously growled after Allende won the 1970 elec-tions: "Make the economy scream." With Allende left dead in the bloody coup, Friedman advised Pinochet that he should not blink when it came to economic transformation, prescribing what he termed the "shock treatment" approach. Under the advice of the famed economist and his former students (known in Latin America as "the Chicago Boys"), Chile replaced its pub-lic school system with vouchers and charter schools, made health care pay-as-you-go, and privatized kindergartens and cemeteries (and did many other things US Republicans have been eyeing for decades). And recall: this was in a country whose people were distinctly hostile to exactly these policies—a country which had, before the coup, democratically chosen socialist policies.

Similar regimes were installed in several Latin American countries during this period. Leading intellectuals in the region drew a direct connection between the economic shock treat-ments that impoverished millions and the epidemic of torture that ravaged hundreds of thousands in Chile, Argentina, Uruguay, and Brazil who believed in a fairer society. As the late Uruguayan historian Eduardo Galeano asked: "How can this inequality be maintained if not through jolts of electric shock?"

Latin America received a particularly strong dose of these twin forms of shock. Most "free-market" makeovers were not so bloody. Radical political transitions such as the collapse of the Soviet Union or the end of South African apartheid have also provided disorienting cover for neoliberal economic transformations. The most frequent midwife by far has been large-scale economic crisis, which time and again has been harnessed to demand radical campaigns of privatization, deregulation, and cuts to safety nets. But in truth, any shock can do the trick—including natural disasters that require large-scale reconstruction and therefore provide an opening to transfer land and resources from the vulnerable to the powerful.

The Opposite of Decency

Most people are appalled by this kind of crisis exploitation, and with good reason. The shock doctrine is the polar opposite of the way decent people, left to their own devices, tend to respond when they see widespread trauma, which is to offer help. Think of the staggering $3 billion privately donated in the aftermath of the 2010 earthquake in Haiti, or the millions offered in response to the 2015 quake in Nepal or the 2004 Asian tsunami. These disasters, like so many others, provoked extraordinary gestures of generosity from individuals around the world. Thousands upon thousands of regular people donated money and volunteered their labor.

As the American historian and writer Rebecca Solnit has so eloquently described, disasters have a way of bringing out the best in us. It is in such moments that we often see some of the most moving displays of mutual aid and solidarity. In Sri Lanka after the 2004 tsunami, despite decades of interethnic civil war, Muslims saved their Hindu neighbors and Hindus saved their Buddhist neighbors. In flooded post-Katrina New Orleans, people put their own lives at great risk to rescue and care for their neighbors. After Superstorm Sandy hit New York, a remarkable network of volunteers fanned out across the city, under the banner of Occupy Sandy—it grew out of the Occupy Wall Street movement—to serve hundreds of thousands of meals, help clear out more than a thousand homes, and provide

clothing, blankets, and medical care to thousands of people in
need.

The shock doctrine is about overriding these deeply human
impulses to help, seeking instead to capitalize on the vulnerability of others in order to maximize wealth and advantage for a
select few.

There are few things more sinister than that.

The Art of the Steal

Shock doctrine logic is entirely in keeping with Trump's view of
the world. He unabashedly sees life as a battle for dominance
over others—and he keeps obsessive track of who is winning. In
his much-self-celebrated negotiations, the questions are always
the same: What's the most that I can get out of this deal? How do
I exploit my adversary's weakness?

In a particularly candid moment on *Fox & Friends* in 2011, he
described a deal he made with former Libyan leader Muammar
Qaddafi like this: "I rented him a piece of land. He paid me more
for one night than the land was worth for the whole year, or for
two years, and then I didn't let him use the land. That's what we
should be doing. I don't want to use the word *screwed*, but I
screwed him. That's what we should be doing."

If Trump extracted predatory terms only from despised dicta-
tors, few tears would be shed. But this is Trump's attitude to all
negotiations. In *Think Big*, one of his how-to-be-like-me manuals, he describes his negotiation philosophy this way: "You hear
lots of people say that a great deal is when both sides win. That
is a bunch of crap. In a great deal you win—not the other side.
You crush the opponent and come away with something better
for yourself."

This cold-blooded enthusiasm for exploiting the weakness of
others has shaped Trump's career as a real estate developer, and

it is a trait he shares with many members of his administration. It's worrying for what it tells us about not only the atmosphere of chaos his team appears to be consciously cultivating but also, far more alarmingly, how they might exploit any larger crises yet to come.

So far, Trump's unending atmosphere of crisis has been sustained largely through his own over-the-top rhetoric — declaring cities "crime-infested" sites of "carnage" when in fact the violent-crime rate has been declining nationwide for decades; hammering away at a manufactured narrative about an immigrant crime wave; and generally insisting that Obama destroyed the country. Soon enough, however, Trump could well have some crises to exploit that are distinctly more real, since crisis is the logical conclusion of his policies on every front.

Given this, it's well worth taking a close look at the ways in which Trump and his team have exploited moments of crisis in the past to achieve their economic and political goals. Understanding this track record will make whatever happens next a whole lot less shocking, and will ultimately help us to resist these tired tactics.

A Career Forged in Shock

In the United States, the neoliberal revolution got a head start in New York City in the mid-1970s. Up until this point, the city had been a bold, if imperfect, experiment in social democracy, featuring the most generous public services in the United States, from libraries to mass transit to hospitals. But in 1975, federal and state cutbacks, combined with a national recession, pushed New York to the brink of all-out bankruptcy, and the crisis was seized upon to dramatically remake the city. Under cover of crisis came a wave of brutal austerity, sweetheart deals to the rich, and privatizations — with the end result of turning the city so many of us love into the temple of speculative finance, luxury consumption, and nonstop gentrification that we know today.

In *Fear City*, a recently published book about this little-understood chapter in America's past, historian Kim Phillips-Fein meticulously documents how the remaking of New York City in the seventies was a prelude to what would become a global tidal wave, one that has left the world sharply divided between the one percent and the rest—and nowhere more so than in the city Donald Trump calls home. It's also a story in which Trump plays a starring, if unflattering, role.

In 1975, with no help forthcoming from President Gerald Ford, it looked so likely that the United States' largest and most storied city would actually go bankrupt that the New York *Daily News* ran a banner headline that said simply: FORD TO CITY: DROP DEAD. At the time, Trump was just twenty-nine years old and still working in the shadow of his wealthy father, who had made his fortune building distinctly unflashy middle-class homes in New York's outer boroughs—and who was notorious as a landlord practicing systemic discrimination against African Americans.

Trump had always dreamed of making his mark in Manhattan, and with the debt crisis he saw his big chance. The opening came in 1976, when the famed Commodore Hotel, a historic midtown landmark, announced that it was losing so much money that it might have to close down. The city government was panicked at the prospect of this iconic building sitting empty, broadcasting a message of urban decay and depriving the city of tax revenue. They needed a buyer, quick, and the mood was sufficiently desperate that, as one local television broadcast put it, "beggars can't be choosers."

Enter Trump, proto–disaster capitalist. Partnering with the Hyatt Corporation, Trump had a plan to replace the Commodore's classic brick facade with "a new skin" of reflective glass, and to reopen it as the Grand Hyatt Hotel (this was in the brief window before the future US president began insisting that all his developments bear his name). He extracted extraordinary terms from a city in crisis. As Phillips-Fein explains:

> Trump would be allowed to purchase the property from the railroad for $9.5 million. Then he would sell it for a dollar to the Urban Development Corporation. . . . Finally, the UDC would lease the property back to Trump and the Hyatt Corporation for ninety-nine years, allowing the developers to pay taxes far below the normal rate for four decades—a windfall worth hundreds of millions of dollars. (As of 2016, Trump's tax break has cost New York City $360 million in uncollected taxes.)

Yes, that's right: for $9.5 million down, Trump extracted a tax-break windfall for the property worth $360 million (and counting) from the city. The new hotel was a blight—what one architectural critic described as "an out-of-towner's vision of city life." In other words, it was vintage Trump, a man who would go on to sell the world on a Russian oligarch's vision of the United States as filtered through bootleg VHS copies of the eighties soap operas *Dynasty* and *Dallas*. In Phillips-Fein's words:

> Donald Trump and the developers who exploited the city's desperation to build their towers had little interest in the rest of New York. The fact that millions of dollars went to subsidize building projects instead of restoring public services or promoting recovery in the poor and working-class neighborhoods of the city never registered as a moral concern.

What is striking about this story is not simply that a young Trump seized on New York's economic catastrophe to boost his own fortune, extracting predatory terms from a government in crisis. It's also that this was not just any deal—it was the one that let Trump emerge from his father's shadow and decisively turned him into a player in his own right. Trump's career was forged in shock, shaped by the unique opportunities for profit presented by moments of crisis. Right from his breakout moment, his attitude toward the public sphere was that it was there to be pillaged, to enrich himself.

It's an attitude that has stayed with him ever since. It's worth remembering that on September 11, 2001, shortly after the Twin Towers came down, Trump gave an interview to a radio station during which he could not help observing that, with the Towers gone, he now had the tallest building in downtown Manhattan. Dead bodies were in the street, lower Manhattan looked like a war zone, and yet, with only a little encouragement from the radio hosts, Trump was thinking about his brand advantage.

When I asked Phillips-Fein what lessons she drew from studying Trump's actions during New York's debt crisis, her reply was all about fear. There was, she said, "this deep level of fear about bankruptcy, fear of the future. And it's that kind of fear that really makes possible the cutbacks of the time, and also the sense that the city needs a savior in the first place." Since the 2016 election, she has been thinking about this a lot. "The way that fear can make things that seem politically impossible suddenly feel as though they're the only alternative. And so I think that is one of the things that we need to fight at this moment, and to find ways to resist that sense of overwhelming fear and chaos, and to find forms of solidarity that can counter it."

fear leads to seeking Savior

It's good advice. Especially since Trump has assembled around him an all-star cast of crisis opportunists.

Meet the Disaster Capitalism Cabinet

Senior members of Trump's team have been at the heart of some of the most egregious examples of the shock doctrine in recent memory. What follows is a brief overview of their exploits (which, by nature of just how many Goldman Sachs executives Trump has appointed, is by no means exhaustive).

Profiting from Climate Change and War

Rex Tillerson, US secretary of state, has built his career in large part around taking advantage of the profitability of war and instability. ExxonMobil profited more than any oil major from the increase in the price of oil that was the result of the 2003 invasion of Iraq. It also directly exploited the Iraq War to defy State Department advice and make an exploration deal in Iraqi Kurdistan, a move that, because it sidelined Iraq's central government, could well have sparked a full-blown civil war, and certainly did contribute to internal conflict.

As CEO of ExxonMobil, Tillerson profited from disaster in other ways as well. As we have already seen, as an executive at the fossil fuel giant, he spent his career working for a company that, despite its own scientists' research into the reality of human-caused climate change, decided to fund and spread misinformation and junk climate science. All the while, according to an *LA Times* investigation, ExxonMobil (both before and after those two companies merged) worked diligently to figure out how to further profit from and protect itself against the very crisis on which it was casting doubt. It did so by exploring drilling in the Arctic (which was melting, thanks to climate change), redesigning a natural gas pipeline in the North Sea to accommodate rising sea levels and supercharged storms, and doing the same for a new rig off the coast of Nova Scotia.

At a public event in 2012, Tillerson acknowledged that climate change was happening—but what he said next was revealing: "as a species," humans have always adapted. "So we will adapt to this. Changes to weather patterns that move crop production areas around—we'll adapt to that."

He's quite right: humans do adapt when their land ceases to produce food. The way humans adapt is by moving. They leave their homes and look for places to live where they can feed themselves and their families. But, as Tillerson well knows, we do not live at a time when countries gladly open their borders to hungry and desperate people. In fact, he now works for a president who has painted refugees from Syria—a country where drought was an accelerant of the tensions that led to civil war—as Trojan horses for terrorism. A president who introduced a travel ban that, if it had not been blocked by the courts, would have barred Syrian migrants from entering the United States. A president who has said about Syrian children seeking asylum, "I can look in their faces and say 'You can't come.'" A president who has not budged from that position even after he ordered missile strikes on Syria, supposedly moved by the horrifying impacts of a chemical weapon attack on Syrian children and "beautiful babies." (But not moved enough to welcome them and their parents.) A president who has announced plans to turn the tracking, surveillance, incarceration, and deportation of immigrants into a defining feature of his administration.

Waiting in the wings, biding their time, are plenty of other members of the Trump team who have deep skills in profiting from all of that.

Profiting from Prisons

Between election day and the end of Trump's first month in office, the stocks of the two largest private prison companies in the USA,

CoreCivic (formerly the Corrections Corporation of America) and the GEO Group, doubled, soaring by 140 percent and 98 percent, respectively.

And why not? Just as Exxon learned to profit from climate change, these companies are part of the sprawling industry of private prisons, private security, and private surveillance that sees wars and migration—both very often linked to climate stresses— as exciting and expanding market opportunities. In the United States, the Immigration and Customs Enforcement agency (ICE) incarcerates up to thirty-four thousand immigrants thought to be in the country illegally on any given day, and 73 percent of them are held in private prisons. Little wonder, then, that these companies' stocks soared on Trump's election. And soon they had even more reasons to celebrate: one of the first things Jeff Sessions did as Trump's attorney general was rescind the Obama administration's decision to move away from for-profit jails for the general prison population.

Profiting from War and Surveillance

Trump appointed as deputy defense secretary Patrick Shanahan, a top executive at Boeing who, at one point, was responsible for selling costly hardware to the US military, including Apache and Chinook helicopters. He also oversaw Boeing's ballistic missile defense program—a part of the operation that stands to profit enormously if international tensions continue to escalate under Trump.

And this is part of a much larger trend. As Lee Fang reported in the *Intercept* in March 2017, "President Donald Trump has weaponized the revolving door by appointing defense contractors and lobbyists to key government positions as he seeks to rapidly expand the military budget and homeland security programs. . . . At least 15 officials with financial ties to defense contractors have been either nominated or appointed so far."

The revolving door is nothing new, of course. Retired military brass reliably take up jobs and contracts with weapons companies. What's new is the number of generals with lucrative ties to military contractors whom Trump has appointed to cabinet posts with the power to allocate funds—including those stemming from his plan to increase spending on the military, the Pentagon, and the Department of Homeland Security by more than $80 billion in just one year.

The other thing that has changed is the size of the Homeland Security and surveillance industry. This sector grew exponentially after the September 11 attacks, when the Bush administration announced it was embarking on a never-ending "war on terror" and that everything that could be outsourced would be. New firms with tinted windows sprouted up like malevolent mushrooms around suburban Virginia, outside Washington, DC, and existing ones, like Booz Allen Hamilton, expanded into brandnew territories. Writing in *Slate* in 2005, Daniel Gross captured the mood of what many called the security bubble: "Homeland security may have just reached the stage that Internet investing hit in 1997. Back then, all you needed to do was put an 'e' in front of your company name and your IPO would rocket. Now you can do the same with 'fortress.'"

That means many of Trump's appointees come from firms that specialize in functions which, not so long ago, it would have been unthinkable to outsource. His National Security Council chief of staff, for instance, is retired Lieutenant General Keith Kellogg. Among the many jobs Kellogg has had with security contractors since going private was one with Cubic Defense. According to the company, he led "our ground combat training business and focus on expanding the company's worldwide customer base." If you think "combat training" is something armies used to do all on their own, you'd be right.

One noticeable thing about Trump's contractor appointees is how many of them come from firms that did not even exist before 9/11: L1 Identity Solutions (specializing in biometrics), the Chertoff Group (founded by Bush's Homeland Security director Michael Chertoff), Palantir Technologies (a surveillance/big data firm cofounded by PayPal billionaire and Trump backer Peter Thiel), and many more. Security firms draw heavily on the military and intelligence wings of government for their staffing. Under Trump, a remarkable number of lobbyists and staffers from these firms are now migrating back to government, where they will very likely push for even more opportunities to monetize the hunt for people President Trump likes to call "bad hombres."

This creates a disastrous cocktail. Take a group of people who directly profit from ongoing war and then put those same people at the heart of government. Who's going to make the case for peace? Indeed, the idea that a war could ever definitively end seems a quaint relic of what during the Bush years was dismissed as "pre–September 11 thinking."

Profiting from Economic Crisis

Ties between the US government and the business world date back to 1776 (several of the Founding Fathers were from wealthy plantation-owning families). The revolving door has been spinning ever since, regardless of whether a Democrat or a Republican was in the Oval Office. The difference with Trump, as is so often the case, is one of volume, and shamelessness.

As of this writing, Donald Trump has appointed five current or former Goldman Sachs executives to senior roles in his administration, including Steve Mnuchin as Treasury secretary, James Donovan (formerly a Goldman Sachs managing director) as deputy Treasury secretary, Gary Cohn (formerly Goldman's chief operating officer) as director of the White House National

Economic Council, and Dina Powell (formerly Goldman's head of impact investing) as the White House senior counselor for economic initiatives. Even Steve Bannon once worked at Goldman. And that's not counting Trump's pick to lead the Securities and Exchange Commission, Jay Clayton, who served as Goldman's lawyer on multibillion-dollar deals, and whose wife is a wealth manager with the company.

Making all these Goldman appointments is particularly brazen given Trump's invocation of the bank to attack his opponents. In a typically vicious salvo at his GOP rival Ted Cruz, he claimed the Goldman guys "have total, total control over him. Just like they have total control over Hillary Clinton."

It's also extremely worrying for what it says about the administration's willingness to exploit the economic shocks that may well reverberate on their watch. Of all the major Wall Street investment banks at the center of the 2008 subprime mortgage crisis, Goldman Sachs was among the most predatory. Not only did Goldman do a huge amount to help inflate the mortgage bubble with complex financial instruments, but it then turned around and, mid crisis, allegedly bet against the mortgage market and earned billions. In 2016, the bank was ordered by the United States Justice Department to pay a settlement of $5 billion—the largest settlement Goldman had ever paid—for these and other malpractices. In 2010, it agreed to a further $550-million fine, the largest ever paid by a Wall Street firm in the then 76-year history of the Securities and Exchange Commission, for its role in the financial crisis.

Democratic senator Carl Levin, who headed the 2010 Senate subcommittee that investigated Goldman Sachs following the financial crisis, summarized their misdeeds:

> The evidence shows that Goldman repeatedly put its own interests and profits ahead of the interests of its clients and our

communities. . . . Goldman Sachs didn't just make money. It profited by taking advantage of its clients' reasonable expectation that it would not sell products that it didn't want to succeed, and that there was no conflict of economic interest between the firm and the customers it had pledged to serve. Goldman's actions demonstrate that it often saw its clients not as valuable customers, but as objects for its own profit. This matters because instead of doing well when its clients did well, Goldman Sachs did well when its clients lost money.

Even among Goldman alumni, Steven Mnuchin has distinguished himself by his willingness to profit off misery. After the 2008 Wall Street collapse, and in the midst of the foreclosure crisis, Mnuchin purchased a California bank. The renamed company, OneWest, earned Mnuchin the nickname "Foreclosure King," reportedly collecting $1.2 billion from the government to help cover the losses for foreclosed homes and evicting tens of thousands of people between 2009 and 2014. One attempted foreclosure involved a ninety-year-old woman who was behind on her payments by 27 cents.

These predatory practices drew fire during Mnuchin's confirmation hearing for Treasury secretary (though not enough for Republicans to vote against him). Oregon Democratic senator Ron Wyden said during the hearing that, "while Mr. Mnuchin was CEO, the bank proved it could put more vulnerable people on the streets faster than just about anybody," and charged "OneWest churned out foreclosures like Chinese factories churned out Trump suits and ties."

Profiting from Natural Disasters

And then there's Vice President Mike Pence, seen by many as the grown-up in Trump's messy room. Yet it is Pence, the former governor of Indiana, who actually has the most disturbing track record when it comes to bloody-minded exploitation of human suffering.

When Mike Pence was announced as Donald Trump's running mate, I thought to myself, "I know that name. I've seen it somewhere." And then I remembered. He was at the heart of one of the most shocking stories I've ever covered: the disaster capitalism free-for-all that followed Katrina and the drowning of New Orleans. Mike Pence's doings as a profiteer from human suffering are so appalling that they are worth exploring in a little more depth, since they tell us a great deal about what we can expect from this administration during times of heightened crisis.

The Katrina Blueprint

Before we delve into Pence's role, what's important to remember about Hurricane Katrina is that, though it is usually described as a "natural disaster," there was nothing natural about the way it impacted the city of New Orleans. When Katrina hit the coast of Mississippi in August 2005, it had been downgraded from a Category 5 to a still-devastating Category 3 hurricane. But by the time it made its way to New Orleans, it had lost most of its strength and been downgraded again, to a "tropical storm."

That's relevant, because a tropical storm should never have broken through New Orleans's flood defense. Katrina did break through, however, because the levees that protect the city did not hold. Why? We now know that despite repeated warnings about the risk, the Army Corps of Engineers had allowed the levees to fall into a state of disrepair. That failure was the result of two main factors.

One was a specific disregard for the lives of poor Black people, whose homes in the Lower Ninth Ward were left most vulnerable by the failure to fix the levees. This was part of a wider neglect of public infrastructure across the United States, which is the direct result of decades of neoliberal policy. Because when you systematically wage war on the very idea of the public sphere and the public good, of course the publicly owned bones of society— roads, bridges, levees, water systems—are going to slip into a state of such disrepair that it takes little to push them beyond the breaking point. When you massively cut taxes so that you don't have money to spend on much of anything besides the police and the military, this is what happens.

It wasn't just the physical infrastructure that failed the city, and particularly its poorest residents, who are, as in so many US cities, overwhelmingly African American. The human systems of disaster response also failed, the second great fracturing. The arm of the federal government that is tasked with responding to moments of national crisis like this is the Federal Emergency Management Agency, with state and municipal governments also playing key roles in evacuation planning and response. All levels of government failed.

It took FEMA five days to get water and food to people in New Orleans who had sought emergency shelter in the Superdome. The most harrowing images from that time were of people stranded on rooftops—of homes and hospitals—holding up signs that said *HELP*, watching the helicopters pass them by. People helped each other as best they could. They rescued each other in canoes and rowboats. They fed each other. They displayed that beautiful human capacity for solidarity that moments of crisis so often intensify. But at the official level, it was the complete opposite. I'll always remember the words of Curtis Muhammad, a longtime New Orleans civil rights organizer, who said this experience "convinced us that we had no caretakers."

The way this abandonment played out was deeply unequal, and the divisions cleaved along lines of race and class. Many people were able to leave the city on their own—they got into their cars, drove to a dry hotel, called their insurance brokers. Some people stayed because they believed the storm defenses would hold. But a great many others stayed because they had no choice—they didn't have a car, or were too infirm to drive, or simply didn't know what to do. Those are the people who needed a functioning system of evacuation and relief—and they were out of luck. It felt like Baghdad all over again, with some people taking shelter in their own private Green Zones while many more were left stranded in the Red Zone—where the worst was yet to come.

Abandoned in the city without food or water, those in need did what anyone would do in those circumstances: they took provisions from local stores. Fox News and other media outlets seized on this to paint New Orleans's Black residents as dangerous "looters" who would soon be coming to invade the dry, white parts of the city and surrounding suburbs and towns. Buildings were spray-painted with messages: "Looters will be shot." Checkpoints were set up to trap people in the flooded parts of town. On Danziger Bridge, police officers shot Black residents on sight (five of the officers involved ultimately pled guilty, and the city came to a $13.3-million settlement with the families in that case and two other similar post-Katrina cases). Meanwhile, gangs of armed white vigilantes prowled the streets looking, as one resident later put it in an exposé by investigative journalist A.C. Thompson, for "the opportunity to hunt Black people." In the Red Zone, apparently, anything goes.

I was in New Orleans and I saw for myself how amped up the police and military were—not to mention private security guards from companies like Blackwater who were showing up fresh from Iraq. It felt very much like a war zone, with poor and Black people in the crosshairs—people whose only crime was trying to survive. By the time the National Guard arrived to organize a full evacuation of the city, it was done with a level of aggression and ruthlessness that was hard to fathom. Soldiers pointed machine guns at residents as they boarded buses, providing no information about where they were being taken. Children were often separated from their parents.

What I saw during the flooding shocked me. But what I saw in the aftermath of Katrina shocked me even more. With the city reeling, and with its residents dispersed across the country and unable to protect their own interests, a plan emerged to ram through a pro-corporate wish list with maximum velocity. Milton Friedman, then ninety-three years old, wrote an article for the *Wall Street Journal* stating, "Most New Orleans schools are in ruins, as are the homes of the children who have attended them. The children are now scattered all over the country. This is a tragedy. It is also an opportunity to radically reform the educational system."

In a similar vein, Richard Baker, at that time a Republican congressman from Louisiana, declared, "We finally cleaned up public housing in New Orleans. We couldn't do it, but God did." I was in an evacuation shelter near Baton Rouge when Baker made that statement. The people I spoke with were just floored by it. Imagine being forced to leave your home, having to sleep in a cot in some cavernous convention center, and then finding out that the people who are supposed to represent you are claiming this was some sort of divine intervention—God apparently really likes condo developments.

Baker got his "cleanup" of public housing. In the months after the storm, with New Orleans's residents—and all their inconvenient opinions, rich culture, and deep attachments—out of the way, thousands of public housing units, many of which had sustained minimal storm damage because they were on high ground, were demolished. They were replaced with condos and townhomes priced far out of reach for most who had lived there.

And this is where Mike Pence enters the story. At the time Katrina hit New Orleans, Pence was chairman of the powerful and highly ideological Republican Study Committee (RSC), a caucus of conservative lawmakers. On September 13, 2005—just fourteen days after the levees were breached and with parts of New Orleans still under water—the RSC convened a fateful meeting at the offices of the Heritage Foundation in Washington, DC. Under Pence's leadership, the group came up with a list of "Pro-Free-Market Ideas for Responding to Hurricane Katrina and High Gas Prices"—thirty-two pseudo relief policies in all, each one straight out of the disaster capitalism playbook.

What stands out is the commitment to wage all-out war on labor standards and the public sphere—which is bitterly ironic, because the failure of public infrastructure is what turned Katrina into a human catastrophe in the first place. Also notable is the determination to use any opportunity to strengthen the hand of the oil and gas industry. The list includes recommendations to "automatically suspend Davis–Bacon prevailing wage laws in disaster areas" (a reference to the law that requires federal contractors to pay a living wage); "make the entire affected area a flat-tax free-enterprise zone"; and "repeal or waive restrictive environmental regulations . . . that hamper rebuilding."

President Bush adopted many of the recommendations within the week, although, under pressure, he was eventually forced to reinstate the labor standards. Another recommendation called for giving parents vouchers to use at private and charter schools (for-profit schools subsidized with tax dollars), a move perfectly in line with the vision held by Trump's pick for education secretary, Betsy DeVos. Within the year, New Orleans became the most privatized school system in the United States.

And there was more. Though climate scientists have directly linked the increased intensity of hurricanes to warming ocean temperatures, that didn't stop Pence and his committee from calling on Congress to repeal environmental regulations on the Gulf Coast, give permission for new oil refineries in the United States, and green-light "drilling in the Arctic National Wildlife Refuge." It's a kind of madness. After all, these very measures are a surefire way to drive up greenhouse gas emissions, the major human contributor to climate change, which leads to fiercer storms. Yet they were immediately championed by Pence, and later adopted by Bush, under the guise of responding to a devastating hurricane.

It's worth pausing to tease out the implications of all of this. Hurricane Katrina turned into a catastrophe in New Orleans because of a combination of extremely heavy weather, possibly linked to climate change, and weak and neglected public infrastructure. The so-called solutions proposed by the group Pence headed at the time were the very things that would inevitably exacerbate climate change and weaken public infrastructure even further. He and his fellow "free-market" travelers were determined, it seems, to do the very things that are guaranteed to lead to more Katrinas in the future.

And now Mike Pence is in a position to bring this vision to the entire United States.

Kleptocracy Free-for-All

NO BID

The oil industry wasn't the only one to profit from Hurricane Katrina. Immediately after the storm, the whole Baghdad gang of contractors—Bechtel, Fluor, Halliburton, Blackwater, CH2M Hill, and Parsons, infamous for its sloppy Iraq work—descended on New Orleans. They had a singular vision: to prove that the kinds of privatized services they had been providing in Iraq and Afghanistan also had an ongoing domestic market—and to collect no-bid contracts totaling $3.4 billion in the process.

The controversies were legion, too many to delve into here. Relevant experience often appeared to have nothing to do with how contracts were allocated. Take, for example, the company that FEMA paid $5.2 million to perform the crucial role of building a base camp for emergency workers in St. Bernard Parish, a suburb of New Orleans. The camp construction fell behind schedule and was never completed. Under investigation, it emerged that the contractor, Lighthouse Disaster Relief, was in fact a religious group. "About the closest thing I have done to this is just organize a youth camp with my church," confessed Lighthouse's director, Pastor Gary Heldreth.

After all the layers of subcontractors had taken their cut, there was next to nothing left for the people doing the work. Author Mike Davis tracked the way FEMA paid Shaw $175 per square foot to install blue tarps on damaged roofs, even though the tarps themselves were provided by the government. Once all the subcontractors took their share, the workers who actually hammered in the tarps were paid as little as two dollars per square foot. "Every level of the contracting food chain, in other words, is grotesquely overfed except the bottom rung," Davis wrote, "where the actual work is carried out." These supposed "contractors" were really—like the Trump Organization—hollow brands, sucking out profit and then slapping their name on cheap or nonexistent services.

In order to offset the tens of billions going to private companies in contracts and tax breaks, in November 2005 the Republican-controlled Congress announced that it needed to cut $40 billion from the federal budget. Among the programs that were slashed: student loans, Medicaid, and food stamps. So, the poorest people in the United States subsidized the contractor bonanza twice: first, when Katrina relief morphed into unregulated corporate handouts, providing neither decent jobs nor functional public services; and second, when the few programs that directly assist the unemployed and working poor nationwide were gutted to pay those bloated bills.

New Orleans is the disaster capitalism blueprint—designed by the current vice president and by the Heritage Foundation, the hard-right think tank to which Trump has outsourced much of his administration's budgeting. Ultimately, the response to Katrina sparked an approval ratings free fall for George W. Bush, a plunge that eventually lost the Republicans the presidency in 2008. Nine years later, with Republicans now in control of Congress and the White House, it's not hard to imagine this test case for privatized disaster response being adopted on a national scale.

The presence of highly militarized police and armed private soldiers in New Orleans came as a surprise to many. Since then, the phenomenon has expanded exponentially, with local police forces across the country outfitted to the gills with military-grade gear, including tanks and drones, and private security companies frequently providing training and support. Given the array of private-military and security contractors occupying key positions in the Trump administration, we can expect all of this to expand further with each new shock.

The Katrina experience also stands as a stark warning to those who are holding out hope for Trump's promised trillion dollars in infrastructure spending. That spending will fix some roads and bridges, and it will create jobs (though—as we'll see in Chapter 10—far less than green infrastructure investment to transition off fossil fuels would). Crucially, Trump has indicated that he plans to do as much as possible not through the public sector but through public-private partnerships—which have a terrible track record for corruption, and may result in far lower wages than true public works projects would. Given Trump's business record, and Pence's role in the administration, there is every reason to fear that his big-ticket infrastructure spending could become a Katrina-like kleptocracy, a government of thieves, with the Mar-a-Lago set helping themselves to vast sums of taxpayer money.

New Orleans provides a harrowing picture of what we can expect when the next shock hits. But sadly, it is far from complete: there is much more that this administration may try to push through under cover of crisis. To become shock resistant, we need to prepare for that too.

CHAPTER NINE

THE TOXIC TO-DO LIST
WHAT TO EXPECT WHEN YOU ARE EXPECTING A CRISIS

In New Orleans after Katrina, some of the key players who now surround Trump showed to what lengths they will go to decimate the public sphere and advance the interests of real estate developers, private contractors, and oil companies. Today, they are in a position to take Katrina national.

What makes this constellation of disaster capitalists all the more worrying is the fact that, though Trump has been able to do a great deal of damage in his first few months in office, he has been repeatedly stymied by the courts and by Congress. And many of the more radical items on this administration's wish list have yet to be attempted at all. His education secretary, Betsy DeVos, for instance, has devoted her life to pushing for a privatized education system like the one in New Orleans after Katrina. Many of the figures who surround Trump are passionate about dismantling Social Security. Several are equally fervent in their distaste for a free press, unions, and political protests. Trump himself has mused publicly about bringing in "the feds" to deal with crime in cities like Chicago, and on the campaign trail he pledged to block all Muslims from entering the US, not just the ones from the countries on his various lists. His attorney general, Jeff Sessions, has been highly critical of police department "consent decrees," an important measure that allows the Justice Department and federal courts to intervene in local and state police forces if they identify a pattern of abuse—for example, repeated shootings of unarmed Black people. Sessions claims these accountability mechanisms "can reduce morale for the police officers," impairing their ability to fight crime (a claim unsupported by the data).

The wealthiest funders of Trump's campaign and of the Far Right more broadly—the multibillionaire Koch Brothers and the Mercer family—have their sights set on eliminating the remaining restrictions on money in politics, while doing away with those laws that require transparency in how such private money is spent. Under the guise of battling a manufactured "voting fraud" crisis, they are also backing groups that have been pushing measures to make it even harder for low-income people and minorities to vote, such as rules requiring photo ID to cast a ballot (some form of these initiatives had already been enacted in at least thirty-two states by the time Trump was elected). If these twin goals are fully realized, progressive challengers will be so outspent by their Republican rivals, and will have so much trouble getting their supporters into voting booths, that the corporate coup Trump represents could well become permanent.

Realizing the full breadth of this antidemocratic vision is not achievable in the current circumstances. Without a crisis, the courts would keep getting in the way, as would several state governments controlled by Democrats, and on some of Trump's more sadistic dreams—like bringing back torture—even Congress might stand up to him.

But the full agenda is still there, lying in wait. Which is why author and journalist Peter Maass, writing in the *Intercept*, described the Trump White House as "a pistol cocked to go off at the first touch"—or rather, the first crisis. As Milton Friedman wrote long ago, "only a crisis—actual or perceived—produces real change. When that crisis occurs, the actions that are taken depend on the ideas that are lying around. That, I believe, is our basic function: to develop alternatives to existing policies, to keep them alive and available until the politically impossible becomes politically inevitable." Survivalists stockpile canned goods and water in preparation for major disasters; these guys stockpile spectacularly antidemocratic ideas.

So the questions we need to focus on are these: What disaster, or series of disasters, could play the enabling role? And what tasks on the toxic to-do list are most likely to rear their heads at these first opportunities?

It's high time for some disaster preparedness.

States of Emergency, States of Exception

During the campaign, some imagined that the more overtly racist elements of Trump's platform were just talk designed to rile up the base, not anything he seriously intended to act on. In Trump's first week in office, when he imposed a travel ban on seven majority-Muslim countries, that comforting illusion disappeared fast. And the response was immediate. In major cities across the United States, thousands upon thousands of people left their homes and flooded to the airports, demanding that the ban be revoked and that the travelers being detained be released. Taxi drivers in New York refused to take fares to or from JFK airport, local politicians and lawyers showed up in droves to help the people under detention, and a federal court judge finally intervened to block the ban. When Trump slightly modified his executive order and reissued it, another judge got in his way.

The whole episode showed the power of resistance, and of judicial courage, and there was much to celebrate. But we can't forget that a terrorist attack in the United States would provide the administration with a pretext to try to override much of this kind of pushback. In all likelihood they would do it swiftly, by declaring protests and strikes that block roads and airports a threat to "national security," and then using that cover to go after protest organizers—with surveillance, arrests, and imprisonment. Many of us well remember the "with us or with the terrorists" atmosphere that descended after September 11—but we don't need to go back that far to see how these dynamics work.

In the immediate aftermath of the Westminster terror attacks in London in March 2017, when a driver plowed into a crowd of pedestrians, deliberately killing four people and injuring dozens more, the Conservative government wasted no time declaring that any expectation of privacy in digital communications was now a threat to national security. Home Secretary Amber Rudd went on the BBC and declared the end-to-end encryption provided by programs like WhatsApp to be "completely unacceptable." And she said that they were meeting with the large tech firms "to ask them to work with us" on providing backdoor access to these platforms.

In France in 2015, after the coordinated attacks in Paris that killed 130 people, the government of François Hollande declared a "state of emergency" that banned political protests. I was in France a week after those horrific events and it was striking that, though the attackers had targeted a concert, a football stadium, restaurants, and other emblems of daily Parisian life, it was only outdoor political activity that was not permitted. Large concerts, Christmas markets, and sporting events—the sorts of places that were likely targets for further attacks—were all free to carry on as usual.

In the months that followed, the state-of-emergency decree was extended again and again—until it had been in place for well over a year. It is currently set to remain in effect until at least July 2017—the new normal. And this took place under a center-left government in a country with a long tradition of disruptive strikes and protests. One would have to be naive to imagine that Donald Trump and Mike Pence wouldn't immediately seize on any attack in the USA to go much further down that same road. We should be prepared for security shocks to be exploited as excuses to increase the rounding up and incarceration of large numbers of people from the communities this administration is already targeting: Latino immigrants, Muslims, Black Lives Matter organizers, climate activists. It's all possible. And, in the name of freeing the hands of law enforcement officials, Sessions would have his excuse to do away with federal oversight of state and local police.

Unfortunately, there is no guarantee that, in the aftermath of an attack, judges would show the same courage in standing up to Trump as they did immediately after his inauguration. As much as they position themselves as neutral arbiters, courts are not immune to public hysteria. And there is no doubt that the President would seize on any domestic terrorist attack to blame the courts. He made this abundantly clear when he tweeted, after his first travel ban was struck down: "Just cannot believe a judge would put our country in such peril. If something happens blame him and court system."

The Dark Prince Is Back

Trump has made no secret of his interest in torture. "Torture works," he said on the campaign, "only a stupid person would say it doesn't work." He also pledged to fill up Guantanamo with new "bad dudes, believe me, we're gonna load it up."

Legally, this won't be easy. Ever since the George W. Bush administration found loopholes it could exploit to take a turn toward sadism, the US courts have made it harder for future administrations to follow suit, as has the Senate, which passed an amendment in 2015 clearly stating that all interrogation techniques must follow the Army Field Manual.

Still, if the country found itself in the grip of a large-enough security crisis, there is no reason to expect that a Republican-controlled House and Senate would refuse the White House the powers it demanded. And Mike Pompeo, Trump's CIA director, has indicated an alarming openness to going backward. After originally stating unequivocally in his confirmation hearing that he would not allow torture tactics to return, he followed up with an addendum: "If experts believed current law was an impediment to gathering vital intelligence to protect the country, I would want to understand such impediments and whether any recommendations were appropriate for changing current law." He has also called for a reversal of the limited restrictions on digital surveillance put in place after Edward Snowden's revelations.

Even without the blessing of Congress or the CIA, an administration that is determined to violate the law can, unfortunately, find a way. The likeliest route for Trump is to outsource this dirty work to private contractors. None other than Blackwater founder Erik Prince (who happens to be the brother of Secretary of Education Betsy DeVos) has been counseling Trump behind the scenes. Investigative journalist Jeremy Scahill, who wrote an award-winning book on Blackwater, reports that Prince not only donated $100,000 to a Trump-friendly political action committee but actively advised the transition team "on matters related to intelligence and defense, including weighing in on candidates for the Defense and State departments." And in April, the *Washington Post* published a report revealing that

the United Arab Emirates arranged a secret meeting in January between Blackwater founder Erik Prince and a Russian close to President Vladimir Putin as part of an apparent effort to establish a back-channel line of communication between Moscow and President-elect Donald Trump, according to U.S., European and Arab officials. The meeting took place around Jan. 11 — nine days before Trump's inauguration — in the Seychelles islands in the Indian Ocean, officials said.

Prince, the *Post* reported, "presented himself as an unofficial envoy for Trump." Through a spokesperson, Prince described the account as "a complete fabrication. The meeting had nothing to do with President Trump."

Prince's appearance in all this is alarming for reasons that go well beyond the revelation of yet another link between the Trump team and Russia. In the wake of a long line of lawsuits and investigations (in 2014, a US federal jury found four Blackwater employees guilty on charges including first-degree murder in a massacre in Baghdad's Nisour Square that left seventeen people dead), Prince attempted to rename Blackwater and finally sold the company. He now has a new firm: Frontier Services Group. He is getting in on the anti-immigrant frenzy sweeping the globe, pitching the company as the most efficient way to keep migrants from successfully crossing borders. In Europe, he makes the case that by paying his company to work in Libya, countries can "secure land borders and so prevent migrants from reaching the Mediterranean." Writing in the *Financial Times* in early 2017, Prince explained that if his plan were implemented, "there would be nowhere for migrant smugglers to hide: they can be detected, detained and handled using a mixture of air and ground operations" — all private, all for-profit.

Prince's resurfacing is a reminder that there are many backdoor ways around constitutional practices. And Trump, as well as other leaders, can turn to companies like his for surveillance, interrogation, and massively ramped-up border controls.

No, They Don't Need to Plan It

Some have warned that Trump has so much to gain from an atmosphere of heightened fear and confusion, and such a blatant disregard for the truth, that we should expect this administration to cook up its own crises. While it would be unwise to put anything past this constellation of characters, the fact is that nefarious conspiracies may well be unnecessary. After all, Trump's reckless and incompetent approach to governance is nothing short of a disaster-creation machine.

Take the administration's incendiary public statements and policies relating to Muslims and "radical Islamic terrorism." A decade and a half into the so-called war on terror, it's not controversial to state the obvious: these kinds of actions and rhetoric make violent responses distinctly more likely. These days, the people warning about this danger most forcefully are not antiracism or antiwar activists, but leading figures in the military and intelligence communities and the foreign policy establishment. They argue that any perception that the United States is at war with Islam as a faith and Muslims as a group is a gift to extremists looking to rationalize bloody attacks on American soldiers and civilians. Daniel L. Bynam, a senior fellow at the Brookings Institution who served on the Joint 9/11 Inquiry Staff of the House and Senate Intelligence Committees, puts it this way: "Trump's actions and rhetoric add credibility to the jihadists' narrative of civilizational war."

Already, ISIS reportedly described Trump's first anti-Muslim-travel executive order as a "blessed ban" that will help to recruit fighters. Iran's foreign minister warned the ban was "a gift to extremists." Even Trump's own national security adviser, Lieutenant General H.R. McMaster, has described Trump's repeated use of the term "radical Islamic terrorism" as unhelpful because, he says, the terrorists are "un-Islamic." Yet nothing

Holy war message

has changed. Trump seems determined to do everything possible to reinforce the holy war message.

The idea that Trump doesn't realize how provocative he's being rings about as hollow as his claims of being unaware that his racist rhetoric has generated a climate ripe for hate crimes.

The Shock of War

The most lethal way that governments overreact to terrorist attacks is by exploiting the atmosphere of fear to embark on a full-blown foreign war. It doesn't necessarily matter if the target has no connection to the original terror attacks. Iraq wasn't responsible for 9/11, and it was invaded anyway.

Trump's likeliest targets are mostly in the Middle East, and they include (but are by no means limited to) the following: Syria; Yemen, where Trump has already increased the number of drone strikes; Iraq, where deadly strikes with high civilian casualties are also on the rise; and, most perilously, Iran. And then, of course, there's North Korea. Already, after visiting the demilitarized zone dividing North and South Korea, Secretary of State Tillerson declared "all options are on the table," pointedly refusing to rule out a preemptive military strike in response to the North Korean regime's missile testing. This was followed by Trump's muscle-flexing announcement of the immediate deployment of a US Navy strike group, including two destroyers, a guided-missile cruiser, and a nuclear-powered aircraft carrier, to the Korean Peninsula (embarrassingly for the administration, the carrier was photographed thousands of miles away, heading in the opposite direction for joint exercises with the Australian Navy). And it was all underlined by a testosterone-fueled tweet from Trump about how, if China doesn't step in, "we will solve the problem without them! U.S.A." North Korean state media, meanwhile, issued a hair-raising declaration that the country was prepared to launch a nuclear attack "in the US mainland."

Trump has openly called for a new nuclear "arms race"—a call we have not heard since the 1980s. He has reportedly asked his foreign policy advisers repeatedly why the United States can't just use nuclear weapons, seemingly not grasping the principle of retaliation. And one of Trump's biggest financial backers, Sheldon Adelson, has talked about needing to threaten Iran with a nuclear strike in the "middle of the desert that doesn't hurt a soul . . . maybe a couple of rattlesnakes. . . . Then you say, 'See! The next one is in the middle of Tehran. So, we mean business.'" Adelson donated $5 million to Trump's inauguration, the largest donation of its kind ever.

I am not saying a nuclear war is likely. But in Trump's very short time in office, there has already been a level of military escalation that is both chilling and bizarrely haphazard. As indicated by his early deployment of the most powerful conventional weapon in the US arsenal—the Massive Ordnance Air Blast, or MOAB—Trump is drunk on the allure of showing the world he's top dog. Which is why Mikhail Gorbachev, who worked toward disarmament when he was Soviet leader, wrote in *Time* magazine that today "the nuclear threat once again seems real. Relations between the great powers have been going from bad to worse for several years now. The advocates for arms build-up and the military-industrial complex are rubbing their hands." (And that was before Trump upped the ante with North Korea.)

There are many reasons why people around Trump, particularly the many who came straight from the defense sector, might decide that further military escalation is in order. As we saw, Trump's April 2017 missile strike on Syria—ordered without congressional approval and therefore illegal according to some experts—won him the most positive news coverage of his presidency, with liberal hawks fawning over him as enthusiastically as his superfans on Fox. His inner circle, meanwhile, immediately pointed to the attacks as proof that there was nothing untoward going on between the White House and Russia. "If there was anything that Syria did, it was to validate the fact that there is no Russia tie," Trump's 33-year-old son Eric told the *Daily Telegraph* (perhaps inadvertently revealing that there might have been more than sympathy for "beautiful babies" behind the decision to stage such a dramatic strike).

Exxon's Wars *oil prices*

There is another reason why this administration might rush to exploit a security crisis to start a new war or escalate an ongoing conflict: there is no faster or more effective way to drive up the price of oil, especially if the violence interferes with oil supplies making it to the world market.

Particularly worrying on this front is Secretary of State Rex Tillerson's relationship with ExxonMobil, one of the oil giants that would benefit most directly from a price spike. Yes, Tillerson agreed to divest from the company, and to recuse himself from decisions that specifically relate to ExxonMobil for one year. But his ties to the company remain deep. Not only was Tillerson at Exxon for forty-one years, his entire working life, but ExxonMobil has agreed to pay him a retirement package worth a staggering $180 million, a sum so large (especially given how far the company's fortunes fell under his leadership) that it may well inspire some feelings of gratitude in the secretary of state. (How would you feel about a corporation that provided you with a $180-million exit package?) As Tom Sanzillo, director of finance at the Institute for Energy Economics and Financial Analysis, puts it, "You can take the boy out of Exxon but you cannot take the Exxon out of the boy."

Moreover, while Tillerson may be excluded from decisions relating to infrastructure in which ExxonMobil has a clear interest (such as approval of the Keystone XL pipeline), he cannot recuse himself from the many foreign policy decisions that could impact oil prices—decisions potentially worth billions to the company. That, after all, would mean recusing himself from any discussion of military conflict in oil-rich regions, or direct discussion with the leaders of petrostates. We have already seen that Tillerson is doing no such thing.

The link between war and oil prices is not hypothetical. When oil prices go down, instability increases in oil-dependent countries such as Venezuela and Russia. Conversely, when conflict breaks out in countries with considerable oil assets—whether Nigeria or Kuwait—the price of oil shoots up as markets anticipate a contraction in supply. (The price of oil even got a small bump when Trump ordered the April missile strike on Syria.) "There is a close correlation between oil prices and conflict," explains Michael Klare, professor of peace and world security studies at Hampshire College. Exhibit A of this phenomenon was the 2003 invasion of Iraq, which helped send the price of oil soaring from around $30 a barrel at the start of the invasion to above $100 by 2008. That, in turn, is what triggered the boom in tar sands investment and the rush to the Arctic. And this dynamic could be repeated. A war that takes large state-owned oil reserves offline, or which significantly weakens the power of OPEC, would be a boon for the oil majors. ExxonMobil, loaded with tar sands reserves and with megaprojects pending in the Russian Arctic, would have a huge amount to gain.

Perhaps the only person who would have more to gain from this kind of instability is Vladimir Putin, head of a vast petro-state that has been in economic crisis since the price of oil collapsed. Russia is the world's leading exporter of natural gas, and its second-largest exporter of oil (after Saudi Arabia). When the price was high, this was great news for Putin: prior to 2014, fully 50 percent of Russia's budget revenues came from oil and gas.

But when prices plummeted, the government was suddenly short hundreds of billions of dollars, an economic catastrophe that has had tremendous human costs. According to the World Bank, in 2015 real wages fell in Russia by nearly 10 percent; Russia's currency, the ruble, depreciated by close to 40 percent; and the population of people classified as poor increased from 3 million to over 19 million. Putin plays the strongman, but this economic crisis makes him vulnerable at home.

Which is why many have speculated that Russia's high-risk military involvement in Syria is partly driven by a desire to get oil prices back up. This theory has been floated most prominently by Alexander Temerko, a right-wing, Ukrainian-born British businessman who works in the oil industry. In 2015, Temerko wrote in the *Guardian*:

> Prolonged war in the Middle East would serve Putin's interests perfectly. The deeper and more widespread the conflict, the more world oil and gas prices are likely to rise, helping him stage an economic recovery at home and render the sanctions useless.
>
> Ushering in better times at home is therefore Putin's ultimate aim as he seeks to prop up a system that takes advantage of people's patriotism and public spirit. The grand plan is for his vital oil and gas revenues to recover so he can buy the loyalty of Russia's 140 million-strong population.

(This is something of an oversimplification: Putin has other reasons for being in Syria as well, including a desire to access the country's ports and potentially its oil and gas fields—and war, as ever, is a great distraction from the misery at home.)

We've also heard a lot about how ExxonMobil made a massive deal with the Russian state oil company Rosneft to drill for oil in the Arctic, which Putin bragged was worth half a trillion dollars. That deal was derailed by US sanctions against Russia imposed under the Obama administration. It is still eminently possible, despite the posturing on both sides over Syria, that Trump could lift those sanctions and clear the way for that deal to go ahead, which would quickly boost ExxonMobil's flagging fortunes. (Months after Trump took office, the company requested a waiver from the US sanctions, and was denied.)

But even if the sanctions are lifted, there is another factor standing in the way of the project moving forward: the depressed price of oil. Tillerson made the deal with Rosneft in 2011, when the price of oil was soaring at around $110 a barrel. Their first commitment was to explore for oil in the sea north of Siberia, under tough-to-extract, icy conditions. Since the oil price collapse, other oil majors, including Shell and France's Total, have backed away from Arctic drilling, in part because frozen conditions drive up costs so much. (The break-even price for Arctic drilling is estimated to be around $100 a barrel, if not more.) So even if sanctions are lifted under Trump, it won't make sense for Exxon and Rosneft to move ahead with their project unless oil prices are high enough. In other words, both parties have significant and multi-layered reasons for wanting the price of oil to shoot back up.

Which is why we need to be very clear that a state of instability and uncertainty is not something that is feared by core figures in and around the Trump administration; on the contrary, many will embrace it. Trump has surrounded himself with masters of chaos—from Tillerson to Mnuchin. And chaos has a long track record of sending the price of oil up. If it rises to $80 or more a barrel, then the scramble to dig up and burn the dirtiest fossil fuels, including those under melting ice, will be back on. A price rebound would unleash a global frenzy in new high-risk, high-carbon fossil fuel extraction, from the Arctic to the tar sands. If that is allowed to happen, it really would rob us of our last chance of averting catastrophic climate change.

So, in a very real sense, preventing war and averting climate chaos are one and the same fight.

Economic Shocks

Just as Trump could not be unaware that his anti-Muslim actions and rhetoric make terror attacks more likely, I suspect that many in the Trump administration are fully cognizant of the fact that their frenzy of financial deregulation makes other kinds of shocks and disasters more likely as well. Trump has announced plans to dismantle Dodd–Frank, the most substantive piece of legislation introduced after the 2008 banking collapse. Dodd–Frank wasn't tough enough, but its absence will liberate Wall Street to go wild blowing new bubbles, which will inevitably burst, creating new economic shocks.

Trump's team are not unaware of this, they are simply unconcerned—the profits from those market bubbles are too tantalizing. Besides, they know that since the banks were never broken up, they are still too big to fail, which means that if it all comes crashing down, they will be bailed out again, just like in 2008. (In fact, Trump issued an executive order calling for a review of the specific part of Dodd–Frank designed to prevent taxpayers from being stuck with the bill for another such bailout—an ominous sign, especially with so many former Goldman executives making White House policy.)

Some members of the administration surely also see a few coveted policy options opening up in the wake of a good market shock or two. During the campaign, Trump courted voters by promising not to touch Social Security or Medicare. But that may well be untenable, given the deep tax cuts on the way. An economic crisis would give Trump a handy excuse for abandoning those promises. In the midst of a moment being sold to the public as economic Armageddon, Betsy DeVos might even have a shot at realizing her dream of replacing public schools with a system based on vouchers and charters.

Trump's gang has a long wish list of policies that do not lend themselves to normal times. In the early days of the new administration, for instance, Mike Pence met with Wisconsin governor Scott Walker to hear how the governor had managed to strip public sector unions of their right to collective bargaining in 2011. (Hint: he used the cover of the state's fiscal crisis, prompting *New York Times* columnist Paul Krugman to declare that in Wisconsin "the shock doctrine is on full display.")

The picture is clear. We will very likely not see this administration's full economic barbarism in the first year. That will only reveal itself later, after the inevitable budget crises and market shocks kick in. Then, in the name of rescuing the government and perhaps the entire economy, the White House will start checking off the more challenging items on the corporate wish list.

Weather Shocks

Just as Trump's national security and economic policies are sure to generate and deepen crises, the administration's moves to ramp up fossil fuel production, dismantle large parts of the country's environmental laws, and trash the Paris climate accord all pave the way for more large-scale industrial accidents—not to mention future climate disasters. There is a lag time of about a decade between the release of carbon dioxide into the atmosphere and the full resulting warming, so the very worst climatic effects of the administration's policies won't likely be felt until they're out of office.

That said, we've already locked in so much warming that no president can complete a term without facing major weather-related disasters. In fact, Trump wasn't even two months in before he was dealing with overwhelming wildfires on the Great

Plains, which led to so many cattle deaths that one rancher described the event as "our Hurricane Katrina."

Trump showed no great interest in the fires, not even sparing them a tweet. But when the first superstorm hits a coast, we should expect a very different reaction from a president who knows the value of oceanfront property, and has only ever been interested in building for the one percent. The worry, of course, is a repeat of Katrina's rip-offs and Iraq's "missing billions," since contracts handed out in a hurry are ripe for corruption, and it is evacuees and workers who pay the price.

Luxury Disaster Response

The biggest Trump-era escalation, however, will most likely be in disaster response services marketed specifically toward the wealthy—what a *New Yorker* headline recently dubbed "Doomsday Prep for the Super-Rich." When I was writing *The Shock Doctrine*, this industry was still in its infancy, and several early companies didn't make it. I wrote, for instance, about a short-lived airline called Help Jet, based in Trump's beloved West Palm Beach. While it lasted, Help Jet offered an array of gold-plated rescue services in exchange for a membership fee.

When a hurricane was on its way, Help Jet dispatched limousines to pick up members, booked them into five-star golf resorts and spas somewhere safe, then whisked them away on private jets. "No standing in lines, no hassle with crowds, just a first-class experience that turns a problem into a vacation," read the company's marketing materials. "Enjoy the feeling of avoiding the usual hurricane evacuation nightmare." With the benefit of hindsight, it seems Help Jet, far from misjudging the market for these services, was simply ahead of its time. These days, luxury real estate developments in New York have begun marketing exclusive private disaster amenities to would-be residents—everything from emergency lighting to private water pumps and generators to thirteen-foot floodgates. One Manhattan condominium boasts of its watertight utility rooms sealed "submarine-style," in case another Superstorm Sandy hits the coast. Trump's golf courses are trying to prepare too. In Ireland, Trump International Golf Links and Hotel applied to build a two-mile-long, thirteen-foot wall to protect the coastal property from rising seas and increasingly dangerous storms.

millionaire Bunkers Evan Osnos recently reported in the *New Yorker* that, in Silicon Valley and on Wall Street, the more serious high-end survivalists are hedging against climate disruption and social collapse by buying space in custom-built underground bunkers in Kansas (protected by heavily armed mercenaries) and building escape homes on high ground in New Zealand. It goes without saying that you need your own private jet to get there—the ultimate Green Zone.

At the ultra-extreme end of this trend is PayPal billionaire Peter Thiel, a major Trump donor and member of his transition team. Thiel underwrote an initiative called the Seasteading Institute, cofounded by Patri Friedman (grandson of Milton) in 2008. The goal of Seasteading is for wealthy people to eventually secede into fully independent nation-states, floating in the open ocean—protected from sea-level rise and fully self-sufficient. Anybody who doesn't like being taxed or regulated will simply be able to, as the movement's manifesto states, "vote with your boat." Thiel recently has appeared to lose interest in the project, saying that the logistics of building floating nation-states were "not quite feasible," but it continues.

What is worrying about the entire top-of-the-line survivalist phenomenon (apart from its general weirdness) is that, as the wealthy create their own luxury escape hatches, there is diminishing incentive to maintain any kind of disaster response infrastructure that exists to help everyone, regardless of income—precisely the dynamic that led to enormous and unnecessary suffering in New Orleans during Katrina. (The survivalists refer to FEMA as "Foolishly Expecting Meaningful Aid"—a joke that is only funny if you have the means to pay cash for your own escape.)

This two-tiered disaster infrastructure is galloping ahead at alarming speed. In fire-prone states such as California and Colorado, insurance companies provide a "concierge" service to their exclusive clients: when wildfires threaten their mansions, the companies dispatch teams of private firefighters to coat them in fire-retardant. The public sphere, meanwhile, is left to further decay.

California provides a glimpse of where this is all headed. For its firefighting, the state relies on upwards of 4,500 prison inmates, who are paid a dollar an hour when they're on the fire line, putting their lives at risk battling wildfires, and about two bucks a day when they're back at camp. By some estimates, California saves about a billion dollars a year through this program—a snapshot of what happens when you mix austerity politics with mass incarceration and climate change.

I Don't Feel Hot—Do You Feel Hot?

The uptick in high-end disaster prep also means there is less reason for the big winners in our economy to embrace the demanding policy changes required to prevent an even warmer and more disaster-prone future. Which might help explain the Trump administration's determination to do everything possible to accelerate the climate crisis.

So far, much of the discussion around Trump's environmental rollbacks has focused on supposed schisms between the members of his inner circle who actively deny climate science, including EPA head Scott Pruitt and Trump himself, and those who concede that humans are indeed contributing to planetary warming, such as Rex Tillerson and Ivanka Trump. But this misses the point: what everyone who surrounds Trump shares is a confidence that they, their children, and indeed their class will be just fine, that their wealth and connections will protect them from the worst of the shocks to come. They will lose some beachfront property, sure, but nothing that can't be replaced with a new mansion in the mountains.

What matters isn't their stated views on the science of climate change. What matters is that not one of them appears to be worried about climate change. The early catastrophic events are playing out mostly in poor parts of the world, where the people are not white. And when disasters do strike wealthy Western nations, there are growing numbers of ways for the wealthy to buy their relative safety. Early in Trump's term, Republican congressman Steve King caused a controversy by tweeting, "We can't restore our civilization with somebody else's babies." It was a revealing comment on many fronts. Climate change is not a concern for the Republican Party because a great many people in positions of power clearly think it'll be "somebody else's babies" who will shoulder the risks, babies who don't count as much as their own. They may not all be climate deniers, but almost every one of them is catastrophically unconcerned.

This insouciance is representative of an extremely disturbing trend. In an age of ever-widening income inequality, a significant cohort of our elites are walling themselves off not just physically but also psychologically, mentally detaching themselves from the collective fate of the rest of humanity. This secessionism from the human species (if only in their minds) liberates them not only to shrug off the urgent need for climate action but also to devise ever more predatory ways to profit from current and future disasters and instability.

What we are hurtling toward is the future I glimpsed in New Orleans and Baghdad all those years ago. A world demarcated into Green Zones and Red Zones and black sites for whoever doesn't cooperate. And it's headed toward a Blackwater-style economy in which private players profit from building the walls, from putting the population under surveillance, from private security and privatized checkpoints.

A World of Green Zones and Red Zones

This is the way our world is being carved up at an alarming rate. Europe, Australia, and North America are erecting increasingly elaborate (and privatized) border fortresses to seal themselves off from people fleeing for their lives. Fleeing, quite often, as a direct result of forces unleashed primarily by those fortressed continents, whether predatory trade deals, wars, or ecological disasters intensified by climate change.

Hands are wrung about the "migrant crisis"—but not nearly so much about the crises driving the migrations. Since 2014, an estimated thirteen thousand people have drowned in the Mediterranean trying to reach European shores. For those who make it, safety is far from assured. The massive migrant camp in Calais, France, was nicknamed "the jungle"—an echo of the way Katrina's abandoned people were categorized as "animals." In late 2016, just before Trump was elected, the Calais camp was bulldozed.

But it's the Australian government that has gone the furthest in treating human desperation as a contagion. For five consecutive years since 2012 migrant boats headed for Australia's coastline have been systematically intercepted at sea and their occupants flown to remote detention camps on the islands of Nauru and Manus. Numerous reports have described the conditions in the camps as tantamount to torture. But the government shrugs. After all, they don't run the camps—private, for-profit contractors do (of course).

Conditions are so degraded on Nauru that in one week in 2016, two refugees set themselves on fire in an attempt to awaken the world to their plight. It hasn't worked. Prime Minister Malcolm Turnbull continues to refuse demands coming from many Australians to welcome the refugees into their vast country. "We cannot be misty-eyed about this," he says, asserting that Australians "have to be very clear and determined in our national purpose."

Nauru, incidentally, is one of the Pacific islands vulnerable to sea-level rise. Its residents, after seeing their home turned into a prison for people fleeing war in places such as Somalia and Afghanistan, will quite possibly be forced to become migrants themselves. It's another glimpse into an already-here future: tomorrow's climate refugees recruited into service as today's prison guards.

Jets, Drones, and Boats

The irony is particularly acute because many of the conflicts driving migration today have already been exacerbated by climate change. For instance, before civil war broke out in Syria, the country faced its deepest drought on record—roughly 1.5 million people were internally displaced as a result. A great many displaced farmers moved to the border city of Daraa, which happens to be where the Syrian uprising broke out in 2011. Drought was not the only factor in bringing tensions to a head, but many analysts, including former secretary of state John Kerry, are convinced it was a key contributor.

In fact, if we chart the locations of the most intense conflict spots in the world right now—from the bloodiest battlefields in Afghanistan and Pakistan, to Libya, Yemen, Somalia, and Iraq—what becomes clear is that these also happen to be some of the hottest and driest places on earth. The Israeli architect Eyal Weizman has mapped the targets of Western drone strikes and found an "astounding coincidence." The strikes are intensely concentrated in regions with an average of just 200 millimeters (7.8 inches) of rainfall per year—so little that even slight climate disruption can push them into drought. In other words, we are bombing the driest places on the planet, which also happen to be the most destabilized.

A frank explanation for this was provided in a US military report published by the Center for Naval Analyses a decade ago: "The Middle East has always been associated with two natural resources, oil (because of its abundance) and water (because of its scarcity)." When it comes to oil, water, and war in the Middle East, certain patterns have become clear over time. First, Western fighter jets follow that abundance of oil in the region, setting off spirals of violence and destabilization. Next come the Western drones, closely tracking water scarcity as drought and conflict mix together. And just as bombs follow oil, and drones follow drought—so, now, boats follow both. Boats filled with refugees fleeing homes ravaged by war and drought in the driest parts of the planet.

And the same capacity to discount the humanity of the "other," which justifies civilian deaths and casualties from bombs and drones, is now being trained on the people in the boats (or arriving on buses or on foot)—casting their need for security as a threat, their desperate flight as some sort of invading army.

The dramatic rise in right-wing nationalism, anti-Black racism, Islamophobia, and straight-up white supremacy over the past decade cannot be pried apart from this maelstrom—from the jets and the drones, the boats and walls. The only way to justify such untenable levels of inequality is to double down on theories of racial hierarchy that tell a story about how the people being locked out of the global Green Zone deserve their fate, whether it's Trump casting Mexicans as rapists and "bad hombres," and Syrian refugees as closet terrorists, or prominent Conservative Canadian politician Kellie Leitch proposing that immigrants be screened for "Canadian values," or successive Australian prime ministers justifying sinister island detention camps as a "humanitarian" alternative to death at sea.

This is what global destabilization looks like in societies that have never redressed their foundational crimes — countries that have insisted slavery and Indigenous land theft were just glitches in otherwise proud histories. After all, there is little more Green Zone/Red Zone than the economy of the slave plantation — of cotillions in the master's house steps away from torture in the fields, all of it taking place on the violently stolen Indigenous land on which North America's wealth was built.

What is becoming clear is that the same theories of racial hierarchy that justified those violent thefts in the name of building the industrial age are visibly resurfacing as the system of wealth and comfort they constructed starts to unravel on multiple fronts simultaneously.

Trump is just one early and vicious manifestation of that unraveling. He is not alone. He won't be the last.

A Crisis of Imagination

Searching for a word to describe the huge discrepancies in privileges and safety between those in Iraq's Green and Red zones, journalists often landed on "sci-fi." And of course, it was. The walled city where the wealthy few live in relative luxury while the masses outside war with one another for survival is pretty much the default premise of every dystopian sci-fi movie that gets made these days, from *The Hunger Games*, with the decadent Capitol versus the desperate colonies, to *Elysium*, with its spa-like elite space station hovering above a sprawling and lethal favela. It's a vision deeply enmeshed with the dominant Western religions, with their grand narratives of great floods washing the world clean, with only a chosen few selected to begin again. It's the story of the great fires that sweep in, burning up the unbelievers and taking the righteous to a gated city in the sky. We have collectively imagined this extreme winners-and-losers ending for our species so many times that one of our most pressing tasks is learning to imagine other possible ends to the human story, ones in which we come together in crisis rather than split apart, take down borders rather than erect more of them.

Because we all pretty much know where the road we are on is leading. It leads to a world of Katrinas, a world that confirms our most catastrophic nightmares. Though there is a thriving subculture of utopian sci-fi, the current crops of mainstream dystopian books and films imagine and reimagine that same Green Zone/Red Zone future over and over again. But the point of dystopian art is not to act as a temporal GPS, showing us where we are inevitably headed. The point is to warn us, to wake us—so that, seeing where this perilous road leads, we can decide to swerve.

"We have it in our power to begin the world over again." So said Thomas Paine many years ago, neatly summarizing the dream of escaping the past that is at the heart of both the colonial project and the American Dream. The truth, however, is that we do *not* have this godlike power of reinvention, nor did we ever. We must live with the messes and mistakes we have made, as well as within the limits of what our planet can sustain.

But we do have it in our power to change ourselves, to attempt to right past wrongs, and to repair our relationships with one another and with the planet we share. It's this work that is the bedrock of shock resistance.

PART IV

HOW THINGS COULD
GET BETTER

She's on the horizon . . . I go two steps, she moves two steps away.
I walk ten steps and the horizon runs ten steps ahead.
No matter how much I walk, I'll never reach her.
What good is utopia? That's what: it's good for walking.

—EDUARDO GALEANO
Walking Words, 1995

CHAPTER TEN

WHEN THE SHOCK DOCTRINE BACKFIRES

When I was in my late teens, my mother had a debilitating series of strokes, which turned out to have been caused by a brain tumor. The first stroke came as a complete shock—she was younger than I am now, physically active and professionally driven. One minute she was biking, the next she was in a neurological ICU, incapable of moving or of breathing without a respirator.

Up until my mother's stroke, I had been a pretty difficult teenager—I was withdrawn from my parents, wild with my friends, serially dishonest. I did well at school for the most part, my one saving grace, but home life was strained or worse.

In the instant that my mother's life changed forever, I did too. I discovered I knew how to be helpful. Affectionate (imagine). I grew up overnight. After brain surgery, she gradually recovered some, though far from all, of her mobility. Watching her adapt to a different life as a disabled person, I learned a lot about the power of humans to find new reserves of strength.

It is true that people can regress during times of crisis. I have seen it many times. In a shocked state, with our understanding of the world badly shaken, a great many of us can become child-like and passive, and overly trusting of people who are only too happy to abuse that trust. But I also know, from my own family's navigation of a shocking event, that there can be the inverse response as well. We can evolve and grow up in a crisis, and set aside all kinds of bullshit—fast.

Resistance, Memory, and the Limits to No

This is true for whole societies as well. Faced with a shared trauma, or a common threat, communities can come together in defiant acts of sanity and maturity. It has happened before, and the early signs are good that it might be happening again.

The Trump administration is coming after huge sectors of the population at once: tens of millions of people impacted by proposed budget cuts, civil rights activists, artists, Indigenous tribes, immigrants, climate scientists . . . Their military belligerence and environmental arson are attacks that reach far outside US borders to wage war on global stability and planetary habitability. It's clear that, like many shock therapists before them, Trump and his gang are betting that this all-at-once strategy will overwhelm their adversaries, sending them scrambling in all directions and ultimately causing them to give up out of sheer exhaustion or a sense of futility.

This blitzkrieg strategy, though it has often worked in the past, is actually quite high-risk. The danger of starting fights on so many fronts is that if it doesn't succeed in demoralizing your opponents, it could very well unite them.

On the day Trump signed the permit approving the Keystone XL oil pipeline, Ponca Nation member Mekasi Camp Horinek shared a version of this theory with reporter Alleen Brown:

> I want to say thank you to the president for all the bad decisions that he's making—for the bad cabinet appointments that he's made and for awakening a sleeping giant. People that have never stood up for themselves, people that have never had their

voices heard, that have never put their bodies on the line are now outraged. I would like to say thank you to President Trump for his bigotry, for his sexism, for bringing all of us in this nation together to stand up and unite.

When Argentina Said No

Because shock tactics rely on the public becoming disoriented by fast-moving events, they tend to backfire most spectacularly in places where there is a strong collective memory of previous instances when fear and trauma were exploited to undermine democracy. Those memories serve as a kind of shock absorber, providing populations with shared reference points that allow them to name what's happening and fight back.

It's a lesson I learned when I glimpsed another kind of future on the streets of Buenos Aires over fifteen years ago. At the end of 2001 and the beginning of 2002, Argentina was in the grips of an economic crisis so severe that it stunned the world.

In the 1990s, the country had opened itself to corporate globalization so rapidly and so thoroughly that the International Monetary Fund held it up as a model student. The iconic logos of global banks, hotel chains, and US fast-food restaurants glowed from the Buenos Aires skyline, and its new shopping malls were so fashionable and luxurious that they frequently drew comparisons with Paris. *Time* magazine, on its cover, declared Argentina's economy a "miracle."

And then it all came crashing down. Amidst a spiraling debt crisis, the government attempted to impose a new round of economic austerity, and all those gleaming global banks had to board up their windows and doors to prevent customers rushing in to withdraw their life savings. Protests spread across the country. In the suburbs, supermarkets (owned by European chains) were looted. In the midst of this chaotic scene, Fernando de la Rúa, then Argentina's president, went on television, his face shiny with sweat, and announced that the country was under attack from "groups that are enemies of order who are looking to spread discord and violence." He declared a thirty-day state of siege—which gave him the power to suspend a range of constitutional guarantees, including freedom of the press—and ordered everyone to stay in their homes.

For many Argentinians, the president's words sounded like a prelude to a military coup—and that proved a fatal misstep. People, no matter their age, knew their history, including the fact that when the military staged its brutal coup in 1976, the need to restore public order against internal enemies had been the pretext. The junta stayed in power until 1983, and in that time it stole the lives of some thirty thousand people.

Determined not to lose their country again, and even while de la Rúa was still on television ordering people to stay in their homes, Buenos Aires's famed central square, Plaza de Mayo, filled up with tens of thousands of people, many banging pots and pans with spoons and forks, a wordless but roaring rebuke to the president's instructions. Argentinians would not give up their basic freedoms in the name of order. Not again, not this time.

And then this great gathering found its voice, and a single rebellious cry rose up from the crowds of grandmothers and high school students, motorcycle couriers and unemployed factory workers, their words directed at the politicians, the bankers, the IMF, and every other "expert" who claimed to have the perfect recipe for Argentina's prosperity and stability: *"¡Que se vayan todos!"*—everyone must go! Demonstrators stayed in the streets even after protesters were killed in clashes with police, bringing the total who lost their lives across the country to more than twenty. Amidst the mayhem, the president was forced to lift the state of siege and flee the presidential palace in a helicopter. As a new president was appointed, the people would rise up and reject him in disgust—again and then again, flipping through three presidents in just three weeks.

Meanwhile, in the rubble of Argentina's democracy, something strange and wonderful started to happen: neighbors poked their heads out of their apartments and houses and, in the absence of a political leadership or a stable government, began to talk to each other. To think together. A month later, there were already some 250 "*asambleas barriales*" (neighborhood assemblies, small and large) in downtown Buenos Aires alone. Picture Occupy Wall Street—but everywhere. The streets, parks, and plazas were filled with meetings as people stayed up late into the night, planning, arguing, testifying—and voting on everything from whether Argentina should pay its foreign debts, to when the next protest should be held, to how to support a group of workers who had turned their abandoned factory into a democratic cooperative.

Many of those first assemblies were as much group therapy as political meetings. Participants spoke about their experience of isolation in a city of 13 million. Academics and shopkeepers apologized for not watching out for each other, publicity managers admitted that they used to look down on unemployed factory workers, assuming they deserved their plight, never imagining that the crisis would reach the bank accounts of the cosmopolitan middle class. And apologies for present-day wrongs soon gave way to tearful confessions about events dating back to the dictatorship. I witnessed a housewife stand up and publicly admit that, three decades earlier, when she heard yet another story about someone's brother or husband being kidnapped by the junta, she had learned to close her heart to the suffering, telling herself, "*Por algo será*"—it must have been for something. They were trying to understand, together, how they had lost so much in the past, and building relationships to prevent those mistakes from ever being repeated.

And from below, they were changing the story of a nation.

The political changes that came out of Argentina's uprising were far from utopian. The government that eventually restored democracy, headed first by Néstor Kirchner and then by his wife Cristina, was masterful at reading the street, and channeled enough of its spirit and demands to preside over more than a decade of progressive (if scandal-marred) rule. To this day, debates rage about how more could have been made from that unique political moment if the popular movements had been ready with their own plan for taking power and governing differently. Yet it's undeniable that, in resisting de la Rúa's austerity plans and defying his order to stay home, Argentinians saved themselves from years of economic bloodletting.

When Spain Said No

Another example of how historical memory can serve as a powerful shock absorber took place a few years later, in Spain. On March 11, 2004, ten bombs ripped through commuter trains and rail stations in Madrid, killing nearly two hundred people. Because it was an attack on a transit system that almost everyone in Madrid used, the sense that anyone could be the next victim spread rapidly through the city, as it would in Paris more than a decade later when simultaneous attacks terrorized that city.

An official investigation found that the attacks had been staged by a terrorist cell inspired by al Qaeda, reportedly in retaliation for Spain's participation in the US-led invasion of Iraq. Yet Spain's prime minister at the time, José María Aznar, immediately went on television and told Spaniards to blame the Basque separatists and—in a bizarre non sequitur—to support his unpopular decision to participate in the Iraq War. "No negotiation is possible or desirable with these assassins who so many times have sown death all around Spain. Only with firmness can we end the attacks," Aznar said.

In the United States after 9/11, many, including most of the media, saw the "with us or with the terrorists" rhetoric of George W. Bush and Dick Cheney as evidence of strong leadership, and handed them enormous new powers to fight what would become the never-ending "war on terror." (Turkey's autocratic president, Recep Tayyip Erdoğan, would pull off something even more draconian after a failed coup attempt in 2016, later locking in sweeping new powers in a referendum.) And yet when Aznar tried similar tactics on his grief-stricken population, they were not seen as evidence of strong leadership but rather as an ominous sign of a resurgent fascism. "We are still hearing the echoes of Franco," said José Antonio Martines Soler, a prominent Madrid newspaper editor who had been persecuted under Francisco Franco's dictatorship, which terrorized the country for thirty-six years. "In every act, in every gesture, in every sentence, Aznar told the people he was right, that he was the owner of the truth and those who disagreed with him were his enemies."

So, over the next two days, remembering a time when fear had governed their country, Spaniards surged into the streets in impressive numbers, saying no to fear and to terrorism—but also to government lies and the Iraq War. All of this happened to be on the eve of national elections, and voters seized the opportunity to defeat Aznar and vote in a party that promised to pull Spanish troops out of Iraq. It was the collective memory of past shocks that made Spain resistant to new ones.

9/11 and the Perils of Official Forgetting

When two planes flew into the World Trade Center in New York and another plowed into the Pentagon, on September 11, 2001, they hit a country which lacked the kind of shared memory of trauma that existed in Spain and Argentina. That's not to say US history is unmarked by repeated traumas. The United States was founded in domestic state terror, from the genocide of Indigenous peoples to slavery through to lynching and mass incarceration; trauma has been ever-present right up to this day. Moreover, very frequently, shocks and crises have been handmaidens to the worst abuses. In the aftermath of the Civil War, the promise of land redistribution as economic reparation to freed slaves was promptly betrayed. The financial crisis of 1873, known as the Great Panic, further entrenched the excuse that the economy was too ravaged and the country too divided—and instead of reparations came a reign of terror against freed slaves in the South. During the Great Depression, amidst economic panic, as many as two million Mexicans and Mexican Americans were expelled. After the attacks on Pearl Harbor, approximately 120,000 Japanese Americans (two-thirds of whom had been born in the United States) were incarcerated in internment camps; just as in Canada almost the entire Japanese-Canadian citizenry was rounded up and forcibly interned.

So the problem after 9/11 was not that the United States had no experience of how shocking events can be harnessed to attack democracy and human rights. The problem, rather, was that these past traumatic events, while very well understood within the communities impacted, were insufficiently understood more broadly: they are not part of a shared national narrative that could have helped all Americans see the difference between reasonable security measures and leaders taking advantage of fear to advance opportunistic agendas.

That's why the Bush administration was able to mercilessly exploit the shock of the September 11 trauma to attack civil liberties at home and launch wars abroad, which we now know were justified through doctored intelligence. That's why the neglect and violence of the state during and after Katrina came as no great surprise to the city's African-American residents—yet seemed unprecedented to so many white Americans.

The split between people who were stunned by Trump's victory and those who saw it coming followed similar racial fault lines.

Shock Resistance in the USA

But one thing that's become clear since Trump took office is that the memory of how terror was exploited after September 11 lives on. Though Trump and his supporters have tried their best to use fear—of Muslims, of Mexicans, of violent "ghettos"—to control and divide the population, the tactic has backfired repeatedly. Since Trump's election, countless people have participated in political actions and gatherings for the first time in their lives, and have rushed to show solidarity with people who have been cast as the "other."

It began on Day One of the new administration. At Trump's inauguration, small groups representing different movements—from climate justice to Black Lives Matter—occupied various street intersections to block access to the ceremony. Then, the next day, came the women's marches: with some six hundred cities participating, this appears to have been the largest coordinated protest in US history, with an estimated 4.2 million people on the streets. And though large women's organizations and established activists helped with the organizing and logistics, the original idea came from a retired attorney and grandmother in Hawaii, who said to a few dozen friends on Facebook: "I think we should march."

I marched in DC with family and friends and was struck by the fact that, though women were in the majority, tens of thousands of men had shown up as well, standing up to defend the rights of their partners, mothers, sisters, daughters, and friends. And while some may have initially thought they were marching only to defend a woman's right to make decisions over her own body, as well as for pay equity, they soon discovered that, in this new era, women's rights are far more expansive, including Black women's right to be free from police violence, and immigrant women's right to be free from fear of deportation, and trans women's right to be free from hate and harassment. As the mission statement declared: "This march is the first step towards unifying our communities, grounded in new relationships, to create change from the grass-roots level up."

This same spirit of unity has been on display when specific communities have been targeted by the administration, or by the wave of hate crimes it has helped unleash. The new activism was most visible after Trump issued the first of his Muslim travel bans, and tens of thousands of people—of all faiths and none—took to the streets and airports to declare "we are all Muslims" and "let them in."

One of the countries included in the travel ban was Yemen. In New York, Yemeni-American families—who own many of the city's ubiquitous corner stores (known locally as "bodegas")—organized swiftly. This is not a community known for being politically active, nor is it one that is represented by big organizations or unions. And yet in a matter of days, the city saw its first "bodega strike," with over a thousand businesses closing down, and some shopkeepers holding outdoor Muslim prayers. Thousands of their family members, friends, and customers came out to support them.

Faith groups have been particularly active in pushing back against the divide-and-conquer tactics. When Jewish cemeteries in St. Louis and Philadelphia were vandalized, for instance, Islamic organizations raised more than $160,000—eight times their initial goal—to help pay for the repairs. And when a white nationalist opened fire in a mosque in Quebec City in January 2017, killing six people and injuring nineteen, the response in the province and across Canada was powerful, including dozens of memorials and vigils, many of them outside mosques—from Vancouver to Toronto to Iqaluit.

Small acts too can assert our common humanity in an atmosphere of fear and division. Trump supporters launched a vicious online campaign to smear Linda Sarsour, a Palestinian American who was one of the organizers of the Women's March on Washington, as a closet supporter of terrorism and an anti-Semite. Such false claims were precisely the kind of attacks that ruined lives and careers after September 11. But this time, it didn't work—an #IStandWithLinda countercampaign rose up almost instantly, so loud and large that it all but buried the smears. And when immigration officers arrested 24-year-old Daniel Ramirez Medina—who had come to the USA from Mexico with his parents as a child—organizers launched a successful campaign for his release, freeing him from a Washington state detention center after more than six weeks in custody.

On a larger scale, hundreds of cities and counties (joined by schools, campuses, churches, and restaurants) have stepped forward to declare themselves "sanctuaries" for immigrants the Trump administration would seek to deport. The sanctuary movement (which began well before the 2016 elections) is inspired by the belief that, by coming together, communities can try to prevent deportations from taking place on their watch. But as many have pointed out, this often does not prevent police and border officials from conducting raids and breaking up families. That's why the American Civil Liberties Union, which raised nearly $80 million through online donations in the first three months after election day, has been coordinating a campaign to pressure state and city governments to adopt a set of nine basic policies aimed at protecting immigrants from Trump's agenda. Within a month, over a thousand communities had already started to push their local law enforcement agencies to make these commitments. (There have been criticisms, it should be noted, that these demands do not go far enough.)

There have also been many actions designed to highlight the interdependence that exists between citizens and immigrants, which mounting xenophobia seeks to deny. In February 2017, workers across sectors and cities participated in a Day Without Immigrants, highlighting how dependent the American economy is on the people Trump is trying to kick out. As one organizer of the day's events told a reporter, "We want to make sure that people understand that this city would stop functioning if we weren't there to build, or cook, or clean." (After twelve restaurant workers in Oklahoma were fired for participating in the demonstration, at least two nearby restaurants immediately offered to hire them.)

The Revenge of Reality

Another hallmark of the Trump era is the war on facts: not only has the press been cast as an enemy of the people, but scientific information has disappeared from government websites and there has been a de facto ban on talking about climate change through official government communications channels. In response, several creative initiatives have emerged to defend objective reality. Days after the inauguration, the Badlands National Park Twitter account was the first to defect from the administration's clampdown on science, tweeting out facts about ocean acidification and the level of carbon dioxide in the atmosphere. The posts were taken down shortly after they were issued, but not before sparking a trend of rogue Twitter accounts.

With key scientific research mysteriously disappearing from government websites, there's been a concerted international effort to save it from the memory hole. Shortly after Trump's win, the Internet Archive, a San Francisco–based nonprofit digital library, which for the last two decades has dedicated itself to preserving Web content for the public (and already has hundreds of billions of webpages archived), announced plans to find a backup server in Canada to preserve US data. In the days before Trump's inauguration, "data rescue" events were held in several cities, as researchers and concerned volunteers met to back up data sets from the EPA and other government websites. And in February 2017, a "hackathon" at UC Berkeley drew two hundred data defenders to help save the knowledge generated by public institutions such as the Department of Energy and NASA's earth sciences programs.

Scientists are often wary of engaging in political activism, since advocacy on the same issue you are researching can be seized upon as evidence of bias. It's an understandable caution, but faced with the Trump administration's open attacks on scientific reality and bald attempts to suppress inconvenient research, many scientists have concluded they have to take a stand. Jane Goodall, the famed primatologist, has described the attacks on science as "a trumpet call" to the scientific community.

Which is why, on Earth Day 2017, tens of thousands of scientists participated in the March for Science in Washington, while upwards of forty thousand joined science marches in Chicago and Los Angeles—and these were just the largest of more than six hundred marches held across the USA and in sixty-eight other countries. "If we cannot discuss facts openly," one Stanford biologist told the *Guardian*, "how can democracy, based on public discussions and trust in our societal truths, survive? And so we will march." (One chant that made the rounds: "What do we want? Evidence-based research. When do we want it? After peer review.") Just one week later, hundreds of thousands of us converged in the blistering heat in Washington (once again, with hundreds of satellite marches elsewhere), coming together under a banner of "climate, jobs, and justice." This time the demand was not just for science to be respected, but for it to form the basis of a bold and urgent economic and social transformation.

What has stood out in this wave of early resistance is how the barriers defining who is and who is not an "activist" or an "organizer" are completely breaking down. People are organizing mass events who have never organized anything political before. A great many are discovering that, whatever their field of expertise, whether they are lawyers or restaurant workers, they have crucial skills to share in this emerging network of resistance. And wherever they live or work, whether it's a laboratory or a bodega or a law firm or inside the home, they have the power, if they organize with others, to throw a wrench into a dangerous system.

At the same time, many of us are realizing that if we're going to rise to the urgency and magnitude of this moment, we need skills and knowledge that we currently lack—about history, about how to change the political system, and even about how to change ourselves. So, in addition to the highly visible campaigns and demonstrations, there has also been a surge of popular education. For many, a first step is relearning how democracy works. When Harvard graduate students announced an online and in-person "Resistance School," meant to equip fledgling organizers with "the tools we need to fight back at the federal, state, and local levels," over fifty thousand people—coming from all fifty states—signed up.

In the days following Trump's election, a handful of former Democratic congressional staffers drafted a twenty-four-page Google Document, distilling lessons learned from seeing the Tea Party challenge Obama's agenda district by district. They called it the Indivisible Guide. In Trump's first hundred days, over seven thousand "Indivisible" chapters were formed—most consisting not of hardened activists but of schoolteachers and retirees, furious that their elected representatives were helping further Trump's agenda. More than a straightforward how-to manual for bottom-up democracy, the Indivisible Guide and the activism that sprang out of it have offered, as one Virginia-based Indivisible recruit and first-time organizer put it, "not just a political community, but a community that cares for you, where what's bringing you together is this shared sense of civic responsibility toward this system that's going off the rails."

There is also a growing desire among white people to do more to challenge racial biases in ourselves, our communities, and our families. Groups like Showing Up for Racial Justice have seen interest in their trainings and workshops surge. The Arab American Association of New York and other groups are hosting reliably packed trainings on how to effectively intervene in hate crimes and racist harassment.

Meanwhile, as the administration prepared the ground for slashing funding to women's shelters, family planning, and violence-against-women programs, grassroots fundraising efforts took off in response. Planned Parenthood reported an astonishing 260,000 donors in the month after the election, with nearly a quarter of the contributions coming in the name of Mike Pence (during the election campaign, the vice president had said he wanted the landmark, pro-choice *Roe v. Wade* Supreme Court decision sent "to the ash heap of history").

All of these acts of solidarity and expressions of unity reflect the fact that, after decades of "siloed" politics, more and more people understand that we can only beat Trumpism in cooperation with one another—no one movement can win on its own. The trick is going to be to stick together, and have each other's backs as never before. That's why over fifty progressive groups, drawn from a dizzying array of struggles, greeted the start of Trump's cabinet hearings with a declaration of "United Resistance"—publicly pledging "to take action to support one another, to be accountable to one another, and to act together in solidarity, whether in the streets, in the halls of power, or in our communities every day. When they come for one, they come for us all."

Nor can we afford to restrict our vision to any one sphere. As Angela Davis put it, concluding a rousing speech at the Women's March on Washington, "The next 1,459 days of the Trump administration will be 1,459 days of resistance: Resistance on the ground, resistance in the classrooms, resistance on the job, resistance in our art and in our music. This is just the beginning and in the words of the inimitable Ella Baker, 'We who believe in freedom cannot rest until it comes.'"

The refusal to be bullied by Trump reaches beyond US borders, across the North American continent. When the Muslim travel ban was announced, thousands of Canadians, led by Muslim and immigrant-rights groups, immediately sprang into action, demanding that Canada provide safe haven to the migrants and refugees being denied entry to the USA. There's also a burgeoning support movement to welcome the growing numbers of immigrants fleeing the States and crossing into Canada by foot, even in subzero weather (with horrifying stories of fingers and toes lost to frostbite).

Canadian refugee law currently treats the United States as a "safe" country, and therefore not a legitimate point from which to flee and seek asylum in Canada. But many are now putting pressure on the Canadian government—through petitions and demonstrations—to change those rules. As a letter from a group of law professors pointed out, Trump's actions "reflect the very bigotry, xenophobia and nativist fear-mongering that the international refugee regime was designed to counteract."

In Mexico, meanwhile, tens of thousands of people across more than a dozen cities have protested Trump's immigration policies, as well as his anti-Mexican ethnic smears. Outside North America, the pressure is on too. In the UK, nearly two million people signed an official petition to block Trump from making a state visit to Britain (Trump, reportedly, is demanding a ride in the golden royal carriage). There is also a growing international movement calling on governments to impose trade sanctions on the United States for violating the emissions reduction pledges it made under the Paris climate accord. And the movement to jam the Trump brand is growing, including a global call to boycott companies that rent space in Trump's various towers, as well as campaigns to push developers to drop the Trump name from cities' skylines.

. . . and around the World

Nearly every country has its own white nationalist or neo-fascist movement to confront, and there are many signs that resistance is rising. In response to the anti-immigrant backlash in Europe, huge demonstrations have been held in cities across the continent—from Berlin to Helsinki—to insist that migrants are welcome. In Barcelona, more than 100,000 people heeded a call from their new mayor (a former housing rights activist) and marched through the streets under the banner *"volem acollir"* (We welcome them).

Many grassroots organizations have sprung up to provide direct aid where governments have failed. When large numbers of migrants began arriving in Greece in 2015, they encountered a people who had "endured five years of austerity shock treatment, who had seen their lives degraded and their social, political and labor rights vanishing," writes sociologist Theodoros Karyotis. And yet, rather than jealously guard what little they had left, locals met migrants with an "outpouring of solidarity." Thousands of Greeks opened their homes to refugees, millions of home-cooked meals were delivered to refugee camps, free health care was provided in community-run clinics, and a warehouse in a worker-run factory was opened to collect donated items such as clothes and baby food.

In Germany, as proposals surfaced that migrants be housed in dodgy conditions that included school gyms, vacant office buildings, empty warehouses, army barracks, and even a former Nazi forced-labor camp, people organized an "Airbnb for refugees," matching migrant families in need of a safe place to stay with spare rooms in local houses. The effort has now spread to thirteen other countries. My country is home to a remarkable pro-refugee movement that has seen thousands of Canadians sponsor Syrian families, taking financial and interpersonal responsibility for the newcomers' needs for one year as they adjusted to a new language, culture, and climate. The *New York Times* described it as "the world's most personal resettlement program."

Most encouragingly, while the early assumption was that Trump's rise could set off a wave of far-right electoral victories, in some countries it seems to be having the opposite effect. Witnessing Trump's ugly administration in action, some electorates are deciding to stop the tide. Ahead of elections in the Netherlands in March 2017, many predicted a win for Geert Wilders and his profoundly anti-Islamic and xenophobic Freedom Party. Instead, Wilders's support suddenly collapsed and the governing party held on to the most seats. But the biggest winner in the election was the GreenLeft party, which went from holding four seats to capturing fourteen. The party's leader, Jesse Klaver, is of Moroccan and Indonesian descent and campaigned with a bold antiracist message. On election day, Klaver had advice for other politicians in Europe facing resurgent right-wing populism and racism: "Don't try to fake the populace. Stand for your principles. Be straight. Be pro-refugee. Be pro-European. . . . You can stop populism."

It's a piece of advice that many heeded in France a couple of months later, though ultimately not enough. Faced with the threat of a victory for the Far Right's Marine Le Pen, many withdrew their support from centrist candidates, fearing a repeat of Clinton vs. Trump, and lent it instead to the left populist candidate, Jean-Luc Mélenchon. He had campaigned on an anti–free trade, pro-peace, and radical economic redistribution agenda and started attracting crowds as large as seventy thousand, more than any other candidate. Against all odds, Mélenchon—who was initially reported to have the support of just 9 percent of voters—managed to capture 19.6 percent of votes cast in the first ballot, putting him within just 2 percentage points of making it to the final runoff. In the final vote, Emmanuel Macron, a neo-liberal former banker, trounced Marine Le Pen, though her extremist party still received a record number of votes. And roughly one-third of eligible voters chose to express their displeasure with both Le Pen and Macron by either abstaining or spoiling their ballots. In Spain, meanwhile, candidates with deep roots in social movements have won mayoralty races in Barcelona and Madrid, and have begun introducing concrete policies that welcome refugees, battle homelessness, and fight pollution at the same time.

Will Solidarity Survive a Major Shock?

These reactions are a vast improvement over the far too successful post–September 11 divide-and-conquer politics. So far, Trump's shock tactics aren't disorienting the opposition. Instead, they are waking people up, in the United States and around the world. But of course the new alliances in the US have not yet had to face a major security crisis or a state of emergency. The real test will be whether the bravery and solidarity seen so far can be sustained when people are being told they are in imminent danger, and that the group they're expressing solidarity with could be harboring the individual who set off a bomb last week.

Nevertheless, there is reason to believe that many of the relationships being built in these early days will be strong enough to counter the fear that inevitably sets in during a state of emergency. If Trump tries to use a crisis event to ram through draconian measures, this emerging resistance is poised to rise up and act as a human barrier to say: "No—not this time."

CHAPTER ELEVEN

WHEN NO WAS NOT ENOUGH

Here's the trouble. Just saying no to shock tactics is often not enough to stop them, at least not on its own. It's a lesson I learned the year after *The Shock Doctrine* came out, when Wall Street suffered its worst crisis since the Great Crash of 1929.

We saw how the 2008 financial crisis—the clear result of unchecked greed in the financial sector—was exploited all around the world, but particularly in southern Europe, to extract punishing, shock doctrine–style concessions from regular people. Europeans resisted these cynical tactics with incredible tenacity and courage (well beyond anything seen so far in the United States under Trump). They occupied squares and plazas and stayed for months. They staged general strikes that shut down cities and, in some cases, even voted to throw the bastards out. Outside Europe, in Tunisia, it was a sudden rise in food prices that became the catalyst for the wave of uprisings that came to be called the Arab Spring.

One of the street slogans in this period, which originated in Italy before spreading to Greece and Spain, was: "We will not pay for your crisis!" Millions of people understood that this was what was being asked of them. They were getting stuck with the bankers' bills, forced to pay for their sins with a higher cost of living and lower wages. And they said no. Loudly, unmistakably, and in tremendous numbers.

But in the vast majority of cases, it wasn't enough—the economic punishments kept coming. At times, a particularly egregious austerity measure might be successfully fought back with street protests. Quebec students fought off a tuition increase in 2012, much as Chilean students fought for an overhaul of their broken education system in 2011. But the austerity agenda ground on.

More importantly, this wave of protest and occupations did not produce a fundamental change in the economic model, one that could shift us off the road headed toward that world of Green Zones and Red Zones. When the failures of our current model revealed themselves in a manner more spectacular than at any point since the Great Depression, we did not collectively seize that moment to grab the wheel of history and swerve.

The responsibility for that is collective. No one person or political party is to blame for the roads not taken. But the failures in the aftermath of the 2008 financial crash were starkest in the United States, because of the remarkable number of factors that seemed aligned in favor of transformative, rather than incremental, change. Which is why it's worth revisiting that moment of crisis in some depth, not to point fingers, but to understand what it looks like to miss such a rare political opening—so we don't repeat those mistakes when the next economic shock hits.

Let's cast our minds back to the beginning of 2009. Barack Obama was entering the White House as the first African-American president, a decisive rebuke to eight years of Bush. He had easily carried the popular vote and for the next two years his fellow Democrats would control Congress.

Obama also had a clear democratic mandate to do more than tinker with the shattered economy. In the final three months before he took office, the country had lost almost two million jobs and the picture going into 2009 looked grim. The idea of taking on Wall Street was incredibly popular (it still is) because the big financial institutions that had tanked the global economy were the reason so many people had lost their homes and jobs and seen their life savings evaporate. The banks had no defenders — their executives were virtually in hiding. On the campaign trail, Obama had talked forcefully about how he would rebuild the economy in favor of "the hard work and sacrifice of folks on Main Street" while standing up to "the greed and irresponsibility of Wall Street."

The new administration had a mandate to battle the climate crisis too. After eight years of denial and obstructionism under George W. Bush, Obama had pledged to put a price on carbon, and to create five million green jobs by making major investments, including in renewable energy and hybrid cars. When Obama won the Democratic primary, he told the cheering crowd that this would be remembered as the moment the rise of the oceans began to slow and "the planet began to heal." Yes, he was weak on the details, but this was no ordinary election, and there is no question that the democratic mandate for boldness was there.

When the Banks Were on Their Knees

Looking back, it's really striking how much economic power Obama and the Democrats had in that short window before they lost Congress. First, they had a free hand to design a stimulus program to rebuild Main Street—and to make it as big as required. After decades of unrelenting cutbacks in social spending, there was suddenly a widespread consensus on the need for the federal government to pull the economy out of recession. The stimulus plan ended up being $800 billion, a staggering sum, although, at the time, it was widely criticized for being too small.

And that was not the only tool that Obama had to make good on his promises to rebuild Main Street. The banks were on their knees, receiving trillions of dollars in public money in direct bailouts and loan guarantees, and there were very lively and heated debates going on, in the United States and around the world, about what governments should demand in exchange for saving the banks from the consequences of their own greed. Should they cap executive salaries? Restore Glass–Steagall, the Depression-era law that separated commercial and investment banks? Should they throw the CEOs responsible for the global crisis in jail? Should the banks be permanently nationalized and run as public trusts? Some of this may sound radical today, but it's worth remembering that these were the actual debates going on in 2009, even in staid publications like the *Financial Times*. And there were similar discussions about the fate of the big auto companies, which were also heading to Washington needing bailouts. Two of the Big Three—General Motors and Chrysler—had to declare bankruptcy that same year and were put under government control.

So, let's zoom out and imagine what might have been. . . . Obama had the electoral mandate for real change, he had a virtual blank check to design a stimulus package, and he had an opportunity to impose much-needed changes on two failing sectors of the US economy—the banks and the auto companies.

Imagine if the Democrats had used the leverage they had in 2009 and 2010 to make serious, substantive restructuring demands of the banks and the auto giants in exchange for continuing to bail them out. Imagine if Obama, who had been elected on a promise to rebuild Main Street, solve climate change, and stabilize the economy, had treated the banking and automotive sectors as components of a unified vision for reviving the economy, while fighting inequality and climate change at the same time.

Obama
mistakes

To be concrete, what if the auto companies had been mandated to restructure themselves so they were producing the vehicles of the low-carbon future—electric cars, electric buses, and light rail? In the midst of the financial crisis, two million manufacturing jobs were lost and hundreds of factories closed down. What if, instead of letting that happen, those factories had been refurbished and retooled? A similar industrial transformation took place during World War II, when US factories were enlisted for the war effort.

It would have been expensive, yes, but the banks could have been required to spend a healthy portion of their bailout money providing the necessary loans for this industrial transformation (as it was, they hoarded the cash). And stimulus money could have been spent to help workers get the training they needed to fully participate in the transition, building the public infrastructure— transit, energy grids—of this same green economy. Obama's infrastructure bill did include important support for green energy and green projects, but the clean infrastructure of the future, including public transit and light rail, was shortchanged in favor of the dirty infrastructure of the past, such as highways. And the opportunities presented by the bank and auto bailouts were squandered almost completely. Even after all their failures, the attitude in Washington was still: the banks know best, the auto companies know best, our job is just to get these industries on their feet as quickly as possible so they can get back to a gently tweaked version of business as usual.

The Jobs Revolution That Wasn't

This road not taken matters because, right now, one of the biggest obstacles to serious action on climate change is the fossil fuel companies' successful positioning of themselves as the only ones capable of creating well-paying jobs and keeping the lights on. Obama and the Democrats could have buried that claim once and for all.

Other countries, in the same period, did bury the claim. Over the past decade, the German government has treated the green economy as the main way to revive its manufacturing sector. In the process, it has created 400,000 jobs, and now 30 percent of the country's energy comes from renewables. And Germany has the strongest economy in Europe by far. The energy transition there is incomplete—Germany remains excessively reliant on coal—and its government has inflicted merciless austerity on other countries while choosing another course for itself. But if the US had followed Germany's domestic example, it would have been so far along the road to a renewables-based economy that it would have been impossible for Trump to undo—no matter how many executive orders he signed. And who knows? The new manufacturing jobs and improved infrastructure might well have been enough to deprive him of his win altogether.

Granted, all of this change and restructuring would have demanded uncommon focus and toughness. If Obama had taken a transformative approach to the failed banks and auto companies and to the reckless energy sector when he came into office, the backlash would have been ferocious and difficult to bear. He would have been painted as a communist, the US's own Hugo Chávez. On the other hand, his mandate for widespread change, along with the outpouring of goodwill that greeted his election, was accompanied by such rare economic powers that it could well have ushered in a new era of economic fairness and climate stability.

The fact that this moment passed Americans by is not a failure that can be pinned on the Democrats alone. During Obama's first years in office, most progressive organizations—relieved to finally be rid of Bush and flattered to have the ear of the governing party for the first time in a decade—confused access with power. As a result, the kind of outside pressure that has leveraged major policy victories in the past was largely MIA during Obama's first term. Despite some valiant attempts, there was no united progressive coalition pressuring Obama to make more of his unique moment in history, pushing him to deliver big on jobs, racial justice, clean air, clean water, and better services. That was a mistake. As the great (and much-missed) historian Howard Zinn once wrote, "The really critical thing isn't who is sitting in the White House, but who is sitting in—in the streets, in the cafeterias, in the halls of government, in the factories. Who is protesting, who is occupying offices and demonstrating. Those are the things that determine what happens."

The bottom line is that in 2009, as theorists and organizers, we weren't ready—too many of us were waiting for change to be delivered from on high. And by the time most of us realized how inadequate that change was, the window had closed and the Tea Party was already on the rise.

Remembering When We Leapt

Before shock doctrine politics became the norm in the eighties, crises that were obviously born of financial greed and corporate malfeasance often sparked very different responses. In fact, they provoked some of the most momentous progressive victories in modern history.

In the United States, after the carnage of the Civil War and the abolition of slavery, Blacks and their radical allies pushed for economic justice and greater social rights. They won major victories, including free public education for all children—although it would take another century before schools were desegregated.

The horrific 1911 fire at the Triangle Shirtwaist Company in New York City, which took the lives of 146 young immigrant garment workers, catalyzed hundreds of thousands of workers into militancy—eventually leading to an overhaul of the state labor code, caps on overtime, new rules for child labor, and break-throughs in health and fire safety regulations.

Most significantly, it was only thanks to the collective response from below to the Great Crash of 1929 that the New Deal became possible. The strike wave of the mid-1930s—the Teamsters' rebellion and Minneapolis general strike, the 83-day shutdown of the west coast by longshore workers, and the Flint sit-down strikes in the auto plants—established the power of industrial unions, and forced owners to share a great deal more wealth with their workers. In this same period, as a response to the suffering brought on by the Great Depression, mass movements demanded sweeping social programs such as Social Security and unemployment insurance (programs from which the majority of African-American and many women workers were notably excluded). In the same period, tough new rules regulating the financial sector were introduced, at real cost to unfettered profit making. Across the industrialized world, pressure from social movements created the conditions for programs like the New Deal, featuring ambitious investments in public infrastructure—utilities, transportation systems, housing, and more—on a scale comparable to what the climate crisis calls for today. (Just as the wreckage of the Second World War provided another such catalyst.)

In 1969, there was an oil spill in Santa Barbara, which coated California's beautiful beaches, and it was something like a Great Crash for the environment—a shock millions responded to by demanding fundamental change. Many of North America's toughest laws protecting air, water, and endangered species can trace their roots back to the popular anger that exploded in response to that disaster.

In all these cases, a painful crisis served as a wake-up call, ushering in meaningful legislation that created a fairer and safer society—thanks in no small part to the hard work of organizers who had been preparing the ground for years before the shocks hit. These were far from perfect reforms, not full-scale transformations, and yet they were directly responsible for winning much of the modern social safety net, as well as the regulatory structures that protect so many workers and public health. Moreover, winning them did not require authoritarian trickery. They were so popular with voters that they didn't have to be snuck in under cover of crisis but rather were loudly demanded by muscular social movements—a deepening of democracy, not its subversion.

So why did those crises produce such visionary change, while more recent ones—Katrina, the subprime mortgage debacle, BP's Deepwater Horizon disaster—have left so little progressive public policy behind?

When Utopia Lends a Hand

Here is one theory: The interplay between lofty dreams and earthly victories has always been at the heart of moments of deep transformation. The breakthroughs won for workers and their families after the Civil War and during the Great Depression, as well as for civil rights and the environment in the sixties and early seventies, were not just responses to crises. They were responses to crises *that unfolded in times when people dared to dream big*, out loud, in public—explosions of utopian imagination.

The Gilded Age strikers of the late nineteenth century, enraged by the enormous fortunes being amassed off the backs of repressed laborers, were inspired by the Paris Commune, when the working people of Paris took over the governing of their city for months. They dreamed of a "cooperative commonwealth," a world where work was but one element of a well-balanced life, with plenty of time for leisure, family, and art. Utopian socialist fiction, including Edward Bellamy's *Looking Backward*, topped the best-seller lists (in sharp contrast to today, when it is classic dystopian fiction—George Orwell's *1984*, Margaret Atwood's *The Handmaid's Tale*, and Sinclair Lewis's *It Can't Happen Here*— that has reappeared on best-seller lists since Trump's inauguration). Working-class organizers in the Great Depression were versed not only in Marx but also in W.E.B. Du Bois, whose vision was of a pan–working class movement that could unite the downtrodden to transform an unjust economic system. As historian Robin D.G. Kelley has written, the end of the nineteenth century was a period of foment for "black-led biracial democratic, populist, and radical movements."

The same is true of the hard-won victories of the civil rights era. It was the movement's transcendent dream—whether articulated in the oratory of Martin Luther King Jr. or in the vision of the Student Nonviolent Coordinating Committee—that created the space for, and inspired, the grassroots organizing that in turn led to tangible wins. A similar utopian fervor in the late sixties and early seventies—emerging out of the countercultural upheaval, when young people were questioning just about everything—laid the groundwork for feminist, lesbian and gay, and environmental breakthroughs.

The New Deal, it is always worth remembering, was adopted by President Roosevelt at a time of such progressive and Left militancy that its programs—radical by today's standards—appeared at the time to be the only way to prevent full-scale revolution. And this was no idle threat. When Upton Sinclair, the muckraking author of *The Jungle*, ran for governor of California in 1934, it was something like the Bernie Sanders campaign of its day. Sinclair was a champion of a more left-wing version of the New Deal, arguing that the key to ending poverty was full state funding of workers' cooperatives. He received nearly 900,000 votes, but fell short of winning the governor's office. (If you didn't learn this in history class, it may not be a coincidence. As the Czech novelist

Milan Kundera famously observed, "the struggle of man against power is the struggle of memory against forgetting.")

Trapped in the Matrix

By the time the 2008 financial fiasco was unfolding, that utopian imagination had largely atrophied. A great many people knew that the appropriate response to the crisis was moral outrage, that gifting the banks with trillions, refusing to prosecute those responsible, and asking the poor and elderly to pay the steepest costs was an obscenity.

Yet generations who had grown up under neoliberalism struggled to picture something, anything, other than what they had always known. This may also have something to do with the power of memory. When workers rose up against the depravities of the industrial age, many had living memories of a different kind of economy. Others were actively fighting to protect an existing way of life, whether it was the family farm that was being lost to predatory creditors or small-scale artisanal businesses being wiped out by industrial capitalism. Having known something different, they were capable of imagining—and fighting for—a radically better future. Even those who have never known anything but enslavement and apartheid have been endlessly creative in finding ways—often through clandestine art forms—to nurture and keep alive the dream of freedom, self-government, and democracy. As the Pulitzer Prize–winning novelist Junot Díaz observed shortly after the 2016 election, forecasting the hard times ahead:

> Those of us whose ancestors were owned and bred like animals know that future all too well, because it is, in part, our past. And we know that by fighting, against all odds, we who had nothing, not even our real names, transformed the universe.

Our ancestors did this with very little, and we who have more must do the same.

It is this imaginative capacity, the ability to envision a world radically different from the present, that has been largely missing since the cry of No first began echoing around the world in 2008. In the West, there is little popular memory of any other kind of economic system. There are specific cultures and communities—most notably Indigenous communities—that have vigilantly kept alive memories and models of other ways to live, not based on ownership of the land and endless extraction of profit. But most of us who are outside those traditions find ourselves fully within capitalism's matrix—so while we can demand slight improvements to our current conditions, imagining something else entirely is distinctly more difficult.

Which is partially why the movements that did emerge—from Europe's "movement of the squares" to Occupy Wall Street and even Egypt's revolution—were very clear on their "no": no to the greed of the bankers, no to austerity, and, in Egypt, no to dictatorship. But what was too often missing was a clear and captivating vision of the world beyond that no.

And in its absence, the shocks kept coming.

With unleashed white supremacy and misogyny, with the world teetering on the edge of ecological collapse, with the very last vestiges of the public sphere set to be devoured by capital, it's clear that we need to do more than draw a line in the sand and say "no more." Yes, we need to do that *and* we need to chart a credible and inspiring path to a different future. And that future cannot simply be where we were before Trump came along (aka the world that gave us Trump). It has to be somewhere we have never been before.

Picturing that place requires a reclaiming of the utopian tradition that animated so many transcendent social movements in the past. It means having the courage to paint a picture of a different world, one which, even if it exists only in our minds, can fuel us as we engage in winnable battles. Because, as Oscar Wilde wrote in 1891, "a map of the world that does not include Utopia is not worth even glancing at, for it leaves out the one country at which Humanity is always landing. And when Humanity lands there, it looks out, and, seeing a better country, sets sail."

Part of that voyage is not just talking and writing about the future we want—but building it as we go.

It's a principle I saw in action (and prayer, and song) in Standing Rock.

Picture of Different World

Holding Hands against the dark

CHAPTER TWELVE

LESSONS FROM STANDING ROCK
DARING TO DREAM

Less than a month after Trump was elected, I went to Standing Rock, North Dakota. The forecast called for an epic snowstorm and it was already starting to come down as we arrived, the low hills and heavy sky a monochromatic white.

Days earlier, the governor had announced plans to clear the camps of the thousands of "water protectors" who had gathered on the outskirts of the Standing Rock Sioux Reservation to try to stop the Dakota Access pipeline. The company was determined to build the oil pipeline under Lake Oahe, the sole source of drinking water for the Standing Rock Sioux, as well as under another section of the Missouri River, which provides drinking water for 17 million people. If the pipeline ruptured, the tribal leaders argued, their people would have no safe water and their sacred sites would be desecrated. The movement's Lakota-language slogan, heard around the world, was *Mni Wiconi*—"water is life."

After months of confrontations with private security and highly militarized police, it seemed the governor now felt, with Trump on the way to the White House, that the coast was clear to crush the movement with force. The blows had been coming for months—about 750 people would be arrested by the time the camps were cleared—and when I arrived, Standing Rock had already become the site of the most violent state repression in recent US history. With the issuing of the eviction order, many were calling December 5, 2016, the Standing Rock Sioux's "last stand," and I along with many others had traveled there to stand with them.

In a surprise development, a convoy of more than two thousand military veterans had also come to Standing Rock to stand with the Sioux, prepared to face off against their fellow uniformed officers if need be. The veterans said they had taken an oath "to serve and protect" the Constitution. And after seeing footage of peaceful Indigenous water protectors being brutally attacked by security dogs, blasted with water cannons in subzero temperatures, and fired on with rubber bullets, pepper spray, and beanbag rounds, these vets had decided that the duty to protect now required that they stand up to the government which had once sent them to war.

By the time I arrived, the network of camps had swelled to roughly ten thousand people, living in hundreds upon hundreds of tents, tepees, and yurts. Dozens of kids were sledding down a snowy hill. The main camp was a hive of calm, nonstop activity. Volunteer cooks served meals to thousands, trucks arriving with fresh ingredients all day. Young media-makers, world-famous musicians, and Hollywood actors were filing continuous dispatches about the latest developments, exposing their huge followings to the drama of the standoff. Seminars on decolonization and nonviolence were happening in the larger tents and a geodesic dome. A group of drummers was gathered around the sacred fire, tending to the flames so they were never extinguished.

Down the road, the newly arrived vets were setting up camp with impressive speed, employing skills honed on the battlefields of Afghanistan, Iraq, and, for a few, Vietnam. It struck me that the last time I had spent this much time with US military personnel was in Baghdad, where young men and women in these same uniforms were sent in to occupy a country that just so happened to have one of the world's largest reserves of crude oil. After all the times American soldiers have been called upon to protect oil and gas wealth and to wage war on Indigenous people at home and abroad, it was unbearably moving to see these soldiers show up, voluntarily and unarmed, to join an Indigenous-led fight to stop yet another water-poisoning, climate-destabilizing fossil fuel project.

One of my first conversations at Standing Rock was with legendary Lakota elder LaDonna Brave Bull Allard, who in many ways had got all this resistance going when she opened the first camp on her land, the Sacred Stone Camp. That was in April 2016. Eight months later, here she was, eyes still sparkling, betraying not a bit of fatigue despite playing den mother to thousands of people who had come from across the world to be part of this historic movement.

She told me that the camp had become a home and a community to hundreds and then thousands. It had also become a field hospital—for those injured by the police attacks, and also those psychically frightened by what Trump's rise was already unleashing.

Learning by Living

Brave Bull Allard, who is the official historian of the Standing Rock Sioux tribe, said that, most of all, the encampment had become a school—for Indigenous youth seeking to connect more deeply with their own culture, to live on the land and in ceremony, and also for non-Indigenous people who realized that the moment called for skills and knowledge most of us don't have.

"My grandkids can't believe how little some of the white people know," she told me, laughing, but without judgment. "They come running: 'Grandma! The white people don't know how to chop wood! Can we teach them?' I say, 'Yes, teach them.'" Brave Bull Allard herself patiently taught hundreds of visitors what she considered basic survival skills: how to use sage as a natural disinfectant, how to stay warm and dry in North Dakota's vicious storms ("everyone needs at least six tarps," she declared sternly).

She told me she had come to understand that, although stopping the pipeline was crucial, there was something greater at work in this convergence. She said the camps were now a place where Indigenous and non-Indigenous people alike were learning to live in relationship and community with the land. And for her, it was not just the hard skills that mattered. This moment was also about exposing visitors to the traditions and ceremonies that had been kept alive despite hundreds of years of genocidal attacks on Indigenous people and culture. This, she told me, is why the traditions survived the onslaught. "We knew this day was coming— the unification of all the tribes. . . . We are here to protect the earth and the water. This is why we are still alive. To do this very thing we are doing. To help humanity answer its most pressing question, how do we live with the earth again, not against it?"

And this teaching needs to happen fast, she said—climate disruption is kicking in. If non-Indigenous people don't start to learn how to take care of earth's life-sustaining systems, then we are all cooked. With this in mind, Brave Bull Allard saw the camps as just the beginning. After the pipeline was defeated, she said, the Standing Rock Sioux needed to turn themselves into a model for green energy and sustainable living.

This vision of a movement not just resisting but modeling and teaching the way forward is shared by many of the movement's key figures, including Standing Rock Sioux tribal council member Cody Two Bears. Dressed in a red sweatshirt with the word Warrior emblazoned in black letters, he talked about the early days of European presence on these lands, when his ancestors educated the visitors on how to survive in a harsh and unfamiliar climate. "We taught them how to grow food, keep warm, build longhouses." But the taking never ended, from the earth and from Indigenous people. And now, Two Bears says, "things are getting worse. So the first people of this land have to teach this country how to live again. By going green, by going renewable, by using the blessings the Creator has given us: the sun and the wind. We are going to start in Native country. And we're going to show the rest of the country how to live."

Age of the Protectors

At Standing Rock, I found myself thinking a lot about what it means to be a protector. Leaders of the movement here had insisted from day one that they were not "protesters" out to make trouble, but "water protectors" determined to stop a whole other order of trouble. And then there were all the vets in t-shirts that said *To Serve and Protect*, deciding that living up to that oath meant putting themselves on the front line to protect the rights of the continent's First Peoples. And I thought about my own duty to be a protector—of my son, and his friends, and the kids yet to come, in the face of the rocky future we've locked in for all of them.

The role of the protector, in the wrong hands, can be lethal. In moments of crisis, strong men step into it with far too much ease, announcing themselves ready to protect the flock from all evil, asking only absolute power and blind obedience in return. Yet the spirit of protection that infused the camp had nothing in common with that all-powerful patriarchal figure. Here was a protection born of intimate knowledge of human frailty, and it was not the one-way, passive kind of protection that can go so very wrong. This protection was reciprocal and it blurred all separation: the water, land, and air protect and sustain all of us—the very least we can do is protect them (or is it us?) when they (or is it we?) are threatened. When the people here faced off against armored tanks and riot police, chanting Mni Wiconi, they were giving voice to that core principle: protect the water, because water protects all of us.

The same sense of vulnerability and reciprocity guided the veterans' presence as well. On December 5, the Obama administration announced it had denied the permit to lay the pipeline under the tribe's water reservoir. That evening, a "forgiveness ceremony" was held on the reservation. For hours, hundreds of vets lined up to beg forgiveness of the elders for crimes committed against Indigenous peoples over centuries by the military institutions they served.

Wesley Clark Jr., one of the main organizers of the veterans' delegation to Standing Rock, began by saying:

Many of us, me particularly, are from the units that have hurt you over the many years. We came. We fought you. We took your land. We signed treaties that we broke. We stole minerals from your sacred hills. We blasted the faces of our presidents onto your sacred mountain. Then we took still more land and then we took your children and then we tried . . . to eliminate your language that God gave you, and the Creator gave you. We didn't respect you, we polluted your Earth, we've hurt you in so many ways but we have come to say that we are sorry.

A Path through Anger

Amidst the tears and the sage smoke, we felt the touch of history. And something else too: a way to deal with rage and grief that went beyond venting. So soon after such a divisive, crude election, it came as a tremendous relief. For weeks, the screens that occupy too much of my life had been engulfed in that unrelenting rage, and in angry circular debates about who, or what, was the one and only true cause of the mess we were now in. Trump won because of the racism of America—end of discussion, some said. No he didn't, it was the elitism of the corporate Dems—Bernie would have fixed everything, others roared. No, he won because of capitalism, the issue above all others—racism and white supremacy are a sideshow. No, identity politics is what destroyed us, you whiners and dividers. No, it was misogyny, you bunch of flaming assholes. No, it was the fossil fuel industry, determined to suck out their last mega-profits, regardless of how much they destabilize the earth. Plenty of good points were made, but it was striking that the goal was rarely to change minds, or find common ground. The goal was to win the argument.

And then, within minutes, all that venom dried up. Those battles suddenly made as little sense as putting an oil pipeline under this community's drinking water source—a pipeline that was originally supposed to pass through the majority-white city of Bismarck, where it was widely rejected over concerns about safety. In the camps, surrounded by people who had been fighting the most powerful industries on earth, the idea that there was any kind of competition between these issues dropped away. In Standing Rock, it was just so clear that it was *all* of it, a single system. It was ecocidal capitalism that was determined to ram that pipeline through the Missouri River—consent and climate change be damned. It was searing racism that made it possible to do in Standing Rock what was deemed impossible in Bismarck, and to treat water protectors as pests to be blasted away with water cannons in frigid weather. Modern capitalism, white supremacy, and fossil fuels were strands of the same braid, inseparable. And they were all woven together here, on this patch of frozen land.

As the great Anishinaabe writer and organizer Winona LaDuke wrote of the standoff, "This is a moment of extreme corporate rights and extreme racism faced with courage, prayers and resolve." It's a battle that knows no borders. All around the world, the people doing the sacred work of protecting fragile ecologies from industrial onslaught are facing dirty wars. According to a report from the human rights watchdog Global Witness, "More than three people were killed a week in 2015 defending their land, forests and rivers against destructive industries. . . . Increasingly communities that take a stand are finding themselves in the firing line of companies' private security, state forces and a thriving market for contract killers." About 40 percent of the victims, they estimate, are Indigenous.

Since the election, I had been longing for some kind of gathering of progressive thinkers and organizers—to strategize, unite, and find a way through the next four years of Trump's daily barrage, the kind of discussion that had been so abruptly interrupted in Australia on the day/night of the election. I pictured it happening at a university, in big halls. I didn't expect to find that space at Standing Rock. But that is indeed where I discovered it, in the camps' combination of reaction and contemplation, and in the constant learning-by-doing modeled by Brave Bull Allard and so many other leaders here.

At Standing Rock, they did not, in the end, manage to stop the pipeline—at least not yet. In a flagrant betrayal of the treaty and land rights, Trump immediately reversed Obama's decision and allowed the company—flanked by layers of militarized police—to ram the pipe under Lake Oahe, without the consent of the Standing Rock Sioux. As I write, oil is flowing beneath the community's drinking water reservoir, and the pipe could burst at any time. That outrage is being challenged in the courts, and extensive pressure is being put on the banks that financed the project. Roughly $80 million (and counting) has been pulled from the banks that have invested in the pipeline.

But the oil still flows.

I will never forget the experience of being at the main camp when the news arrived, after the months of resistance, that the Obama administration had finally denied the pipeline permit. I happened to be standing with Tokata Iron Eyes, a fiercely grounded yet playful thirteen-year-old from Standing Rock who had helped kick-start the movement against the pipeline. I turned on my phone video and asked her how she felt about the breaking news. "Like I have my future back," she replied, and then she burst into tears. I did too.

Thanks to Trump, Tokata has again lost that sense of safety. And yet his action cannot and does not erase the profound learning that took place during all those months on the land. The modeling of a form of resistance that, with one hand, said *no* to an imminent threat and, with the other, worked tirelessly to build the *yes* that is the world we want and need.

CHAPTER THIRTEEN

A TIME TO LEAP
BECAUSE SMALL STEPS WON'T CUT IT

"We can't keep asking our members to sacrifice. They are losing so much. They need those pipeline jobs—we have to offer them something."

The man making this plea was an executive of a major trade union, with many members in Canada's oil and gas sector.

Sitting in a large circle, sixty people listened and shifted in their chairs. What he was saying was undeniable. Everyone has a right to a decent job. And energy workers are hurting badly.

But the people in the room knew too that the case for even one more pipeline was not a matter of bargaining with environmentalists; it was a doomed attempt to bargain with science and chemistry. It is impossible to both keep building new fossil fuel infrastructure and have a chance of keeping temperatures at anything like safe levels.

That's when Arthur Manuel took the floor. A highly respected Indigenous intellectual and former chief from the Secwepemc Nation in British Columbia, Manuel leaned forward, looked the union leader in the eye, and spoke just above a whisper. "Do you think you are the only people who have had to sacrifice? Do you know how much money, how many jobs, my people have turned down from oil and gas and mining companies? Tens of millions of dollars.

"We do it because there are things that are more important than money."

It felt as if the whole room was holding its breath. It was one of several wrenchingly honest exchanges that happened over the course of a two-day gathering in Toronto in May 2015. In the room were leaders and organizers from Haida Gwaii on the west coast to Halifax on the east coast, representing movements across a huge spectrum of issues and identities.

We had come together to figure out what connects the crises facing us, and to try to chart a holistic vision for the future that would overcome many of the overlapping challenges at the same time. Just as in Standing Rock, more and more people are start-ing to see and speak about these connections—pointing out, for instance, that the economic interests pushing hardest for war, at home and abroad, are the very same forces most responsible for warming the planet. And that the economic precariousness that the union representative was speaking about, and the attacks on Indigenous land rights and on the earth itself that were refer-enced by Arthur Manuel (who died suddenly at the start of 2017), also flow from the same place: a corrosive values system that places profit above the well-being of people and the planet. The same system has allowed the pursuit of money to so corrode the political process in the United States that a gang of scandal-plagued plutocrats could seize control of the White House.

The connections between so many of the emergencies that compete for our time and care are clear. Glaring, even. And yet, for so many reasons—pressure from funders, a desire for "click-able" campaigns, a fear of seeming too radical and therefore doomed—many of us have learned to sever those natural con-nections, and work in terms of walled-off "issues" or silos. Anti-austerity people rarely talk about climate change. Climate change people rarely talk about war or occupation. Too seldom within the environmental movement are connections made between the guns that take Black lives on the streets of cities such as Ferguson and Ottawa and the rising seas and devastating droughts destroying the homelands of Black and brown people around the world. Rarely are the dots connected between the powerful men who think they have the right to use and abuse women's bodies and the widespread notion that humans have the right to do the same thing to the earth.

So many of the crises we are facing are symptoms of the same underlying sickness: a dominance-based logic that treats so many people, and the earth itself, as disposable. We came together out of a belief that the persistence of these disconnections, of this siloed thinking, is why progressives are losing ground on virtually every front, left fighting for scraps when we all know that our historical moment demands transformative change. These divisions and compartmentalizations—the hesitancy to identify the *systems* we are up against—are robbing us of our full potential, and have trained too many to believe that lasting solutions will always be out of reach.

We also came together out of a belief that overcoming those divisions—finding and strengthening the threads that run through our various issues and movements—is our most pressing task. That out of those connections would emerge a larger and more fired-up progressive coalition than we have seen in decades, one capable of taking on not only the symptoms of a failed system, but maybe even the system itself. Our goal, and it wasn't modest, was to try to map not just the world we don't want but the one we want instead.

The diversity in the room led to plenty of tough exchanges. But with long, painful histories of failed collaborations and too much broken trust, tough is what happens when people finally decide to make space to dream together. You'd think imagining the world we want would be fun and easy. In fact, it's the hardest work of all. It also happens to be our only hope. As we have seen, Trump and his cohorts are intent on pushing the world backward on every front, all at once. Only a competing vision that is pushing us forward on multiple fronts has a chance against a force like that. Our experiment in mapping these intersectional agendas began in Canada, but it's part of an international conversation — in the US, the UK, Australia, across Europe, and beyond — in which more and more people are arriving at the same conclusion: it's time to unite around a common agenda that can directly battle the political poison spreading through our countries. No is not enough — it's time for some big, bold yeses to rally around.

Time for a People's Shock

Ever since the 2008 financial meltdown, I have been puzzling over the question of what it would take to pull off a truly progressive populist response to the crises we face.

I had thought, at one point, that the factual revelations of climate science — if we truly understood them — might be the catalyst. After all, there couldn't be a clearer indication that our current system is failing: if business as usual is allowed to continue, ever-larger expanses of our planet will cease to be hospitable to human life. And as we've seen, responding effectively to climate change requires throwing out the entire pro-corporate economic playbook — which is one of the main reasons so many right-wing ideologues are determined to deny its reality. So it seemed to me that, just as the aftermath of the Great Crash and World War II became periods of massive social transformation, so could the climate crisis — an existential threat for humanity — become an opportunity for once-in-a-century social and economic change.

The urgency of the climate crisis also gives us something that can be very helpful for getting big things done: a firm, unyielding science-based deadline. We are, it bears repeating, out of time. We've been kicking the can down the road for so many decades that we are just plain out of road. Which means if we want a shot at avoiding catastrophic warming, we need to start a grand economic and political transition *right now*.

And yet, as we all know, climate change doesn't play out like a market collapse or a war. With the exception of increasingly common monster storms, it's slow and grinding, making the warming dangerously easy to push away into our subconscious, behind more obvious daily emergencies. Which is why what brought us together for that meeting in the spring of 2015 wasn't only the climate crisis, but something that was grabbing front-page headlines: the collapse in oil prices, which has been such a problem for ExxonMobil, Rex Tillerson, and Vladimir Putin. For us in Canada—where governments had bet the farm on the expensive tarry oil in Alberta—the sudden drop in price was proving a devastating economic blow. Investors started fleeing from the tar sands, tens of thousands of workers were losing their jobs, and there was no Plan B—whether for creating jobs or raising government revenues.

For years, Canadians had been hearing that we had to choose between a healthy environment and a robust economy—now it turned out we had neither. Huge swaths of Alberta had been logged and contaminated to get at that heavy oil, Indigenous land rights had been grossly betrayed, and the economy was tanking anyway. Indeed, it was tanking precisely because we had pinned so much on a commodity whose price was on a roller coaster ride nobody seemed able to control.

Which was why a few of us had started discussing the idea of a national meeting, wondering if perhaps the oil price collapse, combined with the urgency of the climate crisis, might provide the catalyst for the deep transformation our society and economy needs on so many fronts. We began imagining that we could seize this juncture of overlapping crises to advance policies that dramatically improve lives, close the gap between rich and poor, create large numbers of well-paying, low-carbon jobs, and reinvigorate democracy from the ground up. This would be the inverse of the shock doctrine. It would be a People's Shock, a blow from below.

So we sent out a letter, headed "From price shock to energy shift," and invited leaders from across the country to meet in a circle for two days and dream big. I'm sharing what happened next in the hope that the experience might be useful at a time when so many are looking for ways to bridge divides.

A Platform without a Party

In response to our invitation, they came. Heads of labor federations and unions, directors of major green groups, iconic Indigenous and feminist leaders, key organizers and theorists focused on migrant rights, open technology, food justice, housing, faith, and more. The fact that we were able to bring so many players together with only a few weeks' notice reflected a shared understanding that this was a rare political opening— not unlike the 2008 financial crisis. Only this time, people were determined not to let the opportunity pass us by.

The other factor lending urgency to our gathering was a looming federal election campaign. The Conservative Party, led by the extremely pro-oil Stephen Harper, had been in power for a decade, but the national mood was shifting and the political landscape looked likely to change. Yet, at that stage in the campaign, there wasn't a political party that had succeeded in exciting voters with a different vision for the country. On climate, both principal opposition parties—the centrist Liberals under Justin Trudeau and the center-left New Democratic Party—were running conventional campaigns that called for new tar sands pipelines, still failing to honestly reckon with either the price collapse or the climate crisis.

So, at our gathering, we decided to do something that movements in our country had not attempted for several decades: intervene in a national election by writing a "people's platform," one that would attempt to reflect the needs not of one particular constituency, but of a great many at once.

We saw this as a chance to begin to heal not only our relationship with the planet but the colonial and racial wounds that date back to our country's founding.

We kept something else in mind too: the way of life that is leading to both climatic and economic destabilization is creating other crises as well. It's giving rise to an epidemic of anxiety and despair, expressed through everything from rising prescription drug dependence to high suicide rates, from road rage to screen addiction. So we asked ourselves to imagine: what would it take to build happier, healthier communities? And could those be the same things that would make the planet healthier?

In short, we aimed high. It felt, on some cellular level, like the only moral thing to do: for everyone in the room, whether they were working on migration or homelessness or Indigenous land rights or the climate, there had rarely been so much at stake.

The goal was to come up with a vision so concrete and inspiring that voters could, practically speaking, do two things at once. They could go to the polls to vote against what they didn't want (the disastrous government of the day); and they would still have a space, even if it was outside electoral politics, to say yes to a vision we hoped would reflect what many actually do want, by adding their names to our people's platform or otherwise voicing public support.

We figured that if we built up enough momentum behind the platform, it might exert some pressure on our elected representatives. But before that could happen, we first had to agree on the planks of the document—and that wasn't going to be easy.

Connections, Not Competition

There were a few ground rules in that initial meeting, some unspoken, some not. The first was that no one was allowed to play "my crisis is bigger than your crisis," nor argue that, because of the urgency and scope of the climate crisis, it should take precedence over fighting poverty or racism or other major concerns. Instead of ranking issues, we started from the premise that we live in a time of multiple, intersecting crises, and since all of them are urgent, we cannot afford to fix them sequentially. What we need are *integrated* solutions, concrete ideas for how to radically bring down emissions while creating huge numbers of unionized jobs and delivering meaningful justice to those who have been abused and excluded under the current extractive economy.

Another ground rule was that respectful conflict is healthy and a necessary part of getting to new territory. Arguments mean it's working!

Many of the groups and people in the room talked about how, while they had formed coalitions before, most had been coalitions of "no"—no to a lousy pro-corporate trade deal, no to a punishing austerity agenda, no to a particularly egregious politician, no to oil pipelines or fracking. But we realized that it had been a long time since the progressive side of the political spectrum had assembled to say yes, let alone yes to a sweeping vision for the next economy. So conflicts were inevitable, especially since, like all gatherings, ours was imperfect, with people missing from the room who should have been there.

There were moments of ease and joy too, where ideas for a "just transition" flowed fast and furious. Whiteboards grew crowded with suggestions and questions:

- Free high-quality child care.

- Less driving.

- Less work, more music and gardens and family.

- Super-fast trains. Solar roads.

We also heard challenges we knew we couldn't resolve in two days but would continue puzzling over for years:

- If we don't address ownership, how can we move toward equitable justice?

- How do we move beyond the idea that what we own is what protects us? Security comes from community, from solidarity. Security is based on how solid my ties are, not how much I own.

- How do we build the public sector so we, the *public*, feel part of it? We should all feel ownership over public housing, public resources.

- How can we ensure that informal and unpaid work around caregiving, domestic work, and land care is recognized and valued in a just transition?

- What should a guaranteed basic income look like?

- Climate justice is indivisible from decolonization. How do we imagine reparations to the people most impacted by extractive industries and climate change?

And on all our minds as so many thousands of refugees continued to flee their homes in search of safety:

- Migrants are not looking at the climate crisis. They are in the climate crisis.

Lead with Values, Not Policies

My role in all this was to listen closely to the two days of conversations, notice common themes, and come up with a rough first draft, which everyone would have an opportunity to revise. It was the most challenging assignment of my writing life (I struggle to cowrite with one other person, let alone sixty). And yet some very clear common themes emerged that made a synthesis possible.

One such theme was that we have a system based on limitless taking and extracting, on maximum grabbing. Our economy takes endlessly from workers, asking more and more from them in ever-tighter time frames, even as employers offer less and less security and lower wages in return. Many of our communities are being pushed to a similar breaking point: schools, parks, transit, and other services have had resources clawed back from them over many decades, even as residents have less time to fill in the gaps. And of course we are all part of a system that takes endlessly from the earth's natural bounty, without protecting cycles of regeneration, and while paying dangerously little attention to where we are offloading pollution, whether it be into the water systems that sustain life or the atmosphere that keeps our climate system in balance.

Listening to the stories—workers being laid off after a lifetime of service, immigrants facing indefinite detention under deplorable conditions, Indigenous knowledge and culture ignored and attacked—it was clear to all of us that this is what a system addicted to short-term profits and wealth is structurally required to do: it treats people and the earth either like resources to be mined to their limits or as garbage to be disposed of far out of sight, whether deep in the ocean or deep in a prison cell.

In sharp contrast, when people spoke about the world they wanted, the words *care* and *caretaking* came up again and again—care for the land, for the planet's living systems, and for one another. As we talked, that became a frame within which everything seemed to fit: the need for a shift from a system based on endless taking—from the earth and from one another—to a culture based on caretaking, the principle that when we take, we also take care and give back. A system in which everyone is valued, and we don't treat people or the natural world as if they were disposable.

Acting with care and consent, rather than extractively and through force, became the idea binding the whole draft together, starting with respect for the knowledge and inherent rights of Indigenous peoples, the original caretakers of the land, water, and air. Though many of us (including me) had originally thought we were convening to draft a list of policy goals, we realized that this shift in values, and indeed in morality, was at the core of what we were trying to map.

The specifics of policy all flowed from that shift. For example, when we talk about "green jobs," we usually picture a guy in a hard hat putting up a solar array. And that is one kind of green job, and an important one. But it's not the only one. Looking after elderly and sick people doesn't burn a lot of carbon. Making art doesn't burn a lot of carbon. Teaching is low-carbon. Day care is low carbon. And yet this work, overwhelmingly done by women, tends to be undervalued and underpaid, and is frequently the target of government cutbacks. So we decided to deliberately extend the traditional definition of a green job to anything useful and enriching to our communities that doesn't burn a lot of fossil fuels. As one participant said: "Nursing is renewable energy. Education is renewable energy." It was an attempt, in short, to show how to replace an economy built on destruction with an economy built on love.

Red Lines

We tried to touch on as many issues as possible that reflected the values shift people were calling for (from welcoming many more migrants to putting an end to trade deals that force us to choose between "growth" on the one hand and protecting the environment and creating local jobs on the other). But we also decided to resist the temptation to make laundry lists that would cover every conceivable demand. Instead, we emphasized the frame that showed how so many of our challenges—and solutions— are interconnected, because the frame could then be expanded in whatever place or community the vision was applied.

At the same time, there were certain demands, specific to different groups in the room, that needed to be in the platform. For the Indigenous participants, it was crucial to call for the full implementation of the United Nations Declaration on the Rights of Indigenous Peoples, which states that no development can take place on the land of Indigenous peoples without their "free, prior and informed consent." For the climate activists, there needed to be an acknowledgment that no new fossil fuel infrastructure can be built. For trade union participants, it was critical to call for workers to be not only retrained for new green jobs but democratic participants in that retraining.

For many people in the room, a bright red line was a rejection of nostalgia. The platform could not fall back on an idealized memory of a country that had always relied on land theft and the systematic economic and social exclusion of many communities of color. The inspiration would have to come from the picture of the future that we painted together. Ellen Gabriel, one of the coauthors of the draft and a well-known Indigenous rights activist from Kanehsatà:ke in the province of Quebec, said the process for her represented "a rebirth of humanity." Rebirth, not a resurrection.

Christina Sharpe, a Tufts professor of English who wrote a powerful book called *In the Wake* about the ongoing reverberations of the slave trade, participated in a recent discussion inspired by the platform and offered an important warning on this score: the task, she said, was "to connect but not collapse." This means that though we can and must look for points of unity and commonality across very different experiences and issues, everything cannot be blended into an indecipherable mush of lowest-common-denominator platitudes. The integrity of individual movements, the specificities of community experiences, must be reflected and protected, even as we come together in an attempt to weave a unified vision.

In It Together

In a way, we asked ourselves this: what are the qualities that we value most in people? Those included: generosity, hospitality, warmth, and wisdom. And then we asked ourselves: what do those qualities look like when expressed in public, as policy? We discovered that one of the things those qualities reflect is openness. Which means nurturing a culture that welcomes those in need, rather than greeting strangers with fear and suspicion; that values elders and the knowledge they have accumulated over lifetimes, as well as the ways of knowing that long predate this very recent invention called Canada.

Bianca Mugyenyi, who co-leads the organization that came out of the gathering, boils that principle down when it comes to climate and migration:

> The refugee flows we're seeing now are just a glimpse of what's to come. Climate change and migration are intimately linked, and we're going to see massive displacement of people caused by sea-level rise and extreme weather in the decades to come,

all around the world. So there's a question facing all of us: are we all in this together? We think most people, given the opportunity, believe that we are. You see it over and over in times of crisis, when people step up for others in their communities, but also for complete strangers. But we need our immigration, border and social support systems to catch up with this idea. The Leap is about speaking to our better selves.

Energy Reparations

Today, the energy most of us use is owned by a tiny number of corporations that generate it for the profit of their shareholders. Their primary goal, indeed their fiduciary duty, is to produce maximum profit—which is why most energy companies have been so reluctant to switch to renewables. But what, we asked, if the energy we use was owned by ordinary citizens, and controlled democratically? What if we changed the nature of the energy *and* the structure of its ownership?

So we decided that we didn't want to be buying renewable power from ExxonMobil and Shell, even if they were offering it—we wanted that power generation to be owned by the public, by communities, or by energy cooperatives. If energy systems are owned by us, democratically, then we can use the revenues to build social services needed in rural areas, towns, and cities—day cares, elder care, community centers, and transit systems (instead of wasting it on, say, $180-million retirement packages for the likes of Rex Tillerson). This turn toward community-controlled energy was pioneered in Denmark in the eighties, with government policies that encouraged and subsidized co-operatively owned wind farms, and it has been embraced on a large scale in Germany. (Roughly half of Germany's renewable energy facilities are in the hands of farmers, citizen groups, and almost nine hundred energy cooperatives; in Denmark in 2000, roughly 85 percent of the country's wind turbines were owned by small players such as farmers and co-ops.) Both countries have shown that this model carries immense social benefits and is compatible with a very rapid transition. There are some days when Denmark generates far more power from its wind farms than it can use—so it exports the surplus to Germany and Sweden.

We were inspired by these models—and by the hundreds of thousands of jobs they have created—but we were equally inspired by examples in the United States, where, through networks like the Climate Justice Alliance, low-income communities of color have been fighting to make sure the places that have been most polluted and neglected benefit *first* from a large-scale green energy transition. In Canada, the same patterns are clear: our collective reliance on dirty energy over the past couple of hundred years has taken its highest toll on the poorest and most vulnerable people, overwhelmingly Indigenous and immigrant. That's whose lands have been stolen and poisoned by mining. That's who gets the most polluting refineries and power plants in their neighborhoods. So in addition to calling for "energy democracy" on the German model, we placed reparative justice at the center of the energy transition, calling for Indigenous and other front-line communities (such as immigrant neighborhoods where coal plants have fouled the air) to be first in line to receive public funds to own and control their own green energy projects—with the jobs, profits, and skills staying in those communities.

A justice-based transition also means that workers in high-carbon sectors—many of whom have sacrificed their health in coal mines and oil refineries—must be full and democratic participants. Our guiding principle was: no worker left behind.

In summary, our plan argued that in the process of fundamentally changing our country to make it cleaner, we also have a historic opportunity to make it a lot fairer. As we move to get off fossil fuels, we can simultaneously begin to redress the terrible wrongs done to Indigenous peoples; radically reduce economic, racial, and gender inequalities; eliminate glaring double standards for immigrant workers; and we can create a whole lot of stable, well-paying jobs in green sectors, in land and water remediation, and in the caring professions. Kids would have an opportunity to be healthier because they wouldn't be breathing toxic air; our increasingly aging society could be provided with healthier community living; and we could spend less time stuck in traffic, working long hours, and more time with our friends and families. A happier, more balanced society, in other words, with the definition of happiness liberated from the endless cycle of ever-escalating consumption that underlies the logic of branding (and fueled the rise of Donald Trump). It sounded good to us and—in very un-Canadian fashion—we even dared to hope that the manifesto might become a model for similar broad-based alliances beyond our country's borders.

Yes, We Can Afford to Save Ourselves

We knew that the greatest obstacle our platform would face was the force of austerity logic—the message we have all received, over decades, that governments are perpetually broke, so why even bother dreaming of a genuinely equitable society? With this in mind, we worked closely with a team of economists to cost out how we could raise the revenues to pay for our plan.

The key tools included: ending fossil fuel subsidies (worth about $775 billion globally); getting a fairer share of the financial sector's massive earnings by imposing a transaction tax (which could raise $650 billion globally, according to the European Parliament); increasing royalties on fossil fuel extraction; raising income taxes on corporations and the wealthiest people (lots of room there—a one-percent billionaire's tax alone could raise

$45 billion globally, according to the United Nations); a progressive carbon tax (a $50 tax per metric ton of CO_2 emitted in developed countries would raise an estimated $450 billion annually); and making cuts to military spending (if the military budgets of the top ten military spenders globally were cut by 25 percent, that would free up $325 billion, according to numbers reported by the Stockholm International Peace Research Institute). To our chagrin, we neglected to include a call to shut down tax havens, perhaps the greatest potential revenue source of all.

The math is clear: the money for this great transition is out there—we just need governments with the guts to go after it.

So that, in summary, was our vision—to invest in those sectors that tangibly improve our quality of life and create more caring societies, rather than hacking away at them in the name of that manufactured crisis called "austerity." And we were committed to embedding justice in every aspect of the transition.

The Opposite of *The Art of the Deal*

As I look back on the drafting process, it strikes me that it is about as far away from Trump's "how can I screw you" art of the deal as you can get. No one got everything they wanted, or even sought to. There were serious disagreements, but to arrive at the final document, everyone made concessions; nobody went to the wall. This give-and-take reflected the principles and values that emerged from our discussions: if the goal is to move from a society based on endless taking and depletion to one based on caretaking and renewal, then all of our relationships have to be grounded in those same principles of reciprocity and care— because our relationships with one another are our most valuable resource of all. And that's the antithesis of bullying one another into submission.

Yes to the "Yes"

After a few weeks of back-and-forth over wording, we had a final draft of the platform, acceptable to almost everyone at the original gathering. (The full text appears at the end of the book.) We also agreed on a name: *The Leap Manifesto—A Call for a Canada Based on Caring for the Earth and One Another*. We chose *leap* because it raises a defiant middle finger to centrist incrementalism—the kind that calls itself "cautious" but is in fact exquisitely dangerous at this late stage in the climate crisis. The gap between where we are and where we need to go is so great, and the time left is so short, that small steps are not going to cut it—we need to leap.

My partner, Avi Lewis, who is one of the document's coauthors, puts it like this:

> With The Leap, the scale of the plan matches the scale of the crisis. And for many of us, this comes as a cosmic relief—at last, a set of demands that actually acknowledges how much and how fast we need to change. The Leap rings true because it sees the climate crisis not as a technical problem to be solved by engineers, but as a crisis of a system and an economic philosophy. The Leap identifies the root cause of the climate crisis—and it's the dominant economic logic of our time: extractivism to feed perpetual growth rooted in ever-increasing consumption. . . . That's a scary level of change, but it's honest. And people know in their bones that it's the kind of change we need.

Before releasing it to the public, we asked many organizations and trusted public figures to become initiating signatories. Again and again, we heard: *Yes. This is who we want to be. Let's push our politicians. Cautious centrism be damned.* National icons stood with us without hesitation: Neil Young. Leonard Cohen (then still with us). The novelist Yann Martel wrote back that it should "be shouted in every square by every town crier this country has."

This was a rare document that could be signed by large organizations such as Greenpeace and Oxfam, the Canadian Union of Public Employees (the largest in the country), the head of the Canadian Labour Congress (the union of unions), as well as truly grassroots groups such as Black Lives Matter–Toronto and No One Is Illegal–Coast Salish Territories and the country's largest membership-based advocacy organization, the Council of Canadians. Original endorsers included supporters of all parties, and some who support none. All shared the belief that if the major political parties weren't offering voters a plan commensurate with the multiple crises we face, then it would have to come from outside electoral politics.

Within days of The Leap's launch, thousands of people had added their names, soon tens of thousands, and well over two hundred endorsing organizations. We were stunned. It was clear that a whole lot of people, after decades of fighting against what they don't want—tar sands pipelines, money in politics, corporate trade deals, draconian security bills—were ready to rally around the world they do want. The outpouring reminded me of a slogan I first heard in Argentina, during a raucous election campaign: "Our dreams don't fit on your ballot." That's what people were saying by signing The Leap: Yes, I am going to cast a ballot in this deeply flawed and constricted electoral system, but do not mistake that vote as an expression of the world I want. The Leap was creating a space in which to register that electoral politics at this point in history so often fails to reflect both the dreams and the very urgent needs of huge numbers of people. (But the real trick, in Canada, the United States, and everywhere else, is going to be to get those dreams *on* the ballot with a winning strategy as quickly as possible. . . .)

Exploding the Box

The reaction from the corporate press ranged from confusion (how can there be a platform without a party? why drop it in the middle of an election campaign?) to rage. One of Canada's national newspapers declared The Leap's call for a country based on caring for each other and the planet "madness"; another one deemed it "national suicide."

We weren't surprised. We knew that what we were proposing did not fit inside the box of what is considered politically possible in mainstream political discussions. But what we are trying to do with The Leap—quite explicitly—is explode the box. Because if the box doesn't leave room for the safety and possibly the survival of our species, then there is something very, very wrong with that box. If what is considered politically possible today consigns us to a future of climate chaos the day after tomorrow, then we have to change what's politically possible.

And many clearly agreed. Despite some mystified mainstream reporting, people kept signing, kept asking us for Leap lawn signs, kept self-organizing local Leap chapters in their cities, towns, schools, and unions. And they kept sending us photos of their Leap teach-ins, sit-ins, and rallies—even audio of the songs it was inspiring. A national poll found that a clear majority of support-ers of all three center and center-left parties—the Liberals, the NDP, and the Green Party—were in agreement with The Leap's key demands. Even 20 percent of Conservatives said they were on board.

In the end, Canadians did vote out Stephen Harper, but the biggest loser in the election was the NDP, our center-left party. It had run an extremely cautious campaign and been outflanked on the left by Justin Trudeau's Liberals (who made up for what they lacked in specifics with dazzling progressive PR). At the NDP convention a few months later, young delegates led an internal revolt: convinced that the party could have won if it had gone bold, they called on delegates to officially endorse the spirit of The Leap Manifesto. The resolution passed—a rare example of a major political party even considering a platform offered by outside social movements.

The Living Leap

In the months since its launch, The Leap has become a living, evolving project, with an ever-growing community of supporters constantly enriching and revising the work. Our team is also working closely with organizers around the world who are kicking off similar experiments—from the Australian group I met with on the eve of Trump's election win, to a coalition of green parties in Europe who have written their own Leap-inspired manifesto, to communities from Nunavut in the Arctic to the US Gulf South and the Bronx that are exploring how to adapt the document's framework to their local needs and most pressing crises. There is even a community of "Leapers" in prison: at a Connecticut detention facility for teenaged boys tried as adults, a group of incarcerated students has been exploring ways that a justice-based transition off fossil fuels could be part of a process that keeps young people like them out of prison.

My favorite example of what our team now calls "the Living Leap" involves the Canadian Union of Postal Workers. Like postal employees around the world, these workers have been coping with a push to shut down their workplaces, restrict mail delivery, and maybe even sell off the public postal service to FedEx. In other words, austerity and privatization as usual. But instead of fighting for the best deal they can get under this failed logic, they worked with The Leap team and a group called Friends of Public Services to put together a visionary plan for every post office in the country to become a local hub for the green transition.

Combined with the union's long-standing demand for postal banking, the proposal, called "Delivering Community Power," reimagines the post office as a twenty-first-century network where residents can recharge electric vehicles; individuals and businesses can do an end run around the big banks and get a loan to start an energy co-op; and postal workers do more than deliver the mail—they also deliver locally grown produce and check in on the elderly. In other words, they become care workers, and climate workers—and they do it all in vehicles that are electric and made in Canada.

At first there was a lot of pressure on The Leap team to start our own party, or run candidates in existing ones, using the manifesto as its platform. We resisted those calls, wanting to protect The Leap's movement roots, and not wanting it to be owned by any one party. The vitality of The Leap today, especially since Trump's election, lies in the people, inside Canada and out, who are using it more and more as the basis for their own local work and electoral platforms. For instance, in Thunder Bay, a northern Canadian city with a long reliance on logging, a local Leap group has decided to run a slate of candidates for city council, writing their own version of the manifesto and using it to lay out how their city could be a hub for green manufacturing while battling homelessness and defending Indigenous land rights. And in March 2017, in a hard-fought campaign for state representative in Pennsylvania, legendary housing and anti-poverty activist Cheri Honkala ran on a pledge to create "a platform derived from the Leap Manifesto," citing the need to address the "crises of climate change, inequality, and racism together."

Utopia—Back by Popular Demand

The Leap is part of a shift in the political zeitgeist, as many are realizing that the future depends on our ability to come together across painful divides, and to take leadership from those who traditionally have been most excluded. We have reached the limits of siloed politics, where everyone fights in their own corner without mapping the connections between our various struggles, and without a clear idea of the concepts and values that must form the moral foundation of the future we need.

That recognition doesn't mean that resisting the very specific attacks—on families, on people's bodies, on communities, on individual rights—is suddenly optional. There is no choice but to resist, just as there is no choice but to run insurgent progressive candidates at every level of government, from federal down to the local school board. In the months and years to come, the various resistance tactics described in this book are going to be needed more than ever: the street protests, the strikes, the court challenges, the sanctuaries, the solidarity across divisions of race, gender, and sexual identity—all are going to be essential. And we will need to continue pushing institutions to divest from the industries that profit off various forms of dispossession, from fossil fuels to prisons to war and occupation. And yet even if every one of these resistance fights is victorious—and we know that's not going to be possible—we would still be standing in the same place we were before the Far Right started surging, with no better chance of addressing the root causes of the systemic crises of which Trump is but one virulent symptom.

A great many of today's movement leaders and key organizers understand this well, and are planning and acting accordingly. Alicia Garza, one of the founders of Black Lives Matter, said on the eve of Trump's inauguration that after five years of swelling social movements,

> whether it be Occupy Wall Street, whether it be the DREAMers movement or Black Lives Matter . . . there's a particular hope that I have that all of those movements will join together to become

the powerful force that we can be, that will actually govern this country. So that's what I'm focused on, and I hope that everybody else is thinking about that too.

Many people are, and as they do, we're seeing a rekindling of the kind of utopian dreaming that has been sorely missing from social movements in recent decades. More and more frequently, immediate, pressing demands—a $15-an-hour living wage, an end to police killings and deportations, a tax on carbon—are being paired with calls for a future that is not just better than a violent, untenable present, but . . . wonderful.

In the United States, the boldest and most inspiring example of this new utopianism is the Vision for Black Lives, a sweeping policy platform released in the summer of 2016 by the Movement for Black Lives. Born of a coalition of over fifty Black-led organizations, the platform states, "We reject false solutions and believe we can achieve a complete transformation of the current systems, which place profit over people and make it impossible for many of us to breathe." It goes on to place police shootings and mass incarceration in the context of an economic system that has waged war on Black and brown communities, putting them first in line for lost jobs, hacked-back social services, and environmental pollution. The result has been huge numbers of people exiled from the formal economy, preyed upon by increasingly militarized police, and warehoused in overcrowded prisons. And the platform makes a series of concrete proposals, including defunding prisons, removing police from schools, and demilitarizing police. It also lays out a program for reparations for slavery and systemic discrimination, one that includes free college education and forgiveness of student loans. There is much more—nearly forty policy demands in all, spanning changes to the tax code to breaking up the banks. The *Atlantic* magazine remarked that the platform—which was dropped smack in the middle of the

US presidential campaign—"rivals even political-party platforms in thoroughness."

In the months after Trump's inauguration, the Movement for Black Lives played a central role in deepening connections with other movements, convening dozens of groups under the banner "The Majority." The new formation kicked off with a thrilling month-long slate of actions between April 4 (the anniversary of Dr. Martin Luther King's assassination) and May Day. Nationwide "Fight Racism, Raise Pay" protests linked racial justice to the fast-growing workers' campaign for a $15 minimum wage and the mounting attacks on immigrants. "In the context of Trump's presidency," the new coalition argues, "it is imperative that we put forth a true, collective vision of economic justice and worker justice, for all people."

And in June 2017, thousands of activists from diverse constituencies are descending on Chicago for the second annual People's Summit, organized by National Nurses United, to continue hashing out a broad-based "People's Agenda." Several similar state-level convergences are also under way, in Michigan as well as North Carolina, where "Moral Mondays" have been bringing movements together for several years. As one of its founders, Reverend William Barber, has said, "You have to build a movement, not a moment . . . I believe all these movements—Moral Mondays, Fight for $15, Black Lives Matter— are signs of hope that people are going to stand up and not stand down."

As it has in Canada, the climate crisis is pushing us to put plans for political transformation on a tight and unyielding deadline. A powerful and broad coalition called New York Renews is pushing hard for the state to transition entirely to renewable energy by 2050. If more US states adopt these kinds of ambitious targets, and other countries do the same (Sweden, for instance, has a target of carbon neutrality by 2045), then

Trump and Tillerson's most nefarious efforts may be insufficient to tip the planet into climate chaos.

It's becoming possible to see a genuine path forward—new political formations that, from their inception, will marry the fight for economic fairness with a deep analysis of how racism and misogyny are used as potent tools to enforce a system that further enriches the already obscenely wealthy on the backs of both people and the planet. Formations that could become home to the millions of people who are engaging in activism and organizing for the first time, knitting together a multiracial and intergenerational coalition bound by a common transformational project.

The plans that are taking shape for defeating Trumpism wherever we live go well beyond finding a progressive savior to run for office and then offering that person our blind support. Instead, communities and movements are uniting to lay out the core policies that politicians who want their support must endorse.

The people's platforms are starting to lead—and the politicians will have to follow.

THE CARING MAJORITY WITHIN REACH

The hour calls for optimism; we'll save pessimism for better times.
— JEAN-CLAUDE SERVAIS

I opened this book with the word *shock*, since that's what a great many people said they felt on election day and after. But as I've reflected on the word during the past months of writing, I started to question its accuracy in this context.

A state of shock is produced when a story is ruptured, when we have no idea what's going on. But in so many ways explored in these pages, Trump is not a rupture at all, but rather the culmination—the logical end point—of a great many dangerous stories our culture has been telling for a very long time. That greed is good. That the market rules. That money is what matters in life. That white men are better than the rest. That the natural world is there for us to pillage. That the vulnerable deserve their fate and the one percent deserve their golden towers. That anything public or commonly held is sinister and not worth protecting. That we are surrounded by danger and should only look after our own. That there is no alternative to any of this.

Given these stories are, for many of us, part of the very air we breathe, Trump really shouldn't come as a shock. A billionaire president who boasts he can grab women by their genitals while calling Mexicans "rapists" and jeering at the disabled is the logical expression of a culture that grants indecent levels of impunity to the ultrarich, that is consumed with winner-take-all competition, and that is grounded in dominance-based logic at every level. We should have been expecting him. And indeed, many of those most directly touched by the underbelly of Western racism and misogyny have been expecting him for a long time.

So maybe the emotion beneath what some have been calling shock is really, more accurately, horror. Specifically, the horror of recognition that we feel when we read effective dystopian fiction or watch good dystopian films. All stories of this genre take current trends and follow them to their obvious conclusion—and then use that conclusion to hold up a mirror and ask: Do you like what you see? Do you really want to continue down this road? These nightmare futures are horrifying precisely because they're *not* shocking—not a break with our underlying stories, but their fulfillment. I've come to believe that we should see America's first nuclear-armed reality TV president in a similar fashion, as dystopian fiction come to life. Trump is a mirror, held up not only to the United States but to the world. If we don't like what we see—and throngs of us clearly do not—then it is clear what we need to do.

We have to question not only Trump but the stories that ineluctably produced him. It's not enough to superficially challenge him as an individual, foul and alarmingly ignorant though he may be. We have to confront the deep-seated trends that rewarded him and exalted him until he became the most powerful person in the world. The values that have been sold to us through reality TV, get-rich-quick books, billionaire saviors, philanthrocapitalists. The same values that have been playing out in destroyed safety nets, exploding prison numbers, normalized rape culture, democracy-destroying trade deals, rising seas and privatized disaster response, and in a world of Green Zones and Red Zones.

At the same time, perhaps it's okay—healthy even—for us to be just a little bit shocked by Trump. Here's why: those stories that produced him were always contested. There were always other stories, ones that insisted that money is not all that's valuable, and that all of our fates are intertwined with one another and with the health of the rest of the natural world. The forces Trump represents have always had to suppress those other, older, and self-evidently true stories, so that theirs could dominate against so much intuition and evidence.

The persistence of these other stories should remind us that, while Trump is the logical culmination of the current neoliberal system, the current neoliberal system is not the only logical culmination of the human story. Which is why part of our work now—a key part—is not just resistance. Not just saying no. We have to do that, of course. But we also need to fiercely protect some space to dream and plan for a better world. This isn't an indulgence. It's an essential part of how we defeat Trumpism.

Killing the Trump Within

For me, and this may sound a bit strange, Trump's rise has also prompted a more internal kind of challenge: it has made me determined to kill my inner Trump. We have already seen that the new regime in Washington has led a great many people to try to understand and overcome our own latent biases and prejudices, the ones that have kept us divided in the past. This internal work is crucial as we come together in resistance and transformation.

There are some other, often-overlooked ways that many of us can do more to confront our inner Trump—something, anything, that's just a little bit Trump-ish in our habits. (And to be clear: I'm not saying these omissions make all of us responsible for the outcome of the 2016 elections—this is not about who voted for whom and why.) Maybe it's the part whose attention span is fracturing into 140 characters, and that is prone to confusing "followers" with friends. Maybe it's the part that has learned to see ourselves as brands in the marketplace rather than as people in communities. Or the part that sees other people doing similar work not as potential allies in a struggle that will need all our talents, but as rival products competing for scarce market share. (Given that Trump's presidency is the culmination of corporate branding's insidious colonial logic, perhaps it's past time to leave all that behind.) Or maybe it's the part that can't resist joining a mob to shame and attack people with whom we disagree—sometimes using cruel personal slurs and with an intensity set to nuclear. At the very real risk of bringing on the kinds of attacks I'm describing, is it possible that this habit too is uncomfortably close to the Tweeter-in-Chief?

Or maybe it's the part that is waiting for a billionaire to ride to the rescue, except this one will be kind and generous and concerned about climate change and empowerment for girls. The liberal billionaire savior may appear very far from Trump, but the fantasy still equates great wealth with superhero powers, which, once again, is just a little too close for comfort to the Ministry of Mar-a-Lago.

If some of these impulses and stories seem hardwired inside us, it's not because we're terrible people. It's because so many of us function within systems that are constantly telling us there are not enough resources for everyone to thrive, so we'd better elbow our way to the top, whatever the costs. Willingly or not, anyone who consumes and produces media swims in the cultural waters of reality TV and personal branding and nonstop attention-splintering messages—the same waters that produced Donald Trump. There are different parts of that fetid swimming pool, to be sure, and some people are in zones with no lifeguards and with way more waterborne diseases than others—but it's still hard to get genuinely outside the pool. Recognizing this can help clarify our task: to have a hope of changing the world, we're going to have to be willing to change ourselves.

The good news is that as we de-Trump—perhaps resolving to spend a few more hours a week in face-to-face relationships, or to surrender some ego for the greater good of a project, or to recognize the value of so much in life that cannot be bought or sold—we might just get happier. And that is what will keep us in a struggle that does not have a finish line in sight and indeed will require from us lifetimes of engagement.

The Choice

Because we can try to fight the global rise of right-wing dema-goguery in two possible ways. There's the establishment option embraced by centrist parties the world over. This promises a lit-tle more child care, better representation of women and people of color at the top, and maybe a few more solar panels. But this option also comes with the same old austerity logic, the same blind faith in markets, the same equation of endless consumption with happiness, the same Band-Aids on gaping wounds.

There are many reasons why this limited vision is utterly fail-ing to stop the surge of the Far Right around the world, but the main one is this: it does not have nearly enough to offer. It does nothing to address the real and legitimate grievances that super-charge the search for scapegoats, nor does it give the people most endangered by the rising Right enough hope for a better future. A society with extreme inequality, unmasked neo-fascist tendencies, and an unraveling climate is sick, and neoliberalism, as one of the major drivers of all of these crises, is grossly inadequate medicine. It offers only a weak no to the forces responsible, and it lacks a yes worth seizing.

A great many of us are clearly ready for another approach: a captivating "yes" that lays out a plan for tangible improvements in daily life, unafraid of powerful words such as *redistribution* and *reparation*, and intent on challenging Western culture's equation of a "good life" with ever-escalating creature comforts inside ever-more-isolated consumer cocoons, never mind what the planet can take or what actually leads to our deepest fulfillment.

And perhaps we should thank Trump for this newfound ambition, at least in part. The shamelessness of his corporate coup has done a tremendous amount to make systemic change seem more necessary. If titans of American industry can eagerly line up behind this man—with all of his ugly hatreds, his venality, vanity, and vacuousness—and if Wall Street can cheer on news of his plans to let the planet burn and the elderly starve, and if so much of the media can praise his cruise missiles, ordered over chocolate cake, as "presidential," well then, a great many people are coming to the conclusion that they want no part of a system like that. With this elevation of the basest of figures to the most exalted of positions, the culture of maximum extraction, of endless grabbing and disposing, has reached some kind of breaking point. Clearly, it is the culture itself that must be confronted now, and not policy by policy, but at the root.

What we have seen with insurgent Left candidacies and parties in the United States, France, and elsewhere are not perfect politicians or perfect platforms that have everything figured out. Some of the figures who have led these runs sound more like the past than the future, and the campaigns they have built often do not mirror the diverse countries they seek to govern, or at least not enough. And yet the very fact that these long-shot candidates and often brand-new political formations are coming within an arm's reach of power—repeatedly stunning pollsters and establishment analysts—is proof of a very important fact, one that has been denied and suppressed for the many decades of neoliberalism's stranglehold on public discourse: progressive transformational change is *popular*—more than many of us would have dared imagine as recently as just one or two years ago.

Here is what needs to be understood in our bones: the spell of neoliberalism has been broken, crushed under the weight of lived experience and a mountain of evidence. What for decades was unsayable is now being said out loud by candidates who win millions of votes: *free college tuition, double the minimum wage, 100 percent renewable energy as quickly as technology allows, demilitarize the police, prisons are no place for young people, refugees are welcome here, war makes us all less safe*. And the crowds are roaring their agreement. With so much encouragement, who knows what's next? Reparations for slavery and colonialism? A Marshall Plan to fight violence against women? Prison abolition? Democratic worker co-ops as the centerpiece of a green jobs program? An abandonment of "growth" as a measure of progress? Why not? The intellectual fencing that has constrained the progressive imagination for so long is lying twisted on the ground.

The left-wing almost-wins of the past two years are not defeats. They are the first tremors of a profound ideological realignment from which a progressive majority could well emerge—just as geopolitically significant as the rise of authoritarianism and neo-fascism on the right side of the spectrum. Indeed, the weaknesses and missteps of these Left candidates should be a cause not for despair but for genuine hope. It means that a much larger political tent is possible—it's just a matter of collectively, and carefully, planting the right poles from Day One. As many movement leaders are now arguing, a very good start would be accepting the premise that widening economic inequality and climate disaster are inseparable from systems that have always ranked human life based on race and gender, while the capacity to pit populations against each other based on skin color, religious faith, and sexuality has been the single most potent tool for protecting and sustaining this lethal order. And if the political formation that has the guts to say all that also has a bold plan for humanizing and democratizing new technologies and global trade, then it would quickly seize back populist ground from the Right, while feeling less like a blast from the past and more like a path to an exciting, never-before-attempted future. A deeply diverse and insistently forward-looking campaign like that could well prove unbeatable.

If this sounds overly optimistic, remember: in the United States, the number of people showing up to join political movements is swelling to levels beyond anything organizers say they have seen before. Marches—for women's rights, against deportations, and in defense of Black lives—are seeing record numbers. Progressive political meetings, lectures, town halls, and assemblies are experiencing beyond-capacity participation. Something powerful is at work, and anyone who claims to know how far this can go should be trusted about as much as the pollsters who told us Trump could never win and Brexit would certainly fail. Building this broad tent in a time of siloed politics is hard work, requiring a willingness to honestly confront painful histories before progress is possible. And yet in this moment that combines such fearsome stakes with such fertile potential, what choice do we have but to try? To leap at every new opportunity as it opens?

For instance, after the Republicans' first shot at dismantling Obama's health care program failed, the movement calling for universal public health care surged across the country, with the idea of Medicare-for-all making more sense to more people than it had in decades. Now the push is on for the model to be adopted in large states such as California, no matter what happens in Washington.

As Trump's plans meet his surreal levels of ineptitude in executing them, more such opportunities will emerge. We can expect a similar shifting of the tectonic plates if the North American Free Trade Agreement is opened up for renegotiation. Trump's actions will be a bitter disappointment to his working-class supporters, but the very fact of reopening an agreement we were all told was sealed indefinitely will also be a chance for unions and environmentalists to step forward with a blueprint for genuinely fair trade, and build support behind it. Each one of these openings — and there will be many — is an opportunity to get concrete about what a real alternative to right-wing populism can and should look like. A plank in a true people's platform.

Just one last reminder: Trump's disaster capitalists control a very powerful part of the US government — but they do not control everything. They do not control what cities and states do. They do not even control what Congress does a lot of the time. They certainly do not control what universities and faith institutions and unions do. They do not control what the courts do (yet). They do not control what other sovereign nations do. And they do not control what we do as individuals and in groups around the world.

Precisely because what is happening in Washington is so exquisitely dangerous, what all of us do with our collective power in these non-Trumpified spaces matters now more than ever. At the 2016 Democratic National Convention, Michelle Obama memorably told the crowd that, "When they go low, we go high." She was talking less about deeds than about tone, and her family's refusal to join Trump and his gang in the gutter. It's time to transfer that ethos from tone to deeds: when they go low, everyone needs to aim high. In the many domains Trump does not control, we need to aim higher in our ambitions and accomplish more with our actions. We need to do more to prevent catastrophic climate change. We need to do more to create liberated cities for migrants and refugees. We need to do more to prevent military escalation. We need to do more to protect the rights of women and members of LGBTQ communities. As they go lower and lower, we need to shoot higher and higher.

Reverse Shock

For decades, elites have been using the power of shock to impose nightmares. Donald Trump thinks he'll be able to do it again and again—that we will have forgotten by tomorrow what he said yesterday (which he will say he never said); that we will be overwhelmed by events, and will ultimately scatter, surrender, and let him grab whatever he wants.

But crises, as we have seen, do not always cause societies to regress and give up. There is also the second option—that, faced with a grave common threat, we can choose to come together and make an evolutionary leap. We can choose, as the Reverend William Barber puts it, "to be the moral defibrillators of our time and shock the heart of this nation and build a movement of resistance and hope and justice and love." We can, in other words, surprise the hell out of ourselves—by being united, focused, and determined. By refusing to fall for those tired old shock tactics. By refusing to be afraid, no matter how much we are tested.

The corporate coup described in these pages, in all its dimensions, is a crisis with global reverberations that could echo through geologic time.

How we respond to this crisis is up to us.

So let's choose that second option.

Let's leap.

The Leap Manifesto

A Call for a Canada Based on
Caring for the Earth and One Another

We start from the premise that Canada is facing the deepest crisis in recent memory.

The Truth and Reconciliation Commission has acknowledged shocking details about the violence of Canada's near past. Deepening poverty and inequality are a scar on the country's present. And Canada's record on climate change is a crime against humanity's future.

These facts are all the more jarring because they depart so dramatically from our stated values: respect for Indigenous rights, internationalism, human rights, diversity, and environmental stewardship.

Canada is not this place today—but it could be.

We could live in a country powered entirely by renewable energy, woven together by accessible public transit, in which the jobs and opportunities of this transition are designed to systematically eliminate racial and gender inequality. Caring for one another and caring for the planet could be the economy's fastest-growing sectors. Many more people could have higher-wage jobs with fewer work hours, leaving us ample time to enjoy our loved ones and flourish in our communities.

We know that the time for this great transition is short. Climate scientists have told us that this is the decade to take decisive action to prevent catastrophic global warming. That means small steps will no longer get us where we need to go.

This leap must **begin by respecting the inherent rights and title of the original caretakers of this land. Indigenous communities** have been at the forefront of protecting rivers, coasts, forests and lands from out-of-control industrial activity. We can bolster this role, and reset our relationship, by **fully implementing the United Nations Declaration on the Rights of Indigenous Peoples.**

Moved by the treaties that form the legal basis of this country and bind us to share the land "for as long as the sun shines, the grass grows, and the rivers flow," we want energy sources that will last for time immemorial and never run out or poison the land. Technological breakthroughs have brought this dream within reach. The latest research shows it is feasible for Canada to get 100 percent of its electricity from renewable resources within two decades; by 2050 we could have a 100 percent clean economy.

We demand that this shift begin now.

There is **no longer an excuse for building new infrastructure projects that lock us into increased extraction decades into the future.** The new iron law of energy development must be: **if you wouldn't want it in your backyard, then it doesn't belong in anyone's backyard.** That applies equally to oil and gas pipelines; fracking in New Brunswick, Quebec, and British Columbia; increased tanker traffic off our coasts; and to Canadian-owned mining projects the world over.

The time for energy democracy has come: we believe not just in changes to our energy sources, but that wherever possible communities should collectively control these new energy systems.

As an alternative to the profit-gouging of private companies and the remote bureaucracy of some centralized state ones, we can create innovative ownership structures: democratically run, paying living wages, and keeping much-needed revenue in communities. And **Indigenous Peoples should be first to receive public support for their own clean energy projects. So should communities currently dealing with heavy health impacts of polluting industrial activity.**

Power generated this way will not merely light our homes but redistribute wealth, deepen our democracy, strengthen our economy, and start to heal the wounds that date back to this country's founding.

A leap to a non-polluting economy creates countless openings for similar multiple "wins." We want **a universal program to build energy-efficient homes, and retrofit existing housing, ensuring that the lowest-income communities and neighbourhoods will benefit first** and receive job training and opportunities that reduce poverty over the long term. **We want training and other resources for workers in carbon-intensive jobs, ensuring they are fully able to take part in the clean energy economy.** This transition should involve the democratic participation of workers themselves. **High-speed rail powered by renewables and affordable public transit can unite every community in this country**—in place of more cars, pipelines, and exploding trains that endanger and divide us.

And since we know this leap is beginning late, we need to **invest in our decaying public infrastructure** so that it can withstand increasingly frequent extreme weather events.

Moving to a far more localized and ecologically based agricultural system would reduce reliance on fossil fuels, capture carbon in the soil, and absorb sudden shocks in the global supply—as well as produce healthier and more affordable food for everyone.

We call for an end to all trade deals that interfere with our attempts to rebuild local economies, regulate corporations,

and stop damaging extractive projects. Rebalancing the scales of justice, we should ensure **immigration status and full protection for all workers.** Recognizing Canada's contributions to military conflicts and climate change—primary drivers of the global refugee crisis—we must welcome refugees and migrants seeking safety and a better life.

Shifting to an economy in balance with the earth's limits also means **expanding the sectors of our economy that are already low-carbon: caregiving, teaching, social work, the arts, and public-interest media. Following on Quebec's lead, a national childcare program is long past due.** All this work, much of it performed by women, is the glue that builds humane, resilient communities—and we will need our communities to be as strong as possible in the face of the rocky future we have already locked in.

Since so much of the labour of caretaking—whether of people or the planet—is currently unpaid, we call for a vigorous debate about the introduction of **a universal basic annual income.** Pioneered in Manitoba in the 1970s, this sturdy safety net could help ensure that no one is forced to take work that threatens their children's tomorrow, just to feed those children today.

We declare that "austerity"—which has systematically attacked low-carbon sectors like education and healthcare, while starving public transit and forcing reckless energy privatizations—is a fossilized form of thinking that has become a threat to life on earth.

The money we need to pay for this great transformation is available—we just need the right policies to release it. Like an **end to fossil fuel subsidies. Financial transaction taxes. Increased resource royalties. Higher income taxes on corporations and wealthy people. A progressive carbon tax. Cuts to military spending.** All of these are based on a simple **"polluter pays"** principle and hold enormous promise.

One thing is clear: public scarcity in times of unprecedented private wealth is a manufactured crisis, designed to extinguish our dreams before they have a chance to be born.

Those dreams go well beyond this document. We call on all those seeking political office to seize this opportunity and embrace the urgent need for transformation. We call for **town hall meetings across the country** where residents can gather to democratically define what a genuine leap to the next economy means in their communities.

Inevitably, this bottom-up revival will lead to a renewal of democracy at every level of government, working swiftly toward a system in which **every vote counts and corporate money is removed from political campaigns.**

This is a great deal to take on all at once, but such are the times in which we live.

The drop in oil prices has temporarily relieved the pressure to dig up fossil fuels as rapidly as high-risk technologies will allow. This pause in frenetic expansion should not be viewed as a crisis, but as a gift.

It has given us a rare moment to look at what we have become—and decide to change.

And so we call on all those seeking political office to seize this opportunity and embrace the urgent need for transformation. This is our sacred duty to those this country harmed in the past, to those suffering needlessly in the present, and to all who have a right to a bright and safe future.

Now is the time for boldness.

Now is the time to leap.

ACKNOWLEDGMENTS

Amazing people helped make this book on an absurdly tight timeline. Louise Dennys, Executive Publisher of Penguin Random House Canada, gave her brilliant mind and life over to this project, improving the text in countless ways. Johann Hari insisted I write it before I was convinced, recording long conversations to show me the material was there and sharpening multiple drafts. Derrick O'Keefe turned his life upside down to edit, research and shepherd us along. Sharon Riley provided excellent research and careful fact checking, with indispensable help from Christine Shearer, Allie Tempus, Kate Aronoff and Rajiv Sicora. Jackie Joiner, as always, played orchestra conductor as only she can.

Louise and I are delighted to work with two excellent editors: Helen Conford at Penguin Random House UK and Anthony Arnove at Haymarket Books in the US; he is also representing the book internationally. The impossible schedule required miracles from each of them and from all the publishing teams, especially Rick Meier and Deirdre Molina, and the indefatigable Knopf Canada production group, Brittany Larkin and Terra Page, John Sweet, and Creative Director, Scott Richardson. I am grateful to *The Intercept*, *The Nation* and *The Guardian*, where portions of this text first appeared. Michelle Alexander, Keeanga-Yamahtta Taylor and Eve Ensler read early drafts providing invaluable feedback.

My husband, Avi Lewis, helped think through so many aspects of this argument, and gave me the gift of time and space to immerse myself completely. Thanks also to Michael, Bonnie and Seth Klein; to Michele Landsberg and Stephen Lewis; Sol Guy, Seth MacFarlane, Kyo Maclear, Brit Marling, Katie McKenna, Bianca Mugyenyi, Betsy Reed, Anthony Rogers-Wright, Juliana Saehrig, Katharine Viner and Ofelia Whitely. I am sustained, supported and inspired by the incredible Leap team and by the sixty people who drafted the original document. We are still reeling from the loss of our great collaborator, Arthur Manuel. My deepest thanks are for patient little Toma, who missed his mom over these last months, but feels strongly that, "Donald Trump is too rude to be president."

book:
White Working Class;
Overcoming Clueless
Joan.

Karen R4:

NAOMI KLEIN is an award-winning journalist, syndicated columnist, documentary filmmaker and author of the international
bestsellers *No Logo: Taking Aim at the Brand Bullies*, *The Shock
Doctrine: The Rise of Disaster Capitalism* and *This Changes
Everything: Capitalism vs. the Climate*. She is a senior correspon-
dent for *The Intercept* and her writing appears widely in such
publications as *The New York Times*, *Le Monde*, *The Guardian*
and *The Nation*, where she is a contributing editor. Klein is a
member of the board of directors for climate-action group 350.
org and one of the organizers behind Canada's Leap Manifesto.
In November 2016 she was awarded Australia's prestigious
Sydney Peace Prize for, according to the prize jury, "inspiring us
to stand up locally, nationally and internationally to demand a
new agenda for sharing the planet that respects human rights
and equality."

Her books have been translated into more than thirty lan-
guages.